Transnational Environmental Law in the Anthropocene

Anthropocene is the proposed name for the new geological epoch in which humans have overwhelming impact on planetary processes. This edited volume invites reflection on the meaning and role of law in light of changing planetary realities. Taking the concept of the Anthropocene as a starting point, the contributions to this book address emerging legal issues from a transnational environmental law perspective. How law interacts with, and how law governs, global environmental problems is a challenge that legal scholars have approached with vigour over the last decade.

More recently, the concept of the Anthropocene has become a topic that researchers have also begun to grapple with by engaging with disciplines beyond legal scholarship. One avenue of research that has emerged to address global environmental problems is transnational environmental law. Adopting 'transnational law' as a lens or framework through which to analyse environmental law takes a broader approach to the ways in which law may be assessed and deployed to meet planetary challenges. The chapters within this book provide a timely intervention into the theoretical and practical approaches of transnational environmental law in a time of significant uncertainty and environmental and human crises.

The chapters in this book were originally published as a special issue of *Transnational Legal Theory.*

Emily Webster is Post-Doctoral Associate, Hughes Hall Centre for Climate Change Engagement, University of Cambridge. She is also Senior Research Fellow at the Transnational Law Institute and member of the Climate Law & Governance Centre at King's College London. Her research concerns transnational climate change law and governance, focusing on the transition to a low carbon economy.

Laura Mai is PhD Candidate and Visiting Lecturer at The Dickson Poon School of Law, King's College London, UK and member of the Climate Law & Governance Centre at King's College London.

Transnational Environmental Law in the Anthropocene

Reflections on the Role of Law in Times of Planetary Change

Edited by
Emily Webster and Laura Mai

Routledge
Taylor & Francis Group
LONDON AND NEW YORK

First published 2021
by Routledge
2 Park Square, Milton Park, Abingdon, Oxon OX14 4RN

and by Routledge
52 Vanderbilt Avenue, New York, NY 10017

Routledge is an imprint of the Taylor & Francis Group, an informa business

British Library Cataloguing in Publication Data
A catalogue record for this book is available from the British Library

ISBN: 978-0-367-71557-1 (hbk)
ISBN: 978-0-367-71559-5 (pbk)
ISBN: 978-1-003-15259-0 (ebk)

Typeset in Minion Pro
by Newgen Publishing UK

Publisher's Note
The publisher accepts responsibility for any inconsistencies that may have arisen during the conversion of this book from journal articles to book chapters, namely the inclusion of journal terminology.

Contents

Citation Information

The chapters in this book were originally published in *Transnational Legal Theory*, volume 11, issue 1–2 (June 2020). When citing this material, please use the original page numbering for each article, as follows:

Introduction

Transnational environmental law in the Anthropocene
Emily Webster and Laura Mai
Transnational Legal Theory, volume 11, issue 1–2 (June 2020), pp. 1–15

Chapter 1

Two layers of self-regulation
J. E. Viñuales
Transnational Legal Theory, volume 11, issue 1–2 (June 2020), pp. 16–32

Chapter 2

Ecological law in the Anthropocene
Peter D Burdon
Transnational Legal Theory, volume 11, issue 1–2 (June 2020), pp. 33–46

Chapter 3

Environmental trusteeship and state sovereignty: can they be reconciled?
Klaus Bosselmann
Transnational Legal Theory, volume 11, issue 1–2 (June 2020), pp. 47–61

Chapter 4

Restoration and cooperation for flourishing socio-ecological landscapes
Afshin Akhtar-Khavari
Transnational Legal Theory, volume 11, issue 1–2 (June 2020), pp. 62–74

Chapter 5

Earth system law for the Anthropocene: rethinking environmental law alongside the Earth system metaphor
Louis J. Kotzé
Transnational Legal Theory, volume 11, issue 1–2 (June 2020), pp. 75–104

Chapter 6

(Transnational) law for the Anthropocene: revisiting Jessup's move from 'what?' to 'how?'
Laura Mai
Transnational Legal Theory, volume 11, issue 1–2 (June 2020), pp. 105–120

Chapter 7

Urgent agenda: how climate litigation builds transnational narratives
Phillip Paiement
Transnational Legal Theory, volume 11, issue 1–2 (June 2020), pp. 121–143

Chapter 8

Litigation and regulatory governance in the age of the Anthropocene: the case of fracking in the Karoo
Melanie Murcott and Emily Webster
Transnational Legal Theory, volume 11, issue 1–2 (June 2020), pp. 144–164

Chapter 9

The myth of mermaids and stewardship of the seas
Emily Barritt
Transnational Legal Theory, volume 11, issue 1–2 (June 2020), pp. 165–179

Chapter 10

To the Anthropocene and beyond: the responsibility of law in decimating and protecting marine life
Pierre Cloutier de Repentigny
Transnational Legal Theory, volume 11, issue 1–2 (June 2020), pp. 180–196

Chapter 11

Regimes of waste (im)perceptibility in the life cycle of metal
Tina Beigi and Michael Hennessy Picard
Transnational Legal Theory, volume 11, issue 1–2 (June 2020), pp. 197–218

Notes on Contributors

Afshin Akhtar-Khavari, Professor, Faculty of Law, Queensland University of Technology, Brisbane, Australia.

Emily Barritt, Lecturer and Co-Director, Transnational Law Institute, The Dickson Poon School of Law, King's College London, London, UK.

Tina Beigi, PhD Candidate, Department of Natural Resources Sciences, McGill University, Montreal, QC, Canada.

Klaus Bosselmann, Professor, Faculty of Law, University of Auckland, Auckland, New Zealand.

Peter D Burdon, Associate Professor, Adelaide Law School, Adelaide, Australia.

Pierre Cloutier de Repentigny, PhD Candidate, Centre for Environmental Law and Global Sustainability, Faculty of Law, University of Ottawa, Ottawa, Canada; Pierre Elliott Trudeau Foundation Scholar; Social Sciences and Humanities Research Council Joseph-Armand Bombardier Canada Graduate Scholar.

Michael Hennessy Picard, Junior Research Fellow, Institute of Advanced Studies (IAS), University College London, London, UK.

Louis J. Kotzé, Research Professor, Faculty of Law, North-West University, Potchefstroom, South Africa; Senior Professorial Fellow in Earth System Law, Law School, University of Lincoln, Lincoln, UK.

Laura Mai, PhD Candidate and Visiting Lecturer, The Dickson Poon School of Law, King's College London, London, UK; Member of the Climate Law & Governance Centre, King's College London, London, UK.

Melanie Murcott, Senior Lecturer, Department of Public Law, University of Pretoria, Pretoria, South Africa.

Phillip Paiement, Assistant Professor, Tilburg Law School, Tilburg University, Tilburg, the Netherlands.

J. E. Viñuales, Harold Samuel Professor of Law and Environmental Policy, University of Cambridge, Cambridge, UK.

Emily Webster, Post-Doctoral Associate, Hughes Hall Centre for Climate Change Engagement, University of Cambridge, Cambridge, UK.

INTRODUCTION

Transnational environmental law in the Anthropocene

Emily Webster and Laura Mai

ABSTRACT

Climate change, biodiversity loss, marine degradation and a pandemic have marked 2020. This article introduces a Special Issue that interrogates transnational environmental law in the context of the Anthropocene and invites reflection on the meaning and role of law in light of changing planetary realties. How law interacts with and governs the global environmental problems is a challenge that legal scholars have approached with vigour over the last decade and, more recently, the concept of the Anthropocene has become a topic that researchers have also begun to grapple with. One avenue of research that has emerged to address global environmental problems is transnational environmental law. Adopting 'transnational law' as a lens or framework through which to analyse environmental law takes a broader approach to the ways in which law may be assessed and deployed to meet global environmental challenges. The collection of articles within this Special Issue provide a timely intervention into the theoretical and practical approaches of transnational environmental law in a time of significant global uncertainty and environmental crisis.

> [L]et us call it a conflict between modern humans who believe they are alone in the Holocene, in flight towards the Global or in exodus towards the Local, and the terrestrials who know they are in the Anthropocene and who seek to cohabit with other terrestrials under the authority of a power that as yet lacks any political institution.[1]

1. Towards a new planetary epoch: from Holocene to Anthropocene?

Today, some twenty years after its pronouncement,[2] for some, the term 'Anthropocene' has not lost its profoundness and radical

---

[1] Bruno Latour, *Down To Earth: Politics in the New Climatic Regime* (Polity Press 2018).

[2] Paul J Crutzen and Eugene F Stoermer, 'The "Anthropocene" (2000) 41 *IGBP Global Change Newsletter* 17; see also Paul J Crutzen, 'Geology of Mankind' (2002) 415 *Nature* 23.

potential,[3] while for others, it has retained its controversial and provocative connotations.[4] Intimating a new epoch in the history of the Earth, continued debates and current planetary developments evidence that the idea of the 'Anthropocene' has indeed not lost its relevance. At the core of Anthropocene thinking lies the proposition that humans are now so fundamentally interfering with the biological, geological and chemical systems of our planet, that the effects of these interventions are going to be felt for centuries to come.[5] In other words, in the Anthropocene humans have morphed into 'geologic agents'[6] who meddle with the interconnected planetary processes that make up the Earth System.[7] This proposition aligns with recent scientific evidence, based on the concept of 'planetary boundaries',[8] which suggests that anthropogenic impacts are causing the Earth to move beyond the stable parameters of the Holocene, the geological epoch that began after the last ice age and allowed life on Earth to flourish.[9] While the process of formally recognising the Anthropocene as a new period in the history of the planet is ongoing,[10] it is undeniable that the Earth is changing and that humans are central agents in these transformations. Importantly, however, the concept of the Anthropocene connotes not merely an extension or intensification of

---

[3] See eg Clive Hamilton, 'Anthropocene as Rupture' (2016) *The Anthropocene Review* 93.

[4] See eg Andreas Malm and Alf Hornborg, 'The Geology of Mankind? A Critique of the Anthropocene Narrative' (2014) *The Anthropocene Review* 62; Anna Grear, 'Deconstructing Anthropos: A Critical Legal Reflection on "Anthropocentric" Law and Anthropocene "Humanity"' (2015) *Law and Critique* 225; Christophe Bonneuil and Jean-Baptiste Fressoz, *The Shock of the Anthropocene* (Verso 2015). Critical reflections have also produced alternative names, see eg Donna Harraway, *Staying with the Trouble: Making Kin in the Chthulucene* (Duke University Press 2016). Harraway prefers the term 'Chthulucene' to 'Anthropocene': 'the Chthulucene is made up of ongoing multispecies stories and practices of becoming-with in times that remain at stake, in precarious times, in which the world is not finished and the sky has not fallen – yet … Unlike the dominant dramas of Anthropocene … discourse, human beings are not the only important actors in the Chthulucene, with all other beings able simply to react'. See also Jason Moore, 'The Capitalocene, Part I: On the Nature and Origins of our Ecological Crisis' (2017) *Journal of Peasant Studies* 596; Ivan Vargar Roncancio and others, 'From the Anthropocene to Mutual Thriving: An Agenda for Higher Education in the Ecozoic' (2019) 11 *Sustainability* 3312.

[5] Will Steffen, Paul J Crutzen and John R McNeil, 'The Anthropocene: Are Humans now Overwhelming the Great Forces of Nature?' (2007) 36 *Ambio* 614.

[6] Bruce H Wilkinson, 'Humans as Geologic Agents: A Deep-Time Perspective' (2005) *Geological Society of America* 161.

[7] Will Steffen et al, 'Stratigraphic and Earth System Approaches to Defining the Anthropocene' (2016) *Earth's Future* 324. The Earth System is defined as 'the suite of interacting physical, chemical, and biological global-scale cycles (often called biogeochemical cycles) and energy fluxes which provide the conditions necessary for life on the planet'. It is conceptualised as a materially closed system with the sun as its external energy source; humans are understood to be part of it, see Will Steffen and others, *Global Change and the Earth System: A Planet under Pressure* (Springer 2004) 7.

[8] See Johan Rockström et al, 'Planetary Boundaries: Exploring the Safe Operating Space for Humanity' (2009) 14 *Ecology and Society* 32; Johan Rockström et al, 'A Safe Operating Space for Humanity' (2009) 461 *Nature* 472.

[9] Will Steffen et al, 'Trajectories of the Earth System in the Anthropocene' (2018) *Proceedings of the National Academy of Sciences in the United States of America* online: <https://www.pnas.org/content/115/33/8252> accessed 11 February 2020.

[10] Subcommission on Quaternary Stratigraphy, 'Working Group on the "Anthropocene": Results of binding vote by AWG' (21 May 2019) online: <http://quaternary.stratigraphy.org/working-groups/anthropocene/> accessed 11 February 2020. See also Jan Zalasiewicz and others, 'Are we now living in the Anthropocene?' (2008) 18(2) *GSA Today* 4.

already existing pressures, but a deeper shift towards increased levels of instability, unpredictability and risk.[11] It is in this vein that the concept has moved beyond the natural to the social sciences and the humanities, including law.[12] Engagement with the Anthropocene narrative has prompted scholars across these disciplines to reconsider how 'environmental' problems are properly to be perceived, and to reflect on ensuing implications for their own disciplines and beyond.[13] As the contributions to this Special Issue show, for legal scholarship, engaging with the Anthropocene entails confronting, head-on, theoretical, conceptual and methodological challenges. At the same time, this Special Issue demonstrates, that these challenges can be productively used to foster innovative, cross-disciplinary perspectives which enrich and refresh legal thinking.

This Special Issue of *Transnational Legal Theory*, comes after a year of environmental catastrophes, and is therefore a timely intervention. Between late 2019 and early 2020, unprecedented bush fires have had devastating impacts on the Australian continent.[14] Deforestation in many countries, notably in Brazil,[15] are driven primarily by interests of the agro-forestry sector and continue to severely impact biodiversity and indigenous communities, while also reducing natural carbon sinks which are so central in our efforts to mitigate climate change. Transboundary air pollution, known as 'haze' in South-East Asia, impacts human health, plants, water sources and even weather patterns.[16] The Anthropocene also has a distinctly human

[11] See eg: Patrick W Keys et al, 'Anthropocene Risk' (2019) *Nature Sustainability* 667.

[12] See eg Jamie Lorimer, 'The Anthropo-scene: A Guide for the Perplexed' (2017) *Social Studies of Science* 117.

[13] See Mark A Maslin and Simon L Lewis, 'Anthropocene: Earth System, Geological, Philosophical and Political Paradigm Shifts' (2015) *The Anthropocene Review* 108; Jeremy Baskin, 'Paradigm Dressed as Epoch: The Ideology of the Anthropocene' (2015) *Environmental Values* 9. For perspectives from legal scholarship see eg Kathleen Birrell and Julia Dehm, 'International Law & the Humanities in the 'Anthropocene'' in Shane Chalmers and Sundhya Pahuja (eds), *Routledge Handbook of International Law and the Humanities* (Routledge forthcoming); Tim Stephens, 'What's the Point of International Environmental Law Scholarship in the Anthropocene?' in Ole W Pedersen (ed), *Perspectives on Environmental Law Scholarship: Essays on Purpose Shape and Direction* (Cambridge University Press 2018); Louis Kotzé (ed), *Environmental Law and Governance for the Anthropocene* (Hart Publishing 2017). For perspectives from the political sciences see eg Frank Biermann and Eva Lövbrand (eds), *Anthropocene Encounters: New Directions in Green Political Thinking* (Cambridge University Press 2019); Jedediah Purdy, *After Nature: A Politics for the Anthropocene* (Harvard University Press 2015). For a perspective from geography see eg Jamie Lorimer, 'Multinatural Geographies for the Anthropocene' (2012) *Progress in Human Geography* 593. For a historical perspective see eg Dipesh Chakrabarty, 'The Climate of History: Four Theses' (2009) *Critical Inquiry* 197. For a philosophical perspective see eg Bruno Latour, 'Agency at the Time of the Anthropocene' (2014) *New Literary History* 1.

[14] Adam Morton, 'Yes, Australia has always had bushfires: but 2019 is like nothing we've seen before' *The Guardian* (24 December 2019) online: <https://www.theguardian.com/australia-news/2019/dec/25/factcheck-why-australias-monster-2019-bushfires-are-unprecedented> accessed 28 May 2020.

[15] Herton Escobar, 'Brazil's Deforestation is Exploding – and 2020 will be worse' *Science* (22 November 2019) online: <https://www.sciencemag.org/news/2019/11/brazil-s-deforestation-exploding-and-2020-will-be-worse> accessed 28 May 2020.

[16] Heleen A. de Wit, Jean-Paul Hettelingh, Harry Harmens (eds), Trends in Ecosystem and Health Responses to Long-range Transported Atmospheric Pollutants (*Norwegian Institute for Water Research*, May 2016) 9; 'Indonesia Haze: Why Do Forests Keep Burning? *BBC News* (16 September 2019) online:

dimension. During the first six months of 2019 alone, an estimated total of seven million people had been internally displaced by floods, cyclones, droughts, landslides and earthquakes, making mass displacement due to extreme weather events 'the new norm'.[17] Indeed, the human imprint on Earth is now such that plastics are so abundant in land, freshwater and marine environments that they 'may be considered not only as environmental pollutants, but also as contributors to the character of recent … and contemporary strata … even in remote environments such as that of the deep sea floor and the polar regions'.[18] And the recent spread of COVID-19 across the globe has led commentators to argue that the unfolding pandemic signals that 'by going too far in exploiting the rest of nature, the dominant globalising culture has undone the planet's capacity to sustain life and livelihoods'.[19] It is against this background of planetary turbulence and human struggle that Holocene categories, such as 'global' and 'local', are insufficient to capture Anthropocene realities.[20] Rather a new dimension, the 'Terrestrial',[21] has entered the political—and as the collection of articles in this Special Issue will show, also the (transnational) legal—realm.

2. Transnational environmental law in the context of the Anthropocene

From its very beginnings, transnational law has engaged with the categories of 'global', 'local' and 'territory'—the very concepts which are challenged by Anthropocene realities. In his Storrs Lectures at Yale Law School in 1956, Jessup famously introduced the concept of 'transnational law' to 'include all law which regulates actions or events that transcend national frontiers. Both public and private international law are included, as are other rules that do not wholly fit into such standard categories'.[22] The burgeoning of literature regarding the 'transnational', as evident in the eleven years of *Transnational Legal Theory*, has among other things, encompassed new

---

<https://www.bbc.co.uk/news/world-asia-34265922> accessed 10 March 2020; 'Air Pollution in Southeast Asia Is the Main Cause for Respiratory Disease in Children' (*De Gruyter Science Discoveries*, 20 June 2019) online: <https://sciencediscoveries.degruyter.com/air-pollution-southeast-asia-main-cause-respiratory-disease-children/> accessed 10 March 2020.

[17] Internal Displacement Monitoring Centre, 'Mid-Year Figures: Internal Displacement from January to June 2019' (12 September 2019) online: <https://www.internal-displacement.org/sites/default/files/inline-files/2019-mid-year-figures_for%20website%20upload.pdf> accessed 11 February 2020.

[18] Jan Zalasiewicz et al, 'The Geological Cycle of Plastics and their use as a Stratigraphic Indicator of the Anthropocene' (2016) 13 *Anthropocene* 4, 14.

[19] Ashish Kothari et al, 'Coronavirus and the Crisis of the Anthropocene' (*Ecologist,* 27 March 2020) online: <https://theecologist.org/2020/mar/27/coronavirus-and-crisis-anthropocene> accessed 28 May 2020. For a critical perspective on the socio-economic implications of the Anthropocene see further for example Angela P Harris, 'The Treadmill and the Contract: A Classcrits Guide to the Anthropocene' (2016) 5(1) Tennessee Journal of Race, Gender & Social Justice 1.

[20] Bruno Latour, *Down to Earth: Politics in the New Climatic Regime* (Polity 2018) 40.

[21] *Ibid.*

[22] Philip C Jessup, *Transnational Law* (Yale University Press 1956) 2.

methodological and conceptual lenses with which to view the law,[23] has taken account of the breaking down of barriers between the public and the private,[24] and the national and the international,[25] the erosion of state sovereignty in the context of globalisation,[26] and the powerful impact non-state actors may have on the domestic sphere.[27]

Within environmental law, transnational lenses have been adopted 'through which to study and access a deeper understanding of the relationship between law and environmental protection',[28] particularly in the context of global environmental problems such as climate change and ocean degradation.[29] Concurrently, these global environmental problems—characterised by, among other things, their geographical scale—may be described as '"wicked" problems that [defy] resolution because of the enormous interdependencies, uncertainties, circularities, and conflicting stakeholders implicated by any effort to develop a solution'[30] and as such are 'legally disruptive' in nature,[31] thus posing significant challenges for the law.

Transnational environmental law, on one approach, incorporates international law, yet widens the inquiry to include 'all environmental norms that apply to transboundary activities or that have effects in more than one jurisdiction'.[32] Lin provides a more comprehensive definition of transnational environmental law in this account, that encompasses law 'beyond the state' and provides a theoretical framework with which to assess environmental law

---

23 eg see: Peer Zumbansen, 'Transnational Law, Evolving' in Jan M Smits (ed), *Elgar Encyclopaedia of Comparative Law* (2nd edn, Elgar 2012); Peer Zumbansen, 'Transnational Law' (Comparative Research in Law & Political Economy, Research Report No 9/2008) 24; Peer Zumbansen, 'Defining the Space of Transnational Law: Legal Theory, Global Governance, and Legal Pluralism' (2012) 21 *Transnational Law & Contemporary Problems* 305; Craig Scott, 'Transnational Law as a Proto-Concept: Three Conceptions' (2009) 10(6–7) *German Law Journal* 859; Gregory Shaffer and Daniel Bodansky, 'Transnationalism, Unilateralism and International Law' (2012) 1(1) *Transnational Environmental law* 31; Gregory Shaffer and Carlos Coye, 'From International Law to Jessup's Transnational Law, from Transnational Law to Transnational Legal Orders' in Peer Zumbansen (ed), *The Many Lives of Transnational Law: Critical Engagements With Jessup's Bold Proposal* (Cambridge University Press 2020).

24 eg see: Kenneth Abbott and Duncan Snidal, 'Strengthening International Regulation Through Transnational New Governance: Overcoming the Orchestration Deficit' (2009) 42(2) *Vanderbilt Journal of Transnational Law* 501; Harriet Bulkeley and others, *Transnational Climate Change Governance* (Cambridge University Press 2014); Zumbansen, 'Transnational Law, Evolving', (n 23). In the context of environmental law see: Peter H Sand, 'The Evolution of Transnational Environmental Law: Four Cases in Historical Perspective (2012) 1(1) *Transnational Environmental Law* 183.

25 Veerle Heyvaert and Leslie-Anne Duvic-Paoli, 'The Meanings of Transnational Environmental Law' in Veerle Heyvaert and Leslie-Anne Duvic-Paoli (eds) *Research Handbook on Transnational Environmental Law* (Edward Elgar forthcoming).

26 eg see: Shaffer and Bodansky, (n 23); Zumbansen, 'Transnational Law, Evolving', (n 23).

27 Gregory Shaffer, 'Transnational Legal Process and State Change' (2012) 32(2) *Law & Social Inquiry* 229.

28 Heyvaert and Duvic-Paoli, (n 25); see generally: Veerle Heyvaert and Leslie-Anne Duvic Paoli (eds) *Research Handbook on Transnational Environmental Law* (Edward Elgar forthcoming).

29 Veerle Heyvaert, 'The Transnationalization of Law: Rethinking Law through Transnational Environmental Regulation' (2017) 6(2) *Transnational Environmental Law* 205, 206–7.

30 Richard Lazarus, 'Super Wicked Problems and Climate Change: Restraining the Present to Liberate the Future' (2010) 40 *Environmental Law and Policy Annual Review* 10749, 107050.

31 Elizabeth Fisher, Eloise Scotford and Emily Barritt, 'The Legally Disruptive Nature of Climate Change' (2017) 80(2) *Modern Law Review* 173.

32 Shaffer and Bodansky, (n 23) 32.

and governance. Transnational environmental law, she argues 'recognises that the state is but one of the many actors that ought to be involved in governing human actions *vis-à-vis* the environment. It also recognises the important normative contributions made by non-state actors'.[33] This transnational lens or 'frame' through which to view legal responses to increasingly urgent environmental problems[34] is a useful mechanism with which to ground the search 'for more effective responses to the environmental calamities that threaten the wellbeing and even the survival of present and future generations'.[35]

The study of transnational law has resulted in the emergence of widely differing conceptual and definitional approaches, that within transnational environmental law has left much unsettled.[36] This is evident, for instance, in terms of its understanding and use of the term 'transnational', by its sometime focus on the role of private or subnational actors within the governance of specific issues,[37] and at others the emergence of transnational regulation 'beyond the state',[38] or even the interactions between transnational legal norms and national and international law.[39] As Fisher noted in 2012, transnational environmental law scholarship is in its infancy, there is the need—and as the last decade has proven the appetite for—mapping the field, and attempting to understand the emergence of transnational environmental law and regulation.[40] All this is to say that the divergence of opinions regarding what transnational environmental law consists of and how it should be researched, is a product not merely of the complexity associated with global environmental problems of great scale and the proliferation of actors and norms that have emerged to address them, but also of its more recent emergence as a line of scholarly inquiry[41] which may be exacerbated by the

33 Jolene Lin, 'The Emergence of Transnational Environmental Law' in Louis Kotzé (ed) *Environmental Law and Governance for the Anthropocene* (Hart 2017) 331.
34 Cinnamon Carlarne and Daniel Farber, 'Law Beyond Borders: Transnational Responses to Global Environmental Issues' (2012) 1(1) *Transnational Environmental Law* 13, 14; see also: Natasha Affolder, 'An Unknown Past, an Unequal Present, and an Uncertain Future: Transnational Environmental Law Through Three Research Challenges' in in Veerle Heyvaert and Leslie-Anne Duvic Paoli (eds) *Research Handbook on Transnational Environmental Law* (Edward Elgar forthcoming).
35 Heyvaert and Duvic-Paoli, (n 25).
36 *Ibid.*
37 Eg see: Lin, (n 33).
38 Heyvaert, (n 29) 206; Veerle Hayvaert, *Transnational Environmental Regulation and Governance: Purpose, Strategies and Principles* (Cambridge University Press, 2018).
39 Eg: Olaf Dilling and Till Markus, 'The Transnationalisation of Environmental Law' (2018) 30 *Journal of Environmental Law* 179; Shaffer and Bodansky (n23); For specific examples: of the diffusion of norms though contracts see; Natasha Affolder, 'Contagious Environmental Lawmaking' (2019) 31 *Journal of Environmental Law* 187; and in the context of climate risk disclosure requirements for companies see: Emily Webster, Information Disclosure and the Transition to a Low-Carbon Economy: Climate-Related Risk in the UK and France' (2019) *Journal of Environmental Law* 1; for calls for a the global constitutionalising of international environmental law see: Louis Kotzé, 'A Global Environmental Constitution for the Anthropocene?' (2019) 8(1) *Transnational Environmental Law* 11.
40 Elizabeth Fisher, 'The Rise of Transnational Environmental Law and the Expertise of Lawyers' (2012) 1(1) *Transnational Environmental Law* 43, 45–48.
41 *Ibid.*

perceived methodological 'immaturity' of environmental law scholarship itself.[42]

Taking a transnational perspective provides a diverse array of 'tools and approaches to address environmental challenges'[43] and provides 'a broader and more inclusive' view of law and how it may address environmental problems than international law alone.[44] Thus, transnational environmental law may provide a useful lens through which to assess the role of law and its capacity to address humanity's impact upon the Earth in this new planetary epoch.[45] Indeed, the Anthropocene provides not merely a new context within which to consider transnational environmental law and its response to these new conditions,[46] but a host of conceptual and theoretical approaches within which to ground these analyses.[47]

Even without the Anthropocene as a conceptual hook, transnational environmental law is a fantastically diverse and growing area as scholars grapple with the proliferation of actors involved in both causing and addressing environmental problems and, for example, the evidence of polycentric or multi-levelled governance of environmental problems.[48] Nevertheless, by linking transnational environmental law with the Anthropocene imagery, this Special Issue invites reflection on the meaning and role of law—and transnational legal scholarship—in light of changing planetary realities.

3. Contributions in this special issue

The impact of humanity's large-scale interference with the planet, and the emergence of potentially catastrophic global environmental problems such as climate change, has profoundly shaped transnational environmental law. Yet, as the contributions to this Special Issue demonstrate, the interactions between transnational law and the concept of the Anthropocene go beyond

[42] Elizabeth Fisher, Bettina Lange, Eloise Scotford and Cinnamon Carlarne, 'Maturity and Methodology: Starting a Debate about Environmental Law Scholarship' (2009) 21(2) *Journal of Environmental Law* 213.

[43] Thijs Etty, Veerle Heyveart et al, 'The maturing of Transnational Environmental Law' (2017) 6(2) *Transnational Environmental Law* 193, 194.

[44] Cinnamon Carlarne, 'Delinking International Environmental Law & Climate Change' (2014) 4(1) *Michigan Journal of Environmental & Administrative Law* 1, 26.

[45] Lin, (n 33) 337.

[46] Kotzé (ed), (n 13) viii.

[47] For example, Earth System Governance, see eg: Frank Biermann, *Earth System Governance: World Politics in the Anthropocene* (MIT Press 2014); 'Earth System Governance' online: <https://www.earthsystemgovernance.org/> the Planetary Boundaries, see eg: Will Steffen et al, 'Planetary boundaries: Guiding human development on a changing planet' (2015) 347(6223) *Science* 1259855; Duncan French and Louis Kotzé (eds) *Law, Governance and Planetary Boundaries* (Edward Elgar forthcoming); Earth Jurisprudence, see eg: Peter Burdon (ed), *Exploring Wild Law: The Philosophy of Earth Jurisprudence* (Wakefield Press 2011); for Ecological Law, see eg: Fritjof Capra and Ugo Mattei, *The Ecology of Law: Toward a Legal System in Tune with Nature and Community* (Berrett-Koehler 2015).

[48] Eg see: Kotzé, (n 13); Fisher, (n 40). For responses to climate change see eg: Jacqueline Peel, Lee Godden and Rodney J Keenan, 'Climate Change Law in an Era of Multi-Level Governance' (2012) 1(2) *Transnational Environmental law* 245; Elinor Ostrom, 'A Polycentric Approach for Coping with Climate Change' [2009] The World Bank Policy Research Working Paper 5095.

a law and governance response to humanity's status as biogeological agents, to consider the theoretical and practical implications that this may have for transnational environmental law itself.

The Special Issue opens with a thought-provoking opinion piece by Jorge Viñuales. Viñuales in 'Two Layers of Self-Regulation'[49] identifies two narratives of regulation: human self-regulation and biospheric self-regulation—that is the regulation of the biosphere—and calls for their alignment. Drawing on the history of scholarship concerning these two forms of self-regulation, he addresses the evident disconnect between humans and nature within the narrative of human self-regulation. This he argues, is demonstrated by the erroneous belief of 'human independence from natural conditions'[50] and goes on to show the fallacy of this belief through charting the identification of human dependence on and disruption of, the natural world. Viñuales labels human self-regulation as 'rebellious self-regulation', that is the mechanisms by which humans instigated the industrial revolution thereby accelerating our impact upon the planet. He asks us to question the ways in which this form of regulation is viewed and closes with a warning:

> [w]e may not even realise how rebellious and unsettling our self-regulation is, in its unintended effects, with respect to the wider and deeper self-regulation performed by life on biogeochemical cycles. Dramatically, whether we realise it or not, our rebellion cannot succeed; it would be a secession to nowhere.[51]

Theoretical approaches that adopt an ecological, or multi-disciplinary perspective reconsider how we conceive of, and use law to protect the environment. Five theoretical approaches are adopted within this issue: Peter Burdon addresses ecological law; Klaus Bosselmann Earth Trusteeship, Afshin Akhtar-Khavari takes a socio-ecological approach, Louis Kotzé considers law from an Earth System perspective and finally, Laura Mai rethinks transnational law in the context of the Anthropocene.

Burdon, in 'Ecological Law in the Anthropocene', considers the challenges posed by the Anthropocene paradigm.[52] Burdon argues that rather than constructing a non-anthropocentric ethics, ecological law scholarship should embrace the centrality of human agency in the new geological epoch. The key question for Burdon thus becomes how this agency can be enacted and used with 'humility and responsibility'.[53] Burdon argues that acknowledging the centrality of human agency in the Anthropocene implies that concepts which have been central to ecological scholarship, such as those of ecological integrity and wilderness ethics, can no longer provide accurate frames for

---

[49] Jorge Viñuales, 'Two Layers of Self-Regulation' (2020) 11(1-2) *Transnational Legal Theory*, this issue.
[50] *Ibid*, 13.
[51] *Ibid*, 17.
[52] Peter Burdon, 'Ecological Law in the Anthropocene' (2020) 11(1-2) *Transnational Legal Theory*, this issue.
[53] *Ibid*.

thinking about ecological degradation or planetary reality. Recalling the innovative and critical potential of ecological law scholarship, Burdon calls for 'fresh thinking' and 'a willingness to grapple with uncertainty'.[54]

Bosselmann, in his article 'Environmental Trusteeship and State Sovereignty: Can they be Reconciled?',[55] explores how the concept of 'Earth trusteeship' interacts with the Westphalian paradigm of state sovereignty, including related notions of territoriality and legal ownership of the Earth. Noting inherent inconsistencies, he turns to the concept of fiduciary duties—owed by governments to their citizens—to develop an alternative 'Earth-centred' account of sovereignty under which 'states not only have traditional rights of self-determination and non-intervention but also responsibilities for human rights and the Earth'.[56] Under this new paradigm planetary well-being, rather than the principle of economic growth, would guide both domestic and international environmental protection.

Akhtar-Khavari, in his contribution 'Restoration and Cooperation for Flourishing Socio-ecological Landscapes',[57] draws on the concept of symbiosis to outline a novel cooperative restoration paradigm for environmental law. At the heart of this new paradigm lie cooperative interactions between the human and the more-than-human world, thus implying an ontological shift from the current focus on competition among humans. Akhtar-Khavri argues that this shift prompts environmental law to move from using 'technical measures to fix problems' to creating social institutions that facilitate 'human inputs into the natural environment'.[58] A cooperative approach would benefit both the human and the more-than-human world, creating 'flourishing socio-ecological landscapes'.[59]

Kotzé, in 'Earth System Law for the Anthropocene: Rethinking Environmental Law Along the Earth System Metaphor', reflects on the image of the Earth system and its role in constructing a new paradigm for environmental law in the Anthropocene: Earth System Law.[60] Tracing the development of the Earth system imaginary, Kotzé argues that it provides an epistemic framework for multi-disciplinary research efforts that focus on the planetary scale and take account of the complex interactions between humans and non-humans across multiple levels of organisation. Noting that 'environmental law and environmental lawyers have not yet meaningfully embraced the Earth

54 *Ibid.*
55 Klaus Bosselmann, 'Environmental Trusteeship and State sovereignty: How can they be reconciled' (2020) 11(1-2) *Transnational Legal Theory*, this issue.
56 *Ibid*, 15.
57 Afshin Akhtar-Khavari, 'Restoration and Cooperation for Flourishing Socio-Ecological Landscapes' (2020) 11(1-2) *Transnational Legal Theory*, this issue.
58 *Ibid.*
59 *Ibid.*
60 Louis J Kotzé, 'Earth System Law for the Anthropocene: Rethinking Environmental Law Along the Earth System Metaphor' (2020) 11(1-2) *Transnational Legal Theory*, this issue.

system metaphor',[61] he suggests that taking seriously the Earth system imaginary challenges environmental law scholarship to work in more interdisciplinary manner, to reorganise around systems thinking, acknowledge the adaptive capacities of the Earth system, and navigate ontological shifts to recognise that human and non-human vulnerabilities are connected.

Finally, Mai, in '(Transnational) Law for the Anthropocene: Revisiting Jessup's Move from "What?" to "How?"',[62] argues that legal researchers and practitioners are now tasked to understand how transnational law can be mobilised to navigate Anthropocene realities. Combining perspectives from ecology, sociology and the humanities, Mai identifies the demands which the Anthropocene places on legal thinking. These include changes in spatio-temporal dynamics, emerging new forms of agency and subjectivity as well as the need for law to revisit its normative foundations. She argues that adopting Jessup's practical, progressive and pragmatic perspective is a productive starting point for legal thinking and practice to 'de-familiarise' itself from Holocene orthodoxies and develop new legal forms, strategies and technologies that can help navigate Anthropocene realities.

The issue then moves to an analysis of law directed at specific global environmental problems; namely climate change, marine degradation, and global waste. Taking a broad approach to climate litigation, Phillip Paiement, in his article 'Urgent Agenda: How Climate Litigation Builds Transnational Narratives',[63] identifies common storylines which describe the temporal dimension of climate change and its governance using three climate litigation cases from the Netherlands, Norway, and Ireland as case studies. Paiement finds that the narratives of litigants differ from those of governments. While litigants use linguistic tools to produce a notion of urgency, states describe futures in which technological innovation and economic development alleviate the challenges and costs of the climate crisis. Reaching beyond the traditional legal methodological toolkit, Paiement is able to uncover how competing storylines employed in transnational legal strategies are shaping understandings of climate responsibility and justice.

In 'Litigation and Regulatory Governance in the Age of the Anthropocene: The Case of Fracking in the Karoo',[64] Melanie Murcott and Emily Webster focus in on the role of transnational actors in the contested space of fracking in the ecological sensitive region of the Karoo in South Africa, in which private actors engage in litigation in an attempt to prevent fracking activity in this area. Murcott and Webster identify and assess the constellation of

[61] *Ibid.*
[62] Laura Mai, '(Transnational) Law for the Anthropocene: Revisiting Jessup's Move from 'What?' to 'How?'' (2020) 11(1-2) *Transnational Legal Theory*, this issue.
[63] Phillip Paiement, 'Urgent Agenda: How climate litigation builds transnational narratives' (2020)11(1-2) *Transnational Legal Theory*, this issue.
[64] Melanie Murcott and Emily Webster, 'Litigation and regulatory governance in the age of the Anthropocene: The case of fracking in the Karoo' (2020) 11(1-2) *Transnational Legal Theory*, this issue.

actors involved in what appears to be a purely domestic matter, including the government and transnational fossil fuels promoting fracking on the one hand, and various non-state actors, such as civil society, domestic business as well as the global anti-fracking movement, opposing fracking on the other. They argue that the role and power of the state to regulate fracking activity is significantly impacted by private actors, including by refocusing the minds of transnational corporations and the state on the centrality of public participation, by challenging regulations introduced to govern fracking, and, ultimately, through delaying the operationalisation of fracking, thereby decreasingly its attractiveness to transnational fossil fuel companies.

Moving to marine governance, Emily Barritt in 'The Myth of Mermaids and Stewardship of the Seas'[65] adopts the mythological concept of mermaids to analyse the governance of marine biodiversity beyond national jurisdiction. She does so to prompt us to 'expand our imaginative capacities' and to provide a resource through which to re-examine 'our relationship with the oceans'.[66] Barritt argues that the current regime is fragmented and perceives of ocean ecosystems in a way that does not take into account their ecological complexities. Despite on-going negotiations for a new agreement to govern biodiversity beyond national jurisdictions, she fears that there is little appetite for the reforms needed to adequately address the pressures on ocean ecosystems. In her intervention, she hopes to

> retune and embellish the narrative of ocean space that is told by international law … By appealing to the seductive powers of the mermaids, I hope that some of these warnings might be heard. That, unlike Odysseus' crew, those with the power to effect these changes will not stuff their ears with wax but will pay attention and respond to the song of the sirens.[67]

Staying with marine governance, Pierre Cloutier de Repentigny in 'To the Anthropocene and Beyond: The Responsibility of Law in Decimating and Protecting Marine Life'[68] uses the concept of the Anthropocene to critique the current narrative underpinning the law of the seas; namely economic growth. He demonstrates, through a review of the history of the law of the seas, that the law, rather than being passive, has actively contributed towards the emergence of the Anthropocene. Instead, he argues, there should be a focus on human responsibility towards the marine environment, in a way that recognises humanity's status as geological agents. In this way law would be reformed in this area to incorporate our 'anthropocenic

[65] Emily Barritt, 'The Myth of Mermaids and Stewardship of the Seas' 11(1-2) *Transnational Legal Theory*, this issue.
[66] *Ibid.*
[67] *Ibid.*
[68] Pierre Cloutier de Repentigny, 'To the Anthropocene and Beyond: The Responsibility of Law in Decimating and Protecting Marine Life' (2020) 11(1-2) *Transnational Legal Theory*, this issue.

responsibility'. He concludes, that '[l]aw can and should be used to that end; that is, to impose a framework on our agency that is reflective of our destructive capacity and of the needs of the biosphere'.[69]

The Special Issue ends with a focus on transnational waste. Michael Hennessy Picard and Tina Beigi in 'Regimes of Waste (Im)perceptibility in the Life Cycle of Metal'[70] interrogate the transnational governance of waste and its dominant focus on economic recovery. They argue that within the concept of the circular economy much of waste is imperceptible, thereby limiting the ways in which law may be deployed to govern it. Adopting Latour's binary of 'matters of concern' (the materiality of waste) and 'matters of fact' (legal measures designed to govern waste) they assess the current transnational governance of waste and the visible and invisible life of waste and seek to call 'attention to the blind spots created by the legal categories of mining and electronic waste'.[71] They end by suggesting that reform of the existing 'transnational legal structure' of waste governance based upon ecological law, may be required to move away from the dominant market-based approach that currently prevails.

4. Environmental law and the Anthropocene: an outlook

The emergence of COVID-19 and the global disaster that it has wrought, has exposed the complexities and challenges that have long haunted responses to collective global environmental problems in the context of a global health emergency. During this period the environment initially experienced a decrease in its usual pressures. Emissions of greenhouse gases have reduced significantly in response to the ceasing of everyday life that has accompanied domestic responses to infection control.[72] This has also been accompanied by a reduction in air pollution and consequential health benefits.[73] Indeed, preliminary research has shown a potential link between air pollution and high risk of mortality from the COVID-19 disease, thereby increasing awareness of the significant impacts of air pollution on human health.[74] However, the reduction of air pollutants may have a consequential impact on global temperatures as concentrations of certain anthropogenic aerosols that have a net

[69] *Ibid.*
[70] Michael Hennessy Picard and Tina Beigi, 'Regimes of waste (im)perceptibility in the life cycle of metal' (2020) 11(1-2) *Transnational Legal Theory*, this issue.
[71] *Ibid.*
[72] Corinne Le Quéré et al, 'Temporary reduction in daily global CO2 emissions during the COVID-19 forced confinement' (2020) *Nature Climate Change* online: <https://doi.org/10.1038/s41558-020-0797-x>.
[73] Kai Chen et al, 'Air pollution reduction and mortality benefit during the COVID-19 outbreak in China' *The Lancet* (2020) online: <https://doi.org/10.1016/S2542-5196(20)30107-8>.
[74] Simon Brandon, 'The link between air pollution and COVID-19 deaths' (*World Economic Forum*, 29 April 2020) online: <https://www.weforum.org/agenda/2020/04/link-between-air-pollution-covid-19-deaths-coronavirus-pandemic/>.

cooling effect, are reduced,[75] while long-lived greenhouse gases, such as carbon dioxide, remain in the atmosphere.

While there have been short-term environmental gains in the reduction of pollution, problems such as the disposal of single-use plastic have been exacerbated in the efforts to protect those tasked with caring for the sick and dying and carrying out essential services.[76] This additionally emphasises the importance of plastics in modern life, yet this sector is also supported by the oil and gas sector as the dominant feedstock for plastics production.[77] The immense challenges associated with governing the Anthropocene have been aptly demonstrated in the emergence of this pandemic.[78] Furthermore, it has brought to the fore the implications for humans of our large-scale intervention in the environment; and has raised questions regarding how human encroachment and destruction of the natural world may result in more instances of virus transmission from animals to humans and therefore increased incidences of future disease.[79]

The climate crisis looms large in the background to this current disaster. The need to address climate change and the Paris Agreement's temperature targets,[80] has led, in some quarters, towards linking economic recovery from the pandemic with environmental goals. For instance, the EU's recovery package will include the commitment to reach net zero greenhouse gas

---

[75] Olivier Boucher et al, 'Clouds and Aerosols' in Thomas F Stocker et al (eds), *Climate Change 2013: The Physical Science Basis. Contribution of Working Group I to the Fifth Assessment Report of the Intergovernmental Panel on Climate Change* (Cambridge University Press 2013).

[76] For a discussion of the interactions between the pandemic and international law see: Leslie-Anne Duvic-Paoli, 'COVID-19 Symposium: The COVID-19 Pandemic and the Limits of International Environmental Law' (*OpinioJuris,* 30 March 2020) online: <http://opiniojuris.org/2020/03/30/covid-19-symposium-the-covid-19-pandemic-and-the-limits-of-international-environmental-law/>.

[77] Renee Cho, 'More Plastic is On the Way: What It Means for Climate Change' (*State of the Planet Earth Institute, Columbia University*, 20 February 2020).

[78] Anjay Gambhir, 'Coronavirus and climate change: "There is much uncertainty, and much to play for"' (*Grantham Institute*, 17 March 2020) online: <https://granthaminstitute.com/2020/03/17/coronavirus-and-climate-change-there-is-much-uncertainty-and-much-to-play-for/>; Laurie Goering, 'What COVID-19 can teach us about tackling climate change' (*World Economic Forum*, 15 May 2020) online: <https://www.weforum.org/agenda/2020/05/covid-19-apply-battling-climate-change/>; Kimberly Cartier, 'Eight Lessons from COVID-19 to Guide Our Climate Response' (*EOS, 101*, 24 April 2020) online: <https://eos.org/articles/eight-lessons-from-covid-19-to-guide-our-climate-response>; Matthew Hoffmann et al, 'COVID-19 recovery is a chance to build a greener, more inclusive soceity' (*First Policy Response*, 1 June 2020) online: <http://policyresponse.ca/covid-19-recovery-is-chance-to-build-greener-more-inclusive-society/>.

[79] Eg see: Josef Settele et al, 'IPBES Guest Article: COVID-19 Stimulus Measures Must Save Lives, Protect Livelihoods, and Safeguard Nature to Reduce the Risk of Future Pandemics'(*IPBES*, 27 April 2020) online: <https://ipbes.net/covid19stimulus> The Intergovernmental Science-Policy Platform on Biodiversity and Ecosystem Services is currently undertaking research regarding the link between biodiversity loss and pandemics ('IPBES workshop on biodiversity and pandemics' (*IPBES*, 2020) online: <https://ipbes.net/node/37055>, and it is reported that the Intergovernmental Panel on Climate Change is also considering the links between climate change and pandemics within the confines of its next assessment report in 2021, Alister Doyle, 'Next UN climate science report to consider lessons from coronavirus' (*Climate Home News*, 24 April 2020) online: <https://www.climatechangenews.com/2020/04/23/next-un-climate-science-report-consider-pandemic-risk/>.

[80] Paris Agreement (adopted 12 December 2015, entered into force 4 November 2016) FCCC/CP/2015/10/Add 1 Article 2.1(a).

emissions.[81] Some states have also considered attaching climate conditions to economic bailouts of domestic aviation companies, although many have baulked at this step.[82] For others the recovery from inevitable economic crisis may provide ample justification to further entrench fossil fuel dependency and put off the transition to a low-carbon economy. For instance, in the USA the pandemic has been used to justify relaxing environmental regulations,[83] and in Brazil the Environment Minister suggested in a Ministerial Meeting that the pandemic be used as a distraction to pursue an environmental deregulation agenda.[84]

2020 is a pivotal year for the Paris Agreement, with the agreement formally coming into effect and a hoped-for increase in ambition at COP 26.[85] Yet, international meetings, such as COP 26 and the Convention on Biological Diversity's COP 15 have been postponed, thereby effectively pausing the work of these bodies, potentially undermining attempts to progress on these important issues.[86] Additionally, the economic outfall of the COVID-19 pandemic is yet to fully materialise. Its full impact upon efforts to govern global environmental problems, such as climate change, is likely only to be revealed over the coming months and years.[87]

As demonstrated aptly by the articles in this Special Issue, transnational environmental law scholarship contextualised and drawing on the insights of the Anthropocene, is well placed to grapple with the global environmental challenges that have emerged as a result of human intervention within the planetary system. Research and analyses of law and governance approaches that attempt to reconceptualise our place in the world, to ensure that law not merely serves humans but nature as well, and that critically engage with the

---

[81] 'Covid-19: the EU plan for the economic recovery' (*News European Parliament*, 18 May 2020) online: <https://www.europarl.europa.eu/news/en/headlines/economy/20200513STO79012/covid-19-the-eu-plan-for-the-economic-recovery>.

[82] Sam Morgan, 'Austrian Airlines bailout to be linked to climate targets' (*Euractiv*, 17 April 2020) online: <https://www.euractiv.com/section/aviation/news/austrian-airlines-bailout-to-be-linked-to-climate-targets/>; Sandra Laville, 'Coronavirus: airlines seek €12.8bn in bailouts without environmental conditions attached' *The Guardian* (22 April 2020).

[83] Emily Holden, 'Trump dismantles environmental protections under cover of coronavirus' *The Guardian* (11 May 2020) online: <https://www.theguardian.com/us-news/2020/may/10/trump-environmental-blitzkrieg-coronavirus>.

[84] Jake Spring, 'Brazil minister calls for environmental deregulation while public distracted by COVID' *Reuters* (22 May 2020) online: <https://uk.reuters.com/article/us-brazil-politics-environment/brazil-minister-calls-for-environmental-deregulation-while-public-distracted-by-covid-idUKKBN22Y30Y>.

[85] 'Secretary-General's Briefing to Member States on the 26th Session of the Conference of the Parties (COP26) [as delivered]' (*United Nations Secretary-General*, 6 March 2020) online: <https://www.un.org/sg/en/content/sg/statement/2020-03-06/secretary-generals-briefing-member-states-the-26th-session-of-the-conference-of-the-parties-(cop26)-delivered>.

[86] Chloé Farand, 'Coronavirus delays global efforts for climate and biodiversity action' (*Climate Home News*, 10 March 2020) online: <https://www.climatechangenews.com/2020/03/10/coronavirus-delays-global-efforts-climate-biodiversity-action/>.

[87] Gita Gopinath, 'The Great Lockdown: Worst Economic Downturn Since the Great Depression' (*IMF*, 14 April 2020) online: <https://blogs.imf.org/2020/04/14/the-great-lockdown-worst-economic-downturn-since-the-great-depression/>.

law as it stands and posits what it ought to be, are essential. Although it is in its early stages, transnational environmental law provides a framework for research that contributes to this endeavour. The articles in this Special Issue lay out a range of possible conceptual and methodological tools and perspectives to continue this path of exploration.

Acknowledgements

We would like to thank all the contributors to this Special Issue. Particular thanks go to Phillip Paiement for his invaluable and generous support in producing this Special Issue.

Disclosure statement

No potential conflict of interest was reported by the author(s).

ORCID

Emily Webster http://orcid.org/0000-0003-1360-6071
Laura Mai http://orcid.org/0000-0001-8975-1078

Two layers of self-regulation

J. E. Viñuales

ABSTRACT
Human self-regulation, however conceived, is but a small part of a bigger whole. But that part is becoming more disruptive of the broader self-regulatory system of the biosphere, the Earth system. The purpose of this essay is to connect two narratives. One concerning biospheric self-regulation, which has been formulated in increasing detail, and the other concerning human self-regulation, which remains inchoate and scattered. The starting point of the analysis is the curious fact that, whereas in the past most accounts of the world embedded humans within nature, even if the overall impact of humans on natural cycles was limited, in the last two centuries, the prevailing accounts have assumed or postulated a disconnection between human and natural history, despite the fact that the empirical connection has become inescapable. In this context, this essay first characterises the conceptual disconnection and the empirical connection between human action and geological processes, and then revisits, in this light, the link between biospheric self-regulation and human self-regulation, paying attention to the role of the social practices we call law.

1. Connecting narratives

Human self-regulation, however conceived, is but a small part of a bigger whole. But that part is becoming more disruptive of the broader self-regulatory system of the biosphere, the Earth system. This is an important reason why the social construct that we call law can no longer be understood in the way it is learnt, transmitted and practised today. The link between these two layers of self-regulation was represented in the past in myriad forms, from the diverse expressions of aboriginal law, to the Greek *logos*, to the Western and Eastern traditions of the natural order. The foundations of such representations, however, did not reflect the very concrete and empirical reason that today requires a conceptual representation of the link. This reason is that humans – or, to be fair, some humans and human practices – have become a disruptive force of geological proportions, particularly since the mid-twentieth century.

Most representations of the world from the past embedded humans in it, although the actual impact of human practices was negligible. Over the twentieth century, however, something fundamentally changed. 'Something new under the sun', to borrow the expression of an influential environmental history of the twentieth century, took form[1]; a 'great acceleration', to borrow the words of another influential account,[2] turned human action into a force of geological proportions capable of modifying, both to its advantage and disadvantage, not merely the natural landscape but the very biogeochemical processes on which the biosphere relies. What is odd is that the representations of the world prevailing during this period of transformation separate human history from the natural world. The two are seen as unfolding in different strata, with nature essentially understood as an immutable theatre where human history unfolds as well as a resource to be exploited. To put it in blunt terms: the link was over-represented when it was tenuous and, now that it has become inescapable, it is under- and mis-represented.

In this context, the main purpose of this essay is to connect two narratives. One concerning the impact of living organisms on biogeochemical processes, which has been formulated in increasing detail, both conceptually and empirically. The other concerns human self-regulation, and it remains inchoate and scattered. There are broad accounts, but they differ too widely in focus and scope, ranging from discussions of certain historical processes (such as the rise of agricultural practices at the dawn of the Holocene,[3] the industrial revolution in the late eighteenth century,[4] or the 'great acceleration' after 1945[5]), to specific world-views (eg the influence of Protestant ethic on the rise of capitalism[6] or of Christian beliefs on the domination of nature[7]), to more conceptual accounts of human dynamics at an aggregate level (eg the analysis of 'world systems',[8] ecologically unequal

---

[1] John R McNeill, *Something New Under the Sun : An Environmental History of the Twentieth-Century World* (Norton, 2000).

[2] Will Steffen, Wendy Broadgate, Lisa Deutsch, Owen Gaffney, Cornelia Ludwig, 'The Trajectory of the Anthropocene: The Great Acceleration' (2015) 2 *The Anthropocene Review* 81 [Steffen, *The Great Acceleration*].

[3] Graeme Barker, *The Agricultural Revolution in Prehistory* (Oxford University Press, 2006).

[4] See, among many others, David S Landes, *The Unbound Prometheus. Technological Change and Industrial Development in Western Europe from 1750 to the Present* (Cambridge University Press, 2nd edn 2003 [1969]); Kenneth Pomeranz, *The Great Divergence: China, Europe and the Making of the Modern World Economy* (Princeton University Press, 2000) [Pomeranz, *The Great Divergence*].

[5] Steffen, *The Great Acceleration* (n 2).

[6] Max Weber, *Die protestantische Ethik und der Geist des Kapitalismus* (Mohr, 1934). The study was originally published in two volumes – 20 (1904) and 21 (1905) – of the *Archiv für Sozialwissenschaft und Sozialpolitik*. English translation: *The Protestant Ethic and the Spirit of Capitalism*, trans. by Talcott Parsons (Charles Scribners' sons, 1930).

[7] Lynn White Jr, 'The historical roots of our ecological crisis' (1967) 155/3767 *Science* 1203.

[8] Immanuel Wallerstein, *The Modern World-System, vol. I: Capitalist Agriculture and the Origins of the European World-Economy in the Sixteenth Century* (Academic Press, 1974); *The Modern World-System, vol. II: Mercantilism and the Consolidation of the European World-Economy, 1600–1750* (Academic Press, 1980);

exchanges,[9] integrated assessment models representing human and natural processes[10]). In these accounts, law plays an explicit or implicit role, which I will flesh out in some of them as relevant for the understanding of the broader category of 'human self-regulation'. This is a condition for connecting the two narratives. Human self-regulation has never been as fundamental for the broader biogeochemical processes that regulate the biosphere as it is today. If we call 'law' the conscious or unconscious observance of certain prescriptions of conduct, then, law has never been as fundamental for the Earth system as it is today.

The scope of this brief essay can be described both by what it intends to achieve and by what it explicitly seeks to exclude. The latter first: this essay is not an argument in favour of re-naturalising law, either by reference to past doctrines of the natural order, traditional legal orders or even a new 'natural law' that would genuinely reflect the insertion of human activity in the dynamics of the Earth system. The empirical connection between human activities and global environmental change must be understood as a factual connection from which analytical – not prescriptive – consequences are derived. Prescriptive consequences could also be derived, but they would require an additional normative justification. Nor is this essay an attempt to demonstrate 'causality', whether simple and direct or complex and indirect, between the prevailing form of human self-regulation, ie the laws that organise a world structured around sovereign States and global economic exchanges, and the disruption in biospheric self-regulation. The two exclusions are linked. The two 'layers' of self-regulation are concepts (objects of conception) rather than percepts (objects of perception). Although both global environmental change and social organisation can be empirically observed, this is only possible through complex conceptual aggregations, such as 'biospheric self-regulation' and 'human self-regulation'. In turn, such aggregations entail unspelt normative choices (eg matters of framing, such as speaking of 'humans' rather than of 'some humans' or speaking of 'global environmental change' or 'biogeochemical processes' rather than of more specific phenomena) and so does any attempt at establishing a form of causality, which is also a normative choice. These two exclusions exclude much ground from this essay, but not the core point, which is the connection between the two narratives.

The Modern World-System, vol. III: The Second Great Expansion of the Capitalist World-Economy, 1730–1840's (Academic Press, 1989).

[9] Alf Hornborg, *Global Ecology and Unequal Exchange. Fetishism in a Zero-Sum World* (Routledge, 2013); Alf Hornborg, 'Ecological Economics, Marxism, and Technological Progress: Some Explorations of the Conceptual Foundations of Theories of Ecological Unequal Exchange' (2014) 105 *Ecological Economics* 11; John Bellamy Foster and Hannah Holleman, 'The Theory of Unequal Ecological Exchange: A Marx-Odum Dialectic' (2014) 41 *Journal of Peasant Studies* 199.

[10] See eg: John Weyant, 'Some Contributions of Integrated Assessment Models of Global Climate Change' (2017) 11 *Review of Environmental Economics and Policy* 115.

With these clarifications, this essay will first characterise the conceptual disconnection and the empirical connection between human action and geological processes, and then revisit, in this light, the link between Earth system self-regulation and human self-regulation, paying attention to the role of the social practices we call law.

2. Two separate strata?

As noted in the introduction, in most accounts of the world – 'metaphysical' accounts, to use a comfortable Western shortcut – a link between the human and the natural world was made. Yet, empirically, the actual imprint of humans on the natural world was minor; the link was tenuous. This is not to say that human practices did not lead to vast impacts on landscape or the environment. It means, more specifically, that such practices did not fundamentally affect the operation of the broad biogeochemical processes by which the geological 'epoch' in which humanity has thrived for the last 11,700 years – the Holocene – is characterised. These are differences of scale, akin to that between 'weather' and the 'climate system' or between 'air pollution' and 'atmospheric chemistry'.

Ironically, it is mainly at the time such 'disconnection' started to be formulated or assumed[11] that the seeds for a genuine empirical re-union were sowed. Illustrations of how the disconnection came to be conceptualised can be found in different fields of knowledge. For example, the eminent geologist Charles Llyell, who made a decisive contribution to the realisation of human pre-history,[12] wrote in his influential *Principles of Geology* that, although an 'intelligent being' observing humans may at first gather the impression that they can change nature, on closer scrutiny:

> he would soon perceive that *no one of the fixed and constant laws of the animate or inanimate world was subverted by human agency*, and that the modifications produced were on the occurrence of new and extraordinary circumstances, and those not of a physical, but a moral nature. The deviation permitted, would also appear to be as slight as was consistent with the accomplishment of the new moral ends proposed, and to be in great degree temporary in its nature, so that whenever the power of the new agent was withheld, even for a brief period, a relapse would take place to the ancient state of things.[13]

---

[11] For a historical survey, see Paolo Rossi, *I segni del tempo: storia della Terra e storia delle nazioni da Hooke a Vico* (Feltrinelli, 1979). For a more recent influential account, Dipesh Chakrabarty, 'The Climate of History: Four Theses' (2009) 35 *Critical Inquiry* 197.

[12] Charles Lyell, *The Geological Evidences of the Antiquity of Man* (John Murray, 1863) [Llyell, *Antiquity of Man*].

[13] Charles Lyell, *Principles of Geology, being an Attempt to Explain the Former Changes of the Earth's Surface, by Reference to Causes Now in Operation* (John Murray, 1830) vol. 1, 164 (italics added). I draw in this section on the sources provided by Christophe Bonneuil and Jean-Baptiste Fressoz, *L'événement Anthropocène. La Terre, l'histoire et nous* (Seuil, 2016) [Bonneuil/Fressoz, *Anthropocène*] 41–42, 45.

In poetry, the work of William Wordsworth offers a striking illustration from the early nineteenth century. The sonnet contrasts the villainy, to the human eye, of a lord who has an entire forest cut down, with the unperturbed course of nature:

> Degenerate Douglas! oh, the unworthy Lord!
> Who mere despite of heart could so far please,
> And love of havoc (for which such disease
> Fame taxes him) that he could send forth word
> To level with the dust a noble horde,
> A brotherhood of venerable Trees,
> Leaving an ancient Dome, and Towers like these,
> Beggared and outraged! – Many hearts deplor'd
> The fate of those old Trees; and oft with pain
> The Traveller, at this day, will stop and gaze
> On wrongs, which Nature scarcely seems to heed;
> For shelter'd places, bosoms, nooks and bays,
> And the pure mountains, and the gentle Tweed,
> And the green silent pastures, yet remain.[14]

Similarly, in the fields of history and in the nascent social sciences, the prominent French historian Jules Michelet and the influential philosopher Auguste Comte, founder of 'positivism' as an intellectual movement, placed the disconnection between natural and human history at the foundations of their conceptions. For Michelet:

> Since the beginning of the world a war started that will only end with the end of the world, not before; the war of man against nature, of spirit against matter, of freedom against fatality. History is nothing but the narrative of this everlasting fight… What must encourage us in this fight without end, is the fact that, overall, one of the terms does not change, and the other does change and becomes stronger. *Nature remains the same, whereas every day man takes some advantage over it.*[15]

In the same vein, Comte noted that '[t]he local physical causes, very powerful at the origins of civilisation, have progressively lost their grip as the natural course of human development increasingly allows to neutralise their action'.[16]

In the more specific context of the managerial or policy disciplines, such as a law and economics, the same premise can be found at the foundations of twentieth century legal positivism and growth theory. The overall prevailing conception of a disconnection permeated legal positivism as an intellectual enterprise, which sought to redefine itself as a 'pure' technology detached from both metaphysical and natural science conceptions of reality. In Hans Kelsen's account:

---

[14] William Wordsworth, *Poems in Two Volumes* (Longman et al, 1807) vol. II, 28, 7, Sonnet.

[15] Jules Michelet, *Introduction à l'histoire universelle* (Hachette, 1831) 5–7 (our translation; italics added).

[16] Auguste Comte, *Cours de philosophie positive* (Bachelier, 1839) vol. 4, 251 (our translation).

> If it is necessary to separate the science of law from politics, it is no less necessary to separate it from natural science. One of the most difficult tasks of a general theory of law is that of determining the specific reality of its subject and of showing the difference that exists between legal and natural reality.[17]

Such disconnection also permeated, indeed shaped some important accounts of growth. Robert Solow, whose work on the theory of economic growth became extremely influential in the second half of the twentieth century, saw the human strata as being entirely capable of detaching itself from the possible degradation of the natural strata, assuming that human capital could entirely substitute natural capital. In a piece concerning the use by present generations of exhaustible natural resources, he noted indeed that 'earlier generations are entitled to draw down the pool [of exhaustible resources] (optimally, of course!) so long as they add (optimally, of course) to the stock of reproducible capital'.[18] Of course, a water treatment plant may be as good – or even better and more 'efficient' – than a wetland for the specific purpose of purifying water, but replacing the latter with the former will remove a component of a wider functioning ecosystem, where wetlands play many different roles. To understand this simple point, one must see the limits of such disconnection accounts.

3. Re-united: in harmony or discord?

The few references in the preceding section are only intended as illustrations, albeit carefully selected ones, of an intellectual moment spanning more than two centuries, in which the connection between humans and nature present in most metaphysical accounts was rejected and removed, in an effort perceived as necessary for scientific and human progress. However, at the very same time, another body of work, scattered among different fields, began to hypothesise and later to track a profound connection between the human and natural strata of a different sort, namely one which could be scientifically explained and empirically ascertained.[19]

The historical grounding of this link is deep. The discovery of 'pre-historical' time and of humanity's rooting in it singularly marked intellectual inquiry since the second half of the nineteenth century. Three key works[20] in this

---

[17] Hans Kelsen, *General Theory of Law and the State* (Harvard University Press, 1945) xiv.

[18] Robert Solow, 'Intergenerational Equity and Exhaustible Resources' (1974) 41 *Review of Economic Studies* 29, 41.

[19] For a thorough investigation of the historical sources, see Jacques Grinevald, 'Sketch for a History of the Idea of the Biosphere', in Peter Bunyard and Edward Goldsmith (eds), *GAIA, the Thesis, the Mechanisms and the Implications* (Quintrell & Company, 1988) 1–32 [Grinevald, *Idea of Biosphere*]. This article and, indeed the book, which are inaccessible through digitalised sources, contains a wealth of information of particular interest to those looking for non-mainstream, fresh connections. The same applies to Grinevald's annotated bibliography *La biosphère de l'Anthropocène* (Georg, 2007). My discussion of the link's 'stalkers' relies largely, although not exclusively, on Grinevald's work.

[20] See Daniel Lord Smail, *On Deep History and the Brain* (University of California Press, 2008) 26.

revolution, Darwin's *Origin of Species*,[21] Lubbock's *Pre-Historic Times*[22] and Llyell's *Antiquity of Man*,[23] were immensely influential in other fields, although their implications for the link between human and natural history were ambiguous, as the immensity of the past could also support the idea of an immutable natural theatre which remained unperturbed by human history. Other strands of inquiry, such as those of the Scottish physician James Hutton,[24] some little known work of the famous French naturalist Jean-Baptiste Lamarck,[25] the magnus opus of Lamarck's mentor, the French academician Georges-Louis Leclerc, better known as Buffon,[26] and that of Alexander von Humboldt,[27] all sought to provide an integrated account of life, including humanity, and natural cycles.

These are all predecessors of some contemporary grand narratives of the empirical link, which entertain complex intellectual filiation lines among themselves. I will mention only four of them, which are closely interrelated but do not have the same scope and focus. These are the ideas of 'biosphere', the 'Gaia hypothesis', the 'Anthropocene' epoch and the more limited concept of 'planetary boundaries'. The use of the term 'narrative' to refer to these concepts, ideas and hypotheses should not be over-interpreted. I use it only for ease of reference, to encompass several strands of contributions which share the attempt to chart, scientifically and later on empirically, the connection between life – including humanity – and geological processes.

3.1. The biosphere

The first concept is in many ways the scientific and conceptual umbrella of the other three. The term 'biosphere' was coined by the eminent Austrian geologist Edward Suess,[28] but not with the integrative meaning given to it later

[21] Charles Darwin, *On the Origin of Species* (John Murray, 1859).

[22] John Lubbock, *Pre-Historic Times* (Williams and Norgate, 1865).

[23] Llyell, *Antiquity of Man* (n 12).

[24] James Hutton, *Theory of the Earth with Proofs and Illustrations*, 2 vols. (William Creech, Cadell and Davies, 1795) 11, 545–6 ('the explanation, which is given of the different phenomena of the Earth, must be consistent with the actual constitution of this Earth as a living world, that is, a world maintaining a system of living animals and plants'), reproduced in Grinevald, *Idea of Biosphere*, (n 19) 2.

[25] Jean-Baptiste Lamarck, *Hydrogéologie* (Agasse/Maillard, An X [1802]) 7–8, English translation: *Hydrogeology*, translated by Albert V. Carozzi (Urbana: University of Illinois Press, 1964) 18 ('A sound Physics of the Earth should include all the primary considerations of the Earth's atmosphere, of the characteristics and continual changes of the Earth's external crust, and finally of the origin and development of living organisms. These considerations naturally divide the physics of the Earth into three essential parts, the first being a theory of the atmosphere, or *Meteorology*, the second, a theory of the Earth's external crust, or *Hydrogeology*, and the third, a theory of living organisms, or *Biology*').

[26] Georges-Louis Leclerc, Comte de Buffon, *Histoire naturelle, générale et particulière avec la description du Cabinet du Roi*, 44 volumes (Imprimérie Royale, 1749–1804) (as continued by Lacépède).

[27] Alexander von Humboldt, *Kosmos:* Entwurf einer physischen Weltbeschreibung (JG Cotta, 1844).

[28] Eduard Suess, *Die Entsehung der Alpen* (W Braunmuller, 1875). Suess first used the term in passing to refer to one of the envelopes of the Earth's crust, that encompassing life. He also referred to it in the last chapter of his magnus opus, *Das Antlitz der Erde*, 4 vols (F Tempsky, 1892–1909), Chapter 27 ('Das Leben') appears in the 2nd part of the third volume (published originally as a fourth volume). The

by the work of the Russian/Ukrainian scientist Vladimir Ivanovich Vernadsky.

Vernadsky's book *The Biosphere*,[29] published shortly after a key research stay in Paris, where he met fellow scientists and philosophers Pierre Teilhard de Chardin and Édouard Le Roy, fleshed out an innovative understanding of the 'biosphere'. This understanding goes beyond the descriptive use of this term by Suess, as an Earth 'envelope' encompassing life alongside other envelopes (the 'atmosphere', the 'hydrosphere' and the 'lithosphere'). It emphasises instead the influence of life on the main chemical cycles of the Earth, hence the term '*bio*geochemistry'. And such influence is not merely episodic; life is viewed as a key force giving shape to the entire system. Life – Vernadsky has particularly in mind green plants powered by oxygenic photosynthesis – regulates the oxygen, nitrogen and carbon dioxide cycles. Rather than a 'poor player that struts and frets his hour upon the stage, and then is heard no more', to borrow Macbeth's memorable line, life shapes the entire natural theatre in which its evolution unfolds. Vernadsky notes, for example, that life creates the free oxygen that then combines in the form of ozone (ie, the ozone layer) to provide life shelter from solar radiation. However, Vernadsky did not have humanity in mind as life's spearheading force on geological cycles, as will be later the case under the 'Anthropocene' narrative. At the time he was writing, the human impact on the Earth was far from what it became decades later.

Vernadsky's holistic conception of a global ecology remained somewhat in abeyance, largely due to language and political considerations that made the penetration of Russian science in the West difficult. But it was preserved *inter alia* through the work of British ecologist, George Evelyn Hutchinson,[30] the founder of a major school of global ecology at Yale University. The work of Hutchinson on the anomalies presented by the chemistry of the terrestrial atmosphere[31] was expressly noted in the foundational article of the 'Gaia hypothesis', to which I now turn.

---

work was translated into English by HBC Sollas as: Eduard Suess, *The Face of the Earth*, 5 vols (Clarendon Press, 1904–1924).

[29] Vladamir Ivanonich Vernadsky, *Биосфера* (НХТИ: 1926), translated shortly after into French *La Biosphère* (Alcan, 1929) by Vernadsky and his wife, and only much later into English. After a much criticised first attempt, a translation appeared as *The Biosphere* (New Copernicus/Springer, 1998, trans. by D B Langmuir, foreword by L Margulis, Introduction of J Grinevald, revised and annotated by M McMenamin).

[30] Hutchinson was instrumental in the publication in English of two important works of Vernadsky on the Biosphere, namely 'Problems of Biogeochemistry' (1944) 35 *Transactions of the Connecticut Academy of Arts and Science* 483; 'The Biosphere and the Noosphere' (1945) 33 *American Scientist* 1. In his autobiography, Hutchinson acknowledged the influence of Vernadsky on him and his sincere efforts to have Vernadsky's ideas diffused in the English-speaking world. See George Evelyn Hutchinson, *The Kindly Fruits of the Earth. Recollections of an Embryo Ecologist* (Yale University Press, 1973) 233.

[31] George Evelyn Hutchinson, 'The Biochemistry of the Terrestrial Atmosphere', in Gerard P Kuiper (ed), *The Earth as a Planet* (University of Chicago Press, 1954) 371–433.

3.2. The Gaia hypothesis

Whereas the role of life in shaping biogeochemical cycles was clearly elaborated in Vernadsky's account of the biosphere, its 'self-regulatory' dimension was placed at the forefront of a similar narrative developed by British environmental scientist James Lovelock and American evolutionary biologist Lynn Margulis, the 'Gaia hypothesis'.[32] This narrative was reluctantly received in scientific circles, likely because of prevailing misunderstandings fuelled by the mystical overtones that were added to it over time.

The core idea is no different from that of Vernadsky, but the emphasis is. The 'Gaia hypothesis' holds, in essence, that life is not only a regulator of atmospheric chemistry but that it is a 'self-regulator' or, in other words, that it maintains certain atmospheric conditions precisely for its own benefit. Hence the title '[a]tmospheric homeostasis *by and for* the biosphere' (italics added). This change of emphasis implies a certain unity of purpose in the wide diversity of living organisms of the planet, which generated significant resistance in some quarters. The use of the term 'Gaia' to convey that extremely basic level of 'cooperation' or 'solidarity' among living things, from micro-organisms to plants to animals and humans, and the claim that such basic common impulse (ie the sustaining of atmospheric conditions which would not occur without the effects of living organisms on atmospheric chemistry) is sufficient to consider Gaia (functionally) 'alive', raised many eyebrows. But as noted by Lovelock in a later writing, we should think of it:

> as no more than the capacity of the Earth to regulate itself and to keep cool when things are changing adversely. It as a characteristic which physiologists always refer to by their 'buzz word' homeostasis.[33]

Lovelock further referred to another predecessor, best known for his contribution to the analysis of predator-prey dynamics,[34] namely Alfred Lotka, who in a book contemporary but unconnected to Vernadsky's *Biosphere* wrote:

> It is customary to discuss the evolution of a species of organisms. As we proceed we shall see many reasons why we should constantly take in view the evolution as a whole of the system, organisms plus environment. It may at first sight seem as if this should prove a more complicated problem than the consideration of the evolution of a part only of the system but it will become apparent as we proceed that the physical laws governing evolution in all probability take on a simpler form when referred to the system as a whole than to any portion thereof. It is not so much the

[32] James Lovelock and Lynn Margulis, 'Atmospheric Homeostasis by and for the Biosphere : The Gaia Hypothesis' (1974) 26 *Tellus* 1.

[33] James Lovelock, 'The Gaia Hypothesis', in Peter Bunyard and Edward Goldsmith (eds), *GAIA, the Thesis, the Mechanisms and the Implications* (Quintrell & Company, 1988) 35–45 [Lovelock, *Gaia*], at 45.

[34] The famous Lotka-Volterra model named after Alfred Lotka and Vito Volterra.

> organism or the species that evolves but the entire system, species and environment, the two are inseparable.[35]

It is thus at the level of the entire system, ie at the level of Gaia itself, that the analysis of self-regulation is placed, much like it could be placed at the level of a rainforest, taken as a whole, rather than of that of a specific population of animals or a specimen inhabiting it. Hence the strong accent of this narrative on self-regulation. Living organisms participate in a form of association that, taken as a whole, shapes the atmospheric conditions that enable life. Far from an extraneous play in an immutable theatre, Gaia, including humans, shapes the theatre in which its play unfolds.

An extension of this conception, without the polemical overtones, has been provided by Andrew Watson, Lovelock's doctoral student, and Tim Lenton, Watson's doctoral student, in a superb book on Earth system sciences entitled *Revolutions that Made the Earth.*[36] Lenton and Watson single out two main revolutions undergone by the Earth system, each of which had its origin in life itself. The first revolution concerned the emergence of oxygenic photosynthesis, which filled the Earth's atmosphere with free oxygen. As noted earlier, Vernadsky had seen free oxygen as evidence of a self-regulatory process by life itself. The second grand revolution is that of complexity during the so-called 'Cambrian explosion' of extreme biological innovation and diversification. Interestingly, Lenton and Watson end their account with a present phenomenon which, while stressing the link, specifically the systemic interconnection, between the histories of life and of the planet, points alas in a less hopeful direction. Human-induced climate change and the wider impact of humans on the biosphere may, indeed, be putting an end to the loose association among living beings and becoming a disruptive force of geological proportions.

3.3. The Anthropocene

So far, I have highlighted through the concept of biosphere and the Gaia hypothesis, with their extensions in global ecology and Earth system science, the self-regulatory dimension of life. Life creates the geochemical conditions in which it unfolds. There are, however, other narratives of the connection between life and geological processes which suggest not only that human activity has become a force of geological proportions but that such force is undermining the self-regulatory (the homeostatic) role of life. Unlike the growing warnings against the impending ecological crisis since the 1960s,[37] these narratives are both more encompassing (they do not

---

[35] Alfred Lotka, *Elements of Physical Biology* (Williams and Wilkins Co; Baillière, Tindall and Cox, 1925) 16, reproduced in Lovelock, *Gaia* (n 33) 41.

[36] Tim Lenton and Andrew Watson, *Revolutions that Made the Earth* (Oxford University Press, 2011).

concern only humanity but the wider Earth System) and more descriptive than prescriptive, although their extensions can be strongly political.[38]

One such narrative seeks to replace the current 'epoch' of the Geological Timescale, the Holocene, with a new epoch, the 'Anthropocene', in order to highlight the immense impact of human activity on the Earth system. When compared with the previous narratives, the Anthropocene narrative focusses only on humanity as the segment of life driving geological change and, although there are significant variations in the growing body of literature on this concept, it generally emphasises the adverse impact of human activities on the planet. The idea was initially introduced by the Dutch atmospheric chemist Paul Crutzen and the American ecologist Eugene Stoermer in a brief article[39] and subsequently popularised in Crutzen's 'Geology of Mankind', published in the influential review *Nature*.[40] Since then, it has greatly expanded to a wide range of fields of inquiry from the natural to the social sciences, humanities and law. Some subsequent elaborations provide more detail on the underpinnings of the idea[41] and on the specific project to chart a new epoch of the Geological Timescale.[42]

An important part of the debate relating to the Anthropocene concerns the specific moment in history when this proposed epoch started. Although different views have been expounded, the evolution of the data signals a 'great acceleration' in human impact after the Second World War.[43] Another important and related debate concerns the markers, not only in a stratigraphic sense but, more generally, the phenomena caused by the

---

37 See, among many others: Rachel Carson, *Silent Spring* (Houghton Mifflin, 1962); Kenneth E Boulding, 'The Economics of the Coming Spaceship Earth', in Henry Jarrett (ed), *Environmental Quality in a Growing Economy* (Johns Hopkins University Press, 1966) 3–14; Max Nicholson, *The Environmental Revolution: A Guide for the New Masters of the World* (Hodder & Stoughton, 1969); Barry Commoner, *The Closing Circle: Nature, Man, and Technology* (Alfred Knopf, 1971). See also the greatly influential Donella H Meadows, Dennis L Meadows, Jørgen Randers, and William W Behrens III, *The Limits to Growth* (Universe Books, 1972) [*Limits to Growth*].

38 See, for example, the 'Extinction Rebellion' movement: online: https://rebellion.earth/ (accessed 12 March 2020).

39 Paul J Crutzen and Eugene Stoermer, 'The "Anthropocene"' (2000) 41 IGBP Global Change Newsletter 17.

40 Paul J Crutzen, 'Geology of Mankind' (2002) 415 *Nature* 23.

41 See, among many others: Will Steffen, Jacques Grinevald, Paul J Crutzen and John McNeill, 'The Anthropocene: Conceptual and Historical Perspectives' (2011) 369/1938 *Philosophical Transactions of the Royal Society* 842. For overviews of the relevant literature, see Eduardo S Brondizio et al, 'Re-conceptualizing the Anthropocene: A Call for Collaboration' (2016) 39 *Global Environmental Change* 318; Bonneuil/Fressoz, *Anthropocène* (n 23).

42 Jan Zalasiewicz, Colin Waters, Mark Williams, Colin Summerhayes (eds), *The Anthropocene as a Geological Time Unit* (Cambridge University Press, 2019).

43 Will Steffen, Paul J Crutzen and John R McNeil, 'The Anthropocene: Are Humans now Overwhelming the Great Forces of Nature?' (2007) 36/8 *Ambio* 614. On this debate, see generally Erle C Ellis, 'Anthropogenic transformation of the terrestrial biosphere' (2011) 369/1938 *Philosophical Transactions of the Royal Society* 1010; Simon L Lewis and Mark A Maslin, 'Defining the Anthropocene' (2015) 519 *Nature* 171; Jan Zalasiewicz et al, 'When did the Anthropocene Begin? A Mid-twentieth Century Boundary Level is Stratigraphically Optimal' (2015) 383 *Quaternary International* 196; Colin Waters et al, 'The Anthropocene Is Functionally and Stratigraphically Distinct from the Holocene' (2016) 351/6269 *Science* aad2622-1.

immense growth of human impact. This impact can be measured in several ways, including changes in atmospheric and ocean chemistry[44] but also the devastating influence on other forms of life[45] and on humans themselves.[46] As the debate moves from the stratigraphical proposal to the more general question of impacts of human activities on the planet, other narratives have come into play, as discussed next.

3.4. Planetary boundaries

An influential account of the impact of humanity on major natural cycles – expressly presented as an extension of the Anthropocene narrative – has been provided by a team of researchers, including some of those mentioned earlier,[47] who seek to define the limits of the planet to support human existence. The idea of probing the limits of the planet is not new,[48] but the approach, the estimations and the relative suitability as policy guidance of this research effort are remarkable.

The stated purpose of this research is to contribute to the challenge of maintaining the 'Holocene' conditions in which humanity has thrived, and which would continue for hundreds of thousands of years unless their sustaining cycles are disrupted by human action. In order to do so, the framework identifies nine Earth system processes (climate change, rate of biodiversity loss, interference nitrogen and phosphorous cycles, stratospheric ozone depletion, ocean acidification, global freshwater use, changes in land use, chemical pollution, and atmospheric aerosol loading) and the thresholds of each process, which, if crossed, could tip the balance away from the equilibrium of the Holocene. Such thresholds can be understood as biophysical tipping points beyond which a process transitions to another state. Not every process has a known threshold. As a result, the 'safe operating space' for humanity is described by nine planetary boundaries, which are the values of certain control variables (eg concentration of carbon dioxide) that are at a sufficient distance from thresholds or (when such thresholds are not known) below certain levels of danger.

---

[44] See, eg: Elena M Bennet, Stephen R Carpenter, Nina F Caraco, 'Human Impact on Erodable Phosphorus and Eutrophication: A Global Perspective' (2001) 51/3 *BioScience* 227; James C Orr et al, 'Anthropogenic Ocean Acidification over the Twenty-first Century and its Impact on Calcifying Organisms' (2005) 437 *Nature* 681; James N Galloway et al, 'Transformation of the Nitrogen Cycle: Recent Trends, Questions, and Potential Solutions' (2008) 320/5879 *Science* 889; S Barker and Andy Ridgwell, 'Ocean Acidification' (2012) 3/10 *Nature Education Knowledge* 21.

[45] Robert J Diaz and Rutger Rosenberg, 'Spreading Dead Zones and Consequences for Marine Ecosystems' (2008) 321/5891 Science 926; S L Pimm et al, 'The Biodiversity of Species and their Rates of Extinction, Distribution, and Protection' (2014) 344/6187 *Science* 987.

[46] D Smith, 'Worldwide Trends in DDT Levels in Human Breast Milk' (1999) 28 *International Journal of Epidemiology* 179; QQ Li et al, 'Persistent Organic Pollutants and Adverse Health Effects in Humans' (2006) 69/21 *Journal of Toxicology and Environmental Health/A* 1987.

[47] Johan Rockström et al, 'A Safe Operating Space for Humanity' (2009) 461 *Nature* 472.

[48] See *Limits to Growth* (n 37).

As the authors acknowledge, the determination of planetary boundaries is a normative exercise which cannot be conducted without certain policy and value judgements. In the authors' own quantification, three planetary boundaries – climate change, biodiversity loss, nitrogen and phosphorous cycles – have been crossed. Importantly, these boundaries cannot be considered or addressed in isolation, as they are all interlocked and form part of a system. That means that crossing one boundary has implications for all or at least some of the others.

Planetary boundaries offer a narrative of the biophysical limits within which human action must remain in order to keep its interference with the Earth system under 'safe' levels. Leaving aside the profound value judgements and uncertainties involved in such framing and quantification effort, the broader idea is to define boundaries so that human action does not disrupt the homeostatic power of life on the Earth system. Such disruption is taking place before our very eyes, but the level of conceptual and empirical aggregation required to 'see' it is daunting. We would expect our policy responses to be designed specifically to enable life's ability to self-regulate itself. But, as discussed next, human self-regulation is not merely insufficient to restrain human interference with life's self-regulation; it is likely a contributing factor to such interference.

4. Rebellious self-regulation?

In the previous sections, I have singled out two main points. The first is the assertion of, and perhaps the dogmatic belief in a disconnection between human and natural history, given the immensity of the latter and the increasing powers of humanity over nature. The second point charted the interconnections between humanity and nature, not merely as those of a species with its proximate environment, but as that of a geological force affecting the very biogeochemical processes that enable life on Earth. The two points are connected not only because they are in a collision course with each other but, more profoundly, because the very technological conditions that sustained the idea of human independence from natural conditions have turned humanity into a geological force capable of undermining the Earth-shaping homeostatic action of life.

The idea of 'rebellious self-regulation' refers to the socio-economic mechanisms that enabled the emergence and development of the aforementioned technological conditions and, more specifically, of the thermo-industrial revolution of the late eighteenth century. Law, as a body of social practices, made a substantial part of such mechanisms.[49] 'Self-regulation' thus includes law and

[49] For a broader survey, see Jorge E Viñuales, *The Organisation of the Anthropocene. In Our Hands?* (Brill Research Perspectives, 2018) [Viñuales, *Organisation of the Anthropocene*].

specifically the conception of law that supported the industrial revolution. In this brief piece, I cannot hope to demonstrate that a certain form of legal organisation turned some humans (as the inequalities in such organisation made other humans the victims of these processes) into a disruptive force of geological proportions, interfering with the higher level of self-regulation performed by life in shaping of biogeochemical processes. My hope is only to render plausible the relevance of law in such processes or, in other words, to identify the link between the rebellious self-regulation of humans and the disrupted self-regulation of life. In order to do so, I will briefly characterise, relying on existing studies of the advent, organisation and impact of the industrial revolution, three main points: the triangular trade that rendered possible the industrial revolution, the major role of law in organising the main production transactions and its limited role in addressing their effects, and the rational conception of law that supported this process.

The mechanisms that enabled the process known as the industrial revolution, characterised by the widespread use of automated manufacturing processes and reliance on fossil fuels, mostly coal, has been widely studied.[50] One such study, which offers both a synthesis of existing work and formulates an intriguing hypothesis, is that of American historian Kenneth Pomeranz. In *The Great Divergence*,[51] he compares the proto-industrial conditions prevailing in England and in the Yangzi Delta around 1750 and asks why the industrial revolution took off in the West. His answer points to two rather fortuitous factors, namely the availability of large deposits of coal in England and its ability to rely on the triangular commerce with Africa and the United States, selling manufactures and importing raw materials, cheaply produced in the Southern part of the United States due to the widespread use of African slaves. This explanation thus points to the organisation of the world system dominated by the UK between the late eighteenth and the early twentieth century of asymmetric exchanges. World system analysis, as conceptualised by American sociologist Immanuel Wallerstein,[52] has provided the overall framework for more granular studies of ecologically unequal exchange, which highlight the gains of the UK, in terms of land and resources, in its trade with the Americas. Swedish human ecologist Alf Hornborg has estimated, for example, that cotton exports from the US exchanged for UK manufactures required 6000 times more land for their production than the English goods.[53]

---

[50] See (n 4).

[51] Pomeranz, *The Great Divergence* (n 4).

[52] See (n 8) and, for a summary, Immanuel Wallerstein, *World System Analysis: An Introduction* (Duke University Press, 2004).

[53] Alf Hornborg, *Global Ecology and Unequal Exchange. Fetishism in a Zero-Sum World* (Routledge, 2013) 85–91. For a study looking at patterns of unequal production since 1950, see Anke Schaffartzik et al, 'The Global Metabolic Transition: Regional Patterns and Trends of Global Material Flows, 1950–2010' (2014) 26 *Global Environmental Change* 87.

The law underpinning the organisation of such a world system is a complex patchwork of different legal concepts and institutions, encompassing matters such as the assertion of territorial powers over and the denial of Statehood of non-European political entities,[54] the permission of the use of force,[55] the organisation of trade (market access enabling the exchange of manufactures for raw materials) and investment (foreign investment protection) relations,[56] new forms of business organisation (with tradable shares, unified management, and providing for the protection of investors from the creditors of the juristic person[57] but also, conversely, that of the latter from the creditors of the former[58]), permissive labour laws[59] and, last and alas possibly least, the minimisation of the side effects of production processes.[60] Rather than elaborating on each of these aspects, my purpose is only to identify a pattern in this legal organisation, which, I suspect, has played and continues to play a significant role in making some portions of humanity a disruptive geological force.

This pattern can be described in simple terms by reference to the well-known distinction between transactions and (negative) externalities. In essence, this distinction emphasises the fact that certain transactions can have negative (or positive) side-effects on those not participating in the transaction and, hence, on overall utility. The terminology is highly coded in economic and, more deeply, in utilitarian terms, but the goal is to provide a rationale for governmental intervention either in the form of corrective taxation[61] or of a trading mechanism.[62] In this light, the basic pattern that emerges

---

[54] In his examination of the Berlin Conference, which led to the partition of Africa, Cambridge international law professor John Westlake, noted that '[t]he *moral* rights of all outside the international society [in casu, African territories] against the several members of that society remain intact though they have not and scarcely could have been converted into *legal* rights', *Chapters on the Principles of International Law* (Cambridge University Press, 1894) 139–40 (italics added).

[55] Ian Brownlie, *International Law and the Use of Force by States* (Clarendon Press, 1963), chapter 2.

[56] Anthony Anghie, *Imperialism, Sovereignty and the Making of International Law* (Cambridge University Press, 2004) 141–62; Kate Miles, *The Origins of International Investment Law* (Cambridge University Press, 2013).

[57] Adolf Berle and Gardiner Means, *The Modern Corporation and Private Property* (Macmillan, 1932); Timothy W Guinnane et al, 'Pouvoir et proprieté dans l'entreprise: Pour une histoire international des sociétés à responsabilité limitée' (2008) 63/1 *Annales. Histoire. Sciences Sociales* 73.

[58] Henry Hansmann, Reinier Kraakman and Richard Squire, 'Law and the Rise of the Firm' (2005/2006) 119 *Harvard Law Review* 1335.

[59] O Kahn-Freund, 'Legal Framework', in Allan Flanders and H A Clegg (eds), *The System of Industrial Relations in Great Britain: Its History, Law and Institutions* (Blackwell, 1954), 42–127; Marc Linder, *The Employment Relationship in Anglo-American Law: A Historical Perspective* (Greenwood, 1989); Jacques Le Goff, *Du silence à la parole. Une histoire du droit du travail des années 1830 à nos jours* (Presses universitaires de Rennes, 2004).

[60] A E Dingle, 'The Monster Nuisance of All. Landowners, Alkali Manufacturers, and Air Pollution, 1828–1864' (1982) 35 *Economic History Review* 529; Ben Pontin, 'Tort Law and Victorian Governement Growth: The Historiographical Significance of Tort Law in the Shadow of Chemical Pollution' (1998) 18 *Oxford Journal of Legal Studies* 661; Jean-Baptiste Fressoz, 'Payer pour polluer: l'industrie chimique et la compensation des dommages environnementaux, 1800–1850' (2013) 28 *Histoire & mesure* 145.

[61] Arthur C Pigou, *The Economics of Welfare* (Mcmillan, 1920).

[62] Ronald Coase, 'The Problem of Social Cost' (1960) 3 *Journal of Law and Economics* 1.

from an examination of the above legal mechanisms[63] is, essentially, that the law sustaining the industrial revolution (i) focussed mainly on the organisation of the transaction, ie the definition of powers over the relevant objects (typically resources but also capital, intellectual property rights and even human beings) and the facilitation of production and exchange (capital movements, market access, transit and treatment), (ii) whereas other laws, such as those to improve working conditions, reduce health and other impact on humans, and reduce associated environmental degradation, were organised as an additional layer specifically designed not to interfere with the possibility of continuing the transaction.

The boundary between organising the transaction and mitigating the externality is conceptually porous, but it is ascertainable in context. One striking illustration is the difference between improving the conditions of slaves and an outright ban of slavery. If the transaction is understood as the aforementioned triangular trade, enabled by slave work in the US South, then banning slavery amounted to an outright interference with the transaction rather than the mere mitigation of the 'negative externality' (human suffering). The continuation of the transaction was a consideration – colliding with the British anti-slavery movement – in the position of the UK during the US civil war. It may be recalled that Confederate States in the South, who relied on slaves to produce exports of raw materials to the UK, received recognition of belligerency by the UK within a month of the uprising. At the same time, the UK declared its neutrality but, in the following months and years, failed to prevent the building of warships in its own shipyards, leading to the most important international arbitration of the nineteenth century, the *Alabama claims* arbitration.[64] This specific illustration provides, in my view, a striking reminder of how partial and insufficient it would be to focus on international environmental law to understand the role of law in turning humans into a disruptive geological force. The legal processes organising the transactions at the roots of the novel geological impact of humans must be found well before and beyond international environmental law, which appears, from this perspective, not only as a latecomer but as an epiphenomenon designed to mitigate negative (environmental) externalities without interfering with the transaction.

---

[63] This examination is an ongoing process. I have presented some of the results in Viñuales, *Organisation of the Anthropocene* as well as in Jorge E. Viñuales, 'Comparative Environmental Law: Structuring a Field', in Emma Lees and Jorge E. Viñuales (eds), *The Oxford Handbook of Comparative Environmental Law* (Oxford University Press, 2019) 1–34 (based on a five-year review of the environmental law systems of sixteen specific jurisdictions, as well as many more considered for specific topics). I hope to offer a full analysis of the architecture of environmental law as a mere 'law of externalities' in my forthcoming *The Architecture of Environmental Law: A Comparative Analysis* (Oxford University Press) and, in the area of international law, in my forthcoming *The International Law of Energy* (Cambridge University Press).

[64] See Tom Bingham, 'The Alabama Claims Arbitration' (2005) 54 *International & Comparative Law Quarterly* 1.

Perhaps more fundamentally, it may be the very conception of law prevailing in Europe on the verge of the industrial revolution, with its deliberate and growing detachment from metaphysical accounts and its focus on the autonomy of commerce which may be the deeper enabler of the legal organisation described above. I will end my essay with a brief reference to what remains, in my view, the main exploration of this question, that of German sociologist Max Weber.[65] Weber's thesis is, in essence, that the higher degree of rationality of Western law, itself the result of its own historical processes (the Church/State separation, the bureaucratically organised State, and the need to compose with the increasingly powerful bourgeoisie), was particularly well-suited to support the rise of industrial capitalism, due to the functional specialisation of law and law-making processes. Such specialisation allowed for more predictability (necessary for allocating large capital investments to specific activities) as well as for market organisation, in the form of business organisation, market freedoms and contractual practices. David M Trubek summarises Weber's explanation as follows:

> At least some areas of social life had to be freed of the bonds of kinship, religion, and other foci of traditional authority, and, at the same time, insulated from the arbitrary action of the state. This required that the state, as legal order, be strengthened, so that it superseded other sources of social control, and at the same time be limited, so that it did not encroach upon areas of economic action. The state was to provide a formal order, or facilitative framework within which free economic actors could operate.[66]

To us, such form of human self-regulation still appears modern, reasonable, even desirable. We may not even realise how rebellious and unsettling our self-regulation is, in its unintended effects, with respect to the wider and deeper self-regulation performed by life on biogeochemical cycles. Dramatically, whether we realise it or not, our rebellion cannot succeed; it would be a secession to nowhere. The only alternative is alignment of the two layers of self-regulation. There is ample room within life's self-regulatory processes for human choice, freedom, equality, justice and prosperity; this layer of self-regulation does not and should not require re-naturalising our laws. Our immense task is simply to find self-regulatory mechanisms that remain within that broad space.

Disclosure statement

No potential conflict of interest was reported by the author(s).

---

65 Max Weber, *Wirtschaft und Gesellschaft. Grundriss der verstehenden Soziologie* (Mohr, 4th edn 1956). English translation: *Economy and Society. An Outline of Interpretive Sociology* (University of California Press, edn by G Roth and R Wittich, 1968), part II, section VIII: Economy and Law (The Sociology of Law) 641ff. My discussion follows David M Trubek, 'Max Weber on Law and the Rise of Capitalism' (1972) *Wisconsin Law Review* 720 [Trubek, *Weber*].

66 Trubek, *Weber*, (n 63) 744.

Ecological law in the Anthropocene

Peter D Burdon

ABSTRACT
The issue motivating this article is the extent to which ecological legal thinking needs to change and adapt to the Anthropocene. My contention is that legal scholars tend to use the notion of the 'Anthropocene' as a synonym for the extreme impact human beings are having on the environment. Yet, few go further and consider whether the intellectual foundations or prescriptive proposals of ecological law have been challenged by Earth systems science. This is precisely the gap I intended to address in this article. Part one provides a descriptive summary of key findings in Earth systems science. Following this, part two presents two challenges to ecological lawyers. First I argue that we ought to abandon attempts to formulate a non-anthropocentric theory of law and embrace descriptive and perceptual forms of anthropocentrism. Second, I argue that earth systems science undermines many versions of ecological integrity found in legislation around the world.

Ecological law is an umbrella term that I use to describe a range of theoretical approaches to law which have been influenced by environmental philosophy, ecological science, systems thinking and social ecology.[1] It captures early liberal approaches to environmental law which focused on the precautionary principle, the public trust doctrine and legal rights as well as more recent approaches to law advocated by proponents of Earth Jurisprudence.[2] While there is significant variety between individual approaches to ecological law, each attempts to reconfigure law around the environment. To repurpose a phrase from EF Schumacher: ecological law imagines law as if nature mattered.[3] In pursuing this goal each theory has demonstrated, to varying degrees, a willingness to challenge orthodoxy, confront established doctrine and name the presumptions that underlie orthodox theories of law. For

---

[1] See: Ben Boer 'Social Ecology and Environmental Law' (1984) 1 *Environmental and Planning Law Journal* 233.

[2] Peter Burdon, *Earth Jurisprudence: Private Property and the Environment* (Routledge 2014). In contrast to liberal jurisprudence, Earth Jurisprudence focuses on the concept of law and seeks to make the health and future flourishing of the Earth community a condition for legal authority.

[3] E Schumacher, *Small is Beautiful: Economics as if People Mattered* (Vintage 1993).

example, ecological law has shone a light on the anthropocentrism of western law[4] and the hierarchies of power that leave nature vulnerable to exploitation.[5]

Of all the sources that have influenced ecological law, the most important has been the science of ecology.[6] Ecology provided environmentally conscious lawyers with a firm foundation to advocate for laws that placed human beings as interconnected parts within a broader community of life. It also helped lawyers advocate for the protection of areas which were of no instrumental use. For example, laws for the protection of groundwater were advanced because of the complex role it plays within a broader ecosystem and not because their protection facilitated economic growth or some other human benefit.[7] Interpretations of ecological science also advanced the view that the environment had its own intrinsic value[8] and its own interests that ought to be protected with legal rights.[9] This has been recognised recently with the expansion of laws around the world that grant either 'nature' or specific parts of the environment legal personhood.[10]

While the ecological sciences placed human beings in an ecological context a more recent discipline has emerged that has superseded ecological thinking.[11] Rather than seeing human beings as one part of the Earth community, Earth systems science contends that human beings are unique and have become a force of nature that is able to influence the geological development of the Earth system. The Anthropocene is the proposed name that describes this radical shift in our understanding of Earth. Clive Hamilton provides a concise definition of the Anthropocene: '[a] recent rupture in Earth history arising from the impact of human activity on the Earth System as a whole'.[12] I will unpack these terms in the next section but for now I note that Earth systems science and ecology are not necessarily commensurate. There is overlap[13] but Earth systems science is offering new insights and describing a single integrated system rather than a collection of interconnected ecosystems.

---

4 Klaus Bosselmann, *When Two Worlds Collide: Society and Ecology* (RSVP Publishing 1999).

5 Nicole Graham, *Lawscape: Property, Environment, Law* (Routledge 2010).

6 Sean Coyle and Karen Morrow, *The Philosophical Foundations of Environmental Law: Property, Rights and Nature* (Hart Publishing 2004) 147–51.

7 Gabriel Eckstein, *The International Law of Transboundary Groundwater Resources* (Routledge 2017).

8 See for example, Part 7(1)(a) of the *Natural Resources Management Act 2004* (SA) which notes: 'The objects of this Act include to assist in the achievement of ecologically sustainable development in the State by establishing an integrated scheme to promote the use and management of natural resources in a manner that—(a) recognises and protects the intrinsic values of natural resources … '

9 Peter Burdon and Claire Williams, 'Rights of Nature: A Constructive Analysis' in Douglas Fisher (ed) *Research Handbook on Fundamental Concepts of Environmental Law* (Routledge 2016).

10 For a summary see Peter Burdon and Claire Williams, 'Rights of Nature: A Constructive Analysis in Douglas Fisher (ed), *Research Handbook on Fundamental Concepts of Environmental Law* (Edward Elgar Publishing 2016).

11 Clive Hamilton, 'The Anthropocene Rupture' (2016) 2(1) *The Anthropocene Review* 1.

12 Clive Hamilton, *Defiant Earth: The Fate of Humans in the Anthropocene* (Allen & Unwin 2017) 9.

13 *Ibid*, 12.

While these variances in terminology might appear to be subtle differences, the implications of Earth systems science are immense. The issue motivating this article is the extent to which ecological legal thinking needs to change and adapt to this new vision of reality. Or more precisely, what aspects of ecological science are still relevant to today? And equally important—what do we need to discard to think clearly about law in the Anthropocene? My contention is that legal scholars tend to use the phrase 'Anthropocene' as a synonym for the extreme impact human beings are having on the environment. Yet, few go further and consider whether the intellectual foundations or prescriptive proposals of ecological law have been challenged by Earth systems science.[14]

This is precisely the gap I intended to address in this article. In part one, I provide a summary of key principles in Earth systems science. Here, I stick close to science but I also recognise that no term can (or should) belong to a single discipline. Instead, I acknowledge the burgeoning literature on what we might call the 'cultural' meaning of the Anthropocene in fields ranging from law to musicology.[15] Following this, in part two I present two challenges to ecological law, focusing on anthropocentrism and the notion of ecological integrity. I pose these challenges as a fellow advocate of ecological law and in the spirit of 'self-reflective criticism'[16] so that perhaps we might once again confront orthodoxy and bring fresh thinking to our work.

1. The Anthropocene: key principles

In the introduction, I referred to Clive Hamilton's short description of the Anthropocene as a 'recent rupture in Earth history arising from the impact of human activity on the Earth System as a whole'.[17] In this section my goal is to unpack the key principles in this description so that we can consider their potential impact on legal thinking today.[18]

The first critical point is that the Anthropocene rupture is relatively recent with most accounts dating it to have occurred since the 1950s.[19] Moreover, human beings have only been able to study the Earth as a system since the

---

[14] Two of the best collections on the Anthropocene and Law are Louis Kotzé (ed), *Environmental Law and Governance for the Anthropocene* (Hart Publishing 2017) and Michelle Lim (ed), *Charting Environmental Law Futures in the Anthropocene* (Springer 2017).

[15] Virginia E Whealton, 'Franz Liszt's Album d'un Voyageur: Music, Memorials, and the Anthropocene' (2019) 41(5) *Nineteenth-Century Contexts* 543.

[16] J Ronald Engel, 'Summons to a New Axial Age: The Promise, Limits, and Future of the Earth Charter' in Laura Westra and Mirian Vilela (eds), *The Earth Charter, Ecological Integrity and Social Movements* (Earthscan 2014) xv.

[17] Hamilton (n 11) 9.

[18] Those looking for a detailed description of the scientific underpinnings of the Anthropocene ought to consult Ian Angus, *Facing the Anthropocene: Fossil Capitalism and the Crisis of the Earth System* (Monthly Review Press 2016) 25–106.

[19] *Ibid* 38–47.

1980s. Prior to this we could only grasp aspects of the Earth system through systems modelling[20] and arctic ice-core drilling.[21] While the Gaia hypothesis developed by James Lovelock and Lyn Margulis might be treated as a precursor theory,[22] the study of the Earth as a single integrated system required new technology, such as satellites capable of gathering data around the world and computers that could analyse and transmit that information.[23]

One of the earliest bodies to begin processing and analysing this data was the International Geosphere Biosphere Program (IGBP) which was initiated by the International Council of Scientific Unions in 1986. Drawing on this research, Frank Oldfield and Will Steffen provided the first sophisticated definition of the Earth system: 'the Earth System has come to mean the suite of interacting physical, chemical, and biological global-scale cycles (often called biogeochemical cycles) and energy fluxes which provide the conditions necessary for life on the planet'.[24] The Earth System also incorporates the metabolism of industrial culture. As the authors note:

> Human beings, their societies and their activities are an integral component of the Earth system, and are not an outside force perturbing an otherwise natural system. There are many modes of natural variability and instability within the System as well as anthropogenically driven changes. By definition, both parts of variability are part of the dynamics of the Earth System. They are often impossible to separate completely and they interact in complex and sometimes mutually reinforcing ways.[25]

As noted in the introduction, this definition has ideas in common with those articulated in ecology. And yet it is vital to insist on a distinction. Ecology studies local and regional ecosystems and presents human beings as a dominant animal. By contrast, Earth systems science conceives of the Earth as a total system and presents human beings as capable of influencing and disrupting that whole. This point was captured and expanded upon by Will Steffen:

> the Earth itself is a single system, which the biosphere is an active, essential component ... Second, human activities are no so pervasive and profound in the consequences that they affect the Earth at a global scale in complex, interactive and accelerating ways; humans now have the capacity to alter the Earth

[20] See the work of Donna H Meadows, 'Dana's Writings' (*The Donella Meadows Project: Academy for Systems Change*, 2020) online: http://donellameadows.org/donella-meadows-legacy/danas-writing/ accessed 3 March 2020.

[21] Hamilton, (n 11) 10–11. For more detail see Angus, (n 17) 29–38; Clive Hamilton and Jacques Grinevald, 'Was the Anthropocene Anticipated' (2015) *The Anthropocene Review* 59.

[22] James Lovelock and Lyn Margulis, 'Atmospheric Homeostasis by and for the Biosphere: The Gaia Hypothesis' (1974) 26(1–2) *Tellus* 2; Ferris Jabr, 'The Earth Is Just as Alive as You Are', (*The New York Times*, 20 April 2019) https://www.nytimes.com/2019/04/20/opinion/sunday/amazon-earth-rain-forest-environment.html accessed 19 March 2020.

[23] Angus (n 17) 30.

[24] Frank Oldfield and Will Steffen, 'The Earth System' in Will Steffen et al (eds), *Global Change and the Earth System: A Planet Under Pressure* (Springer 2004) 7.

[25] *Ibid.*

> system in ways that threaten the very processes and components, both biotic and abiotic, upon which humans depend.[26]

I draw out the implications of this shift in more detail below but the differences between ecology and Earth systems science have led commenters to insists that the Anthropocene ought to be compared to a paradigm shift[27] or second Copernican revolution in terms of its importance.[28] Thus, as Hans Joachim Schellnhuber from the Potsdam Institute for Climate Impact Research states: '[t]his new revolution will be in a way a reversal of the first: it will enable us to look back on our planet to perceive one single, complex, dissipative, dynamic entity, far more thermodynamic equilibrium—the Earth system'.[29]

2. Ecological law

In the last section I described key ideas in Earth systems science. Emerging from this literature is an Earth system that has entered a 'non-analog' state or which is '*terra incognita*'.[30] Even if the International Commission on Stratigraphy does not formally add the Anthropocene to the geological time scale, the evidence for its designation is already robust[31] and it requires us to think about our planet and ourselves in new ways. As our descriptions of reality change, so to must our interpretations of the world. As Hamilton writes, 'we are faced with the discomforting choice between groping unsteadily toward new conceptions that attempt to build on a new real, or clinging to old conceptions rooted in a world that has been left behind'.[32] With this in mind, I turn now to engage two ideas that that are important to many advocates of ecological law—anthropocentrism and the concept of ecological integrity.

2.1. Anthropocentrism

> The problem is not that humans are anthropocentric, but that we are not anthropocentric enough.[33]

A dominant strand in ecological law argues that the dominant cause of the environmental crisis lies in the way western culture conceives of the relationship between human beings and nature. More specifically, the argument is

26 Will Steffen et al, *Global Change and the Earth System: A Planet Under Pressure* (Springer 2004) 1.
27 Hamilton, (n 11) 13.
28 Angus (n 17) 28, 32.
29 Hans Joachim Schellnhuber, 'Earth System Analysis and the Second Copernican Revolution' (1999) 402 *Nature* 23.
30 Angus (n 17) 29.
31 *Ibid* 58.
32 Hamilton, (n 11) 38.
33 *Ibid* 43.

that human beings view themselves as separate from and dominant over the natural world.[34] For writers like Lyn White Junior, this 'anthropocentric' perspective has its deepest roots in Christianity.[35] While others trace it from the ancient Greeks,[36] the scientific revolution[37] or the dawning of capitalism.[38] Whatever the source, the argument contends that anthropocentrism needs to be displaced by a new perspective which, drawing on ecological science, positions human beings as one interconnected part of a broader community of life. This gives rise to various kinds of legal analysis, ranging from attempts to reconfigure our concept of law[39] to reform initiatives seeking to place obligations on owners,[40] give effect to the public trust doctrine[41] or attempts to extend legal rights to the environment.[42]

For many writers, anthropocentrism is presented as objectively incorrect and unequivocally harmful. George Sessions, whose writing on deep ecology inspired some of the more idealistic[43] strands of ecological law, described anthropocentrism as a mode of thinking that separates human beings from nature and regards the latter as existing for the use and exploitation of the former.[44] And yet, Ben Mylius reminds us that anthropocentrism has a much more nuanced meaning and which can be broken down into three separate ideas:

1. *Perceptual* anthropocentrism: which characterises paradigms informed by sense-data from human sensory organs;
2. *Descriptive* anthropocentrism: which characterises paradigms that begin from, centre upon, or are ordered around *Homo sapiens*/'the human'; and
3. Normative anthropocentrism: which characterises paradigms that constrain inquiry in a way that somehow privileges Homo sapiens/'the human' [passive normative anthropocentrism]; and which characterises paradigms that make assumptions or assertions about the superiority of Homo sapiens, its capacities, the primacy of its values, its position in the

34 For an early statement see Bosselmann (n 5). See also Fritjof Capra and Ugo Mattei, *The Ecology of Law* (Berrett-Koehler 2018).
35 Lyn White Jnr, 'The Historical Roots of our Ecological Crisis' (1967) 155 (3767) *Science* 1203.
36 Derrick Jensen, *Listening to the Land: Conversations About Nature, Culture and Eros* (Chelsea Green 2005) 5.
37 Carolyn Merchant, *The Death of Nature: Women, Ecology, and the Scientific Revolution* (HarperCollins 1990).
38 David Harvey, *Justice, Nature and the Geography of Difference* (John Wiley & Sons 1997).
39 Burdon (n 2).
40 Eric T. Freyfogle, *The Land We Share: Private Property and The Common Good* (Island Press 2003).
41 Peter Brown, *Restoring the Public Trust* (Beacon Press 1994).
42 Erin L. O'Donnell and Julia Talbot-Jones, 'Creating Legal Rights for Rivers: Lessons from Australia, New Zealand, and India' (2018) 23(1) *Ecology and Society*, online: https://doi.org/10.5751/ES-09854-230107 accessed 3 March 2020.
43 Idealistic in the formal sense ie the notion that ideas determine reality.
44 George S Sessions, 'Anthropocentrism and the Environmental Crisis' (1974) 2(1) *Social Behaviour and Natural Environments* 73.

universe, and/or make prescriptions based on these assertions and assumptions [active normative anthropocentrism].[45]

This is a helpful intervention and allows us to describe ecological law as being concerned primarily with normative anthropocentrism. Perceptual anthropocentrism seems to me to be an inescapable part of the human conditions and writers since Friedrich Nietzsche have regarded it as integral to the way we encounter and interpret the world.[46] Seeing and knowing always takes place from an embodied and situated, existence. There is no such thing as a purely objective presentation of a social phenomenon, a concept, a thinker or a practice. We always see the world from an angle or through a lens, even if that is not immediately perceptible to us.

Further to these observations, I contend that the Anthropocene has rendered descriptive anthropocentrism an objective fact. What other conclusion could one draw from the thesis that human beings have become a geological force, capable of altering the Earth system as a whole? Are we truly just like primates or other large mammals? Surely not. In fact, I would go further and suggest that the Anthropocene matches perfectly Mylius's description of a paradigm that causes our worldview to begin from and become ordered around human beings. Here I am not just saying that environmental thinkers should disentangle the various meanings of anthropocentrism (they should). Rather, I think that we need to come to terms with descriptive anthropocentrism so that we can grapple with its normative implications. We cannot do this if 'anthropocentrism' is regarded as an unequivocal negative. Hamilton expands on this point:

> We can no longer withdraw and expect nature to return to any kind of 'natural' state. There is no going back to the Holocene. We may have acquired it foolishly, but we now have a responsibility for the Earth as a whole and pretending otherwise is itself irresponsible. So the question is not whether human beings stand at the center of the world, but what kind of human being stands at the center of the world, and what is the nature of that world.[47]

To date the most common response to the Anthropocene has been an arrogant normative anthropocentrism as portrayed in documents such as the eco-modernist manifesto.[48] This is not surprising given: (1) the necessity of

[45] Ben Mylius, 'Three Types of Anthropocentrism' (2018) 15(2) *Environmental Philosophy* 159.

[46] Friedrich Nietzsche, *On the Genealogy of Morals*, tr, Walter Kaufmann (Random House 1989) 119: 'There is only a perspective seeing, only a perspective "knowing"; and the more affects we allow to speak about one thing, the more eyes, different eyes, we can use to observe one thing, the more complete will our "concept" of this thing, our "objectivity," be. But to eliminate the will altogether, to suspend each and every affect, supposing we were capable of this—what would that mean but to castrate the intellect?'

[47] Hamilton (n 12) 47.

[48] See: 'An Ecomodernist Manifesto' (*Ecomodernism*, 2020) online: http://www.ecomodernism.org accessed 29 October 2019.

some technological response to problems such as climate change; (2) the compatibility of technological solutions with industrial capitalism; and, (3) how thoroughly environmental thinkers have ceded territory on debates about anthropocentrism or sought to fall back on ideas and arguments formulated from within a Holocene worldview. In saying this, I also need to underline that there is no reason why accepting descriptive anthropocentrism needs to result in an arrogant and hubristic normativity. There is nothing incompatible with putting descriptive anthropocentrism at the centre of ecological law and proceeding with humility, uncertainty and caution. In fact, I suggest that this is our only hope of responding to the environmental crisis in a way that places the value of others at the centre of our moral and legal worldview.

Taking this point further, I contend that a serious reckoning with the Anthropocene ought to result in an emphasis on old ideas such as the precautionary principle and the centrality of obligations to legal relations.[49] One reason to insist on this reading is because the Anthropocene requires a fundamental shift from enlightenment notions of freedom on morality. For example, while Kant considered freedom to be essential to morality and the human condition, such a pure dichotomy no longer holds.[50] Descriptive anthropocentrism suggests a human subject that is embedded in an Earth system (not just an ecosystem). This subject has more power than ever before and our freedom is being exercised on a planet that is not passive, but increasingly hostile and unpredictable. This is an anti-humanist[51] perspective in so far as it recognises that our future will be determined as much by the Earth system as by our own choices. Isabelle Stengers describes the influence of the Earth system on our lives as a kind of intrusion:

> This is perhaps what is most difficult to conceptualize: no future can be foreseen in which she will give back us the liberty of ignoring her. It is not a matter of a 'bad moment that will pass,' followed by any kind of happy ending—in the shoddy sense of a 'problem solved.' We are no longer authorized to forget her. We will have to go on answering for what we are undertaking in the face of an implacable being who is death to our justifications.[52]

We can push this point further to say that in the Anthropocene, the consequences of human agency are planetary. *Contra* Kant, morality is not rooted in freedom but in our embeddedness within the Earth system.[53] The accompanying responsibility to care for the Earth is much greater than

---

[49] Daniel Matthews 'Obligations in the New Climatic Regime' (*Critical Legal Thinking*, 16 July 2018) online: http://criticallegalthinking.com/2018/07/16/obligations-in-the-new-climatic-regime/ accessed 1 October 2019.

[50] Michael Hogue, *The Tangled Bank: Towards an Ecotheological Ethics of Responsible Participation* (Pickwick Publications, 2008) 191.

[51] Hamilton (n 11) 54.

[52] Isabelle Stengers, *In Catastrophic Times: Resisting the Coming Barbarism* (Open Humanities Press 2015) 47.

[53] Hamilton, above (n 11) 52.

traditionally expressed in ecological law and it must be actively discharged. We must own and embrace our new-found power/responsibility.[54] It is far too late to try and relinquish power or fall back on wilderness ethics. Descriptive anthropocentrism also carries a new spin on traditional claims that human beings have a unique moral status. As Hamilton contends: '[i]t elevates human specialness in order to highlight our powers and their dangers, and so the obligations that go with them'.[55] This conclusion shares similarities with the 'ethics of responsibility' proposed by Hans Jonas and his understanding that Kantian notions of responsibility were not designed to mitigate new forms of human power that have been unleashed through technology. However, embracing descriptive anthropocentrism provides a way of thinking about responsibility that does not require a commitment to Jonas's metaphysics or his reliance on arguments about the intrinsic value of nature.[56]

As we grope toward an ethics for the Anthropocene we might (counterintuitively) look backwards to writers who praised human industriousness but couched their praise in tones of caution and modesty. Goethe is such a figure and his injunction to use technology in a morally responsible way feels both contemporary and prescient.[57] Relevant also are Ovid's didactic poems in the *Metamorphoses*. Icarus is an obvious example but more relevant perhaps is Phaethon who tricked his father Helios into letting him steer the chariot of the sun. Phaethon represents the confidence of the young and his hubris blinds him from seeing the power that he possesses at his fingertips. However, once the horses bolt and the chariot goes off its 'well-worn track' Phaethon is forced to confront his arrogance. Ovid writes:

> When unhappy Phaethon looked from the top of the firmament down on the earth and saw it lying so far, far deep beneath him, terror suddenly struck him: has face turned pale and his knees shook; his vision grew darkly blurred in the dazzling, glaring brightness.[58]

Like Phaethon we are also in an unenviable situation. That we have become geological agents is the greatest mistake in human history and the cause of our greatest sorrows. But this is the situation we find ourselves in and all we can do is respond with more humility, responsibility and compassion than we have exhibited thus far. If not, then we only need to follow Phaethon's story a little further:

---

54 *Ibid* 53.

55 *Ibid* 54.

56 Hans Jonas, *Imperative of Responsibility: In Search of an Ethics for the Technological Age* (University of Chicago Press 1984).

57 See: Adrian Wilding, 'Ideas for a Critical Theory of Nature' (2008) 19(4) *Capitalism, Nature Socialism* 48. See also Clive Hamilton, 'The Banality of Ethics in the Anthropocene, Part 2' (*The Conversation*, 14 July 2015) online https://theconversation.com/the-banality-of-ethics-in-the-anthropocene-part-2-44647 accessed 13 March 2020.

58 Ovid, *Metamorphoses* (Translated by David Raeburn, Penguin Books 2004) 55.

> The earth now burst into flames on all of the hills and the mountains,
> split into huge wide cracks, and dried as it lost its moisture.
> The corn turned while and the trees were charred into leafless skeletons;
> parched grain offered the perfect fuel for self-ruination.
> Those losses were trifling. Destruction fell upon great walled cities;
> mighty nations with all their peoples with conflagration
> turned into ashes. Fire swept over the forest-clad mountains.
> ...
>
> Phaethon now looked down on a world in flames;
> Not a region
> remained unscorched. He couldn't endure the force of the heat ...
> Wrapped in the pitchy darkness, he didn't know where he was going
> nor where he might be, as the winged steeds swept him along at their mercy.[59]

2.2. *Ecological integrity*

> It's not the end of the world, but it is the end of pre-history.[60]

In the last section I argued that the Anthropocene requires an active commitment to exercising human power with humility and restraint. In making this argument, I noted that wilderness ethics and calls to step back and allow nature to return to a pristine state are inconsistent with our newfound status as geological agents. The Anthropocene exists 'at the heart of our lives' and cannot be disavowed.[61]

Perhaps the most powerful expression of this idea is Dipesh Chakrabarty's insight that the Anthropocene has undercut the 'artificial but time-honored distinction between natural and human histories'.[62] The traditional view is reflected in the writing of Jacob Burckhardt who argued that 'history is not the same thing as nature' and that history 'is the breach with nature caused by the awakening of human consciousness'.[63] Writers such as Aldo Leopold added some nuance to this perspective by bringing to life the active role the environment has played in human history.[64] However, scholars engaging

---

[59] *Ibid* 58–59.
[60] McKenzie Wark, *Molecular Red: Theory for the Anthropocene* (Verso 2016) xii.
[61] Stengers (n 49) 47.
[62] Dipesh Chakrabarty, 'The Climate of History: Four Theses' (2009) 35(2) *Critical Inquiry* 206.
[63] Jacob Burckhardt, *Reflections on History* (Liberty Fund, 1979 [1868]) 31.
[64] Aldo Leopold, *A Sand County Almanac* (Ballantine Books 1986) 241: 'Many historical events, hitherto explained solely in terms of human enterprise, were actually biotic interactions between people and

the Anthropocene are saying something different and new—the transformation of humankind into geological agents has marked the convergence of human history with geological history.[65] This argument has important implications for ecological theorists that describe human beings as mere biological agents.[66] Chakrabarty explains:

> To call human beings geological agents is to scale up our imagination of the human ... For it is no longer a question simply of man having an interactive relation with nature ... Now it is being claimed that humans are a force of nature in a geological sense. A fundamental assumption of Western (and now universal) political thought has come undone in this crisis.[67]

This is a controversial thesis and not without its critics.[68] However, it is also a compelling extrapolation from the Earth systems science described in the first part of this article. Drawing on Chakrabarty, Hamilton also argues that the social sciences 'have been built on an understanding of the historical processes that is no longer defensible'.[69] As natural history and human history collapse into one another, we must also rethink dichotomies between humans and nature (subjects and objects). This is not interconnectedness in an ecological sense or a homeostatic Gaia system. In the Anthropocene, the human is submerged into the Earth system and both have more power and volatility.

There are several implications that one can draw from this. For one, the Anthropocene challenges popular arguments that suggest that nature has its own independent integrity which exists outside the parameters of human affairs. The notion of ecological integrity derives from wilderness ethics and has also been recognised in legislative instruments such as the *Clean Water Act US* (1972) and the Earth Charter (2000) which has been endorsed by UNESCO. As described by Laura Westra, the generic concept of integrity 'connotes a valuable whole, the state of being whole or undiminished, unimpaired, or in perfect condition'.[70] Because of the extent of human exploitation of the environment, Westra argues further that 'wild nature' provides the paradigmatic example of ecological integrity[71] and James Karr suggests that tools such as the 'multimetric Index of Biological Integrity' might allow

the land. The characteristics of the land determined the facts quite as potently as the characteristics of the men who lived on it.'

65 Chakrabarty (n 59) 206.

66 *Ibid* 205–6.

67 *Ibid* 206–7.

68 Anna Grear, '"Anthropocene, Capitalocene, Chthulucene": Re-encountering Environmental Law and Its "Subject" with Haraway and New Materialism' in Louis Kotze (ed), *Environmental Law and Governance for the Anthropocene* (Hart Publishing 2017).

69 Hamilton (n 11) 8.

70 Laura Westra, 'Ecological Integrity' in Carl Mitcham (ed), *Encyclopaedia of Science, Technology and Ethics* (Macmillan Reference 2005) 574.

71 Laura Westra, *Ecological Integrity and Global Governance: Science, Ethics and the Law* (Routledge 2016) 5.

scientists to provide an approximate description of the extent to which systems deviate from verifiable integrity levels calibrated from a baseline condition of wild nature.[72] It is difficult to see how such ideas can persists in the Anthropocene. Certainly, we must abandon concepts that are grounded in a pristine nature that exists 'out there' and which exist (or can be returned to) a pristine state.

This has led some writers to redefine ecological integrity at a global level[73] and reimagine its parameters for the Anthropocene.[74] For example, Peter Bridgewater, Rakhyun E Kim, and Klaus Bosselmann have sought to define ecological integrity in the following way: '… the ecological integrity of an area of land (including freshwaters) or sea is the combination of the biodiversity and ecosystem processes (functions) that characterized the area at a given point in time'.[75] This is a much more encompassing definition and its insistence on measuring integrity 'at a given point in time' shifts our attention away from notions of pristine nature.[76] As we scale up, the authors have coined the term 'biosphere integrity' to describe the 'combination of the biodiversity and ecosystem processes that characterized the biosphere as a whole'.[77] The authors also propose that 'biosphere integrity' could be measured with reference to planetary boundaries, a concept that seeks to quantify the 'safe limits outside of which the Earth system cannot continue to function in a stale, Holocene-like state'.[78]

This proposal is worthy of further discussion and investigation. The key reason to try and update ecological integrity for the Anthropocene is instrumental—it allows us to 'leverage' a concept that is 'already included in major international instruments in the field of sustainable development'.[79] However, against this rationale we should pay attention to the ways concepts developed for the Holocene carry baggage into the new epoch. Specifically, in so far as integrity connotes purity and wholeness[80] it has no place in the Anthropocene. Relatedly, the seven planetary boundaries were not designed to measure Earth systems integrity or tipping points but the 'safe operating

---

[72] James Karr, 'Health, Integrity and Biological Assessment: The Importance of While Things' in David Pimentel, Laura Westra and Reed Noss (eds), *Ecological Integrity: Integrating Environment, Conservation and Health* (Island Press 2000) 96.

[73] J Ronald Engel, 'Moving Forward: New Approaches and Concluding Thoughts' in Laura Westra, Prue Taylor and Agnès Michelot (eds), *Confronting Ecological and Economic Collapse: Ecological Integrity for Law, Policy and Human Rights* (Routledge 2015) 240.

[74] Peter Bridgewater, Rakhyun E Kim and Klaus Bosselmann, 'Ecological Integrity: A Relevant Concept for International Environmental Law in the Anthropocene?' (2015) 25(1) *Yearbook of international Environmental* 61.

[75] *Ibid* 72.

[76] *Ibid* 73.

[77] *Ibid.*

[78] Johan Rockström et al, 'A Safe Operating Space for Humanity' (2009) 461 *Nature* 472.

[79] Bridgewater et al (n 70) 74.

[80] Westra (n 67) 5.

space for humanity'.[81] Planetary boundaries are more accurately seen as a guard rail, which when crossed, place us in a 'zone of uncertainty'. Steffan explains:

> This zone encapsulates both gaps and weaknesses in the scientific knowledge base and intrinsic uncertainty's in the functioning of the Earth system. At the "safe" end of the zone of uncertainty, current scientific knowledge suggests that there is a very low probability of crossing a critical threshold or significantly eroding the reliance of the Earth system. Beyond the "danger" end of the zone of uncertainty, current knowledge suggests a much higher probability of a change to the functioning of the Earth system that could potentially be devastating for human societies.[82]

Thus, I argue that the difference between ecological integrity and planetary boundaries is more than semantic and any attempt to retrofit the one onto the other must also grapple with these differences. If (as it seems to me) integrity is not a useful concept in the Anthropocene, then I see no reason why we cannot refine our ideas and develop new concepts that match our planetary situation. Here I am calling for nothing more than the same boldness and imagination that characterised the development of ecological law during its inception.

3. Conclusion

In this article, I have posed two challenges to advocates of ecological law. First, I have argued that ecological lawyers should adopt descriptive anthropocentrism as a central fact of the Anthropocene. Our challenge is not to construct a non-anthropocentric ethics but to come to terms with our new-found power and think about how we might act with humility and responsibility as geological agents. Second, I suggested that the concept of ecological integrity no longer provides an accurate model for thinking about ecological degradation or our planetary reality.

The Anthropocene represents a paradigm shift for our world view. We ought to be mindful of the way Holocene concepts are marked and perhaps also limited by the historical and scientific contexts from which they emerged. Today, we need fresh thinking and a willingness to grapple with uncertainty as the ground shifts beneath our feet.[83] As I have argued, a hallmark of ecological law has been its ability to confront orthodoxy and

---

81 Rockström et al (n 74) 472. Although I note that one of the seven boundaries concerns changes to biospheric integrity.

82 Will Steffen et al, 'Planetary Boundaries: Guiding Human Development on a Changing Planet' (2015) 347 *Science* 1259855.

83 Here I am invoking Werner Heisenberg's famous comment about the dawn of quantum physics: 'The violent reaction to the recent development of modern physics can only be understood when one realises that here the foundation of physics have started moving; and that this motion has caused the feeling that the ground would be cut from science.' See: Werner Heisenberg, *Philosophy and Physics* (Harper and Row 1962) 53.

established truths. Yet, we must be mindful of dogma and the way disciplines protect themselves by establishing a bulwark against change. As we enter a period of great uncertainty and volatility, we might take advice from Samuel Alexander: 'let us be pioneers once more!'[84]

Disclosure statement

No potential conflict of interest was reported by the author(s).

[84] Samuel Alexander, *Entropia: Life Beyond Industrial Civilisation* (Simplicity Institute Publishing 2013) 179.

Environmental trusteeship and state sovereignty: can they be reconciled?

Klaus Bosselmann

ABSTRACT

The call for Earth trusteeship cannot easily be reconciled with state sovereignty. The concept of state sovereignty emerged at a time of great distances and absolute national autonomy. In a globalised, interconnected world that utterly depends on the integrity of Earth's ecological systems, absolute territorial sovereignty is counterproductive and potentially life threatening. Arguably, the time is right for reconceptualisation state sovereignty. Sovereignty includes not just fiduciary and trusteeship obligations towards the state's own citizens, but also towards humanity at large and Earth as a whole. The current UN reform process including Agenda 2030 offers a window opportunity for institutionalising Earth trusteeship at international and national levels.

Introduction

The central question of Earth governance is how the protection of Earth and her ecological systems can be expressed in politics, law and governance.[1] If it is true that long-term survival depends on humanity's ability to maintain and restore the integrity of Earth's ecological systems,[2] then how we control and govern ourselves is—literally—vital. So far, our governments have not governed to cause measurable change. Rather they seem to be caught up in crisis management with little vision and commitment to tackling climate breakdown, the plight of the oceans and the massive loss of biological diversity.[3]

True to Albert Einstein's famous definition of insanity ('insanity is doing the same thing over and over again and expecting different results'), states have over and over again relied on negotiating compromises between environmental needs and economic demands. This is routine insanity. Humanity cannot negotiate the physical conditions that life on Earth, including human beings and their economies, depends on.

---

[1] Klaus Bosselmann, *Earth Governance: Trusteeship of the Global Commons* (Edward Elgar, 2015).

[2] Will Steffen and others, 'The Anthropocene: From Global Change to Planetary Stewardship' (2011) 40(7) *AMBIO A Journal of the Human Environment* 739.

[3] Bosselmann, 'Earth Governance: Trusteeship of the Global Commons' (n 1) 155.

It is 'known' that climate change could lead to a world of declining ecological and biological integrity, which threatens the future of all life on the planet.[4] Yet states have been dealing with climate change as just one issue amongst many others, and often competing, concerns, most notably the concern for ongoing economic growth.[5]

What is missing here is a sense of urgency. If you live in the poorer parts of the world the urgency is only too obvious. If you are young, the urgency is equally felt, but the same may be true for the rest of us as we all experience draughts, floods and erratic weather patterns on a regular basis and wherever we happen to live.

Urgency is less felt, however, in institutions of governance. Political leaders may express their concern about climate change at every possible occasion, however real action is a rarity. There are many reasons why governments—despite or, some might say, *because* of the *Paris Agreement*, do not really act.[6] The predominance of economic rationality (of cost efficiency and growth) is certainly a major reason. But there is also a remarkable myopia that economic and political institutions the world over suffer from. Corporations, governments and parliaments are neither willing nor sufficiently equipped to solve global environmental problems.

Why is this so? Again, there may be many reasons, but a main reason is that these institutions have been designed in an age of much narrower space and time horizons.[7] This is particularly true for the institution of the modern sovereign state. The Westphalian idea of nation states was designed at a time when Europe recovered from the trauma of 30-year-long civil war.[8] Creating a peace order of nation states that can be identified as such and held accountable was seen paramount. At the same time, the world outside Europe had been discovered offering highly attractive opportunities for trade and overseas possessions. The best tool for achieving both objectives was the idea of a sovereign state. Once control of a given territory and its people has been physically established, international law recognises this as the establishment (or extension, respectively) of a sovereign state.[9] State sovereignty allowed both mutual control and accountability of nations within Europe,

4 Anders Wijkman and Johan Rockström, *Bankrupting Nature: Denying Our Planetary Boundaries* (Routledge, Revised edn 2012) 44–47.

5 Klaus Bosselmann, *The Principle of Sustainability: Transforming Law and Governance* (Routledge, 2nd edn 2017), 179–180.

6 See generally Simon Copland, 'Anti-politics and Global Climate Inaction: The Case of the Australian Carbon Tax' (2019*) Critical Sociology* 1; Margaretha Wewerinke-Singh and Curtis Doebbler, 'The Paris Agreement: Some Critical Reflections on Process and Substance' (2016) 39(4) *University of New South Wales Law Journal* 1486.

7 Daniel C Est and Maria H Ivanova, 'Making International Environmental Efforts Work: the Case for a Global Environmental Organization' (2001) *Yale Center for Environmental Law and Policy* 1, 7–8.

8 Jason Farr, 'Point: The Westphalia Legacy and the Modern Nation–State' (2005) 80(3/4) *International Social Science Review* 156–159.

9 Margaret Moore, *A Political Theory of Territory* (Oxford University Press, 2015) 15.

to create the peace order, as well as European exploration and exploitation of the rest of the world: America, Africa, parts of Asia, Australia/New Zealand and Antarctica.

The core of state sovereignty was designed as property over their own territory at the exclusion of any foreigners ('territorial sovereignty').[10] This core has largely stayed unchanged until today and has been the legacy under which modern international environmental law was established.[11]

Principle 2 of the 1992 Rio *Declaration on Environment and Development* says: 'States have, in accordance with the Charter of the United Nations and the principles of international law, the sovereign right to exploit their own resources pursuant to their own environmental and developmental policies'.[12] Like a private owner of land, the state has the undisturbed right to exploit its territory. Crucially, the state has no obligation to protect it or protect any areas outside national boundaries such as oceans and the atmosphere.

On the other hand, the second half of Principle 2 says that states have 'the responsibility to ensure that activities within their jurisdiction or control do not cause damage to the environment of other States or of areas beyond the limits of national jurisdiction'. Furthermore, Principle 7 of the *Rio Declaration* reads: 'States shall cooperate in a spirit of global partnership to conserve, protect and restore the health and integrity of the Earth's ecosystem'.[13] So, is there a legal obligation of states to protect the global environment and integrity of the Earth's ecosystem after all?

The short answer is no. The current system of international law does not require the sovereign state to protect the natural environment within or beyond national boundaries.[14] It only expects states to consider—but not necessarily avoid—disastrous environmental consequences of their actions. There is huge discretion involved here, a degree of moral responsibility, but no legal obligations whatsoever. Only negotiated treaties and fundamental principles of international law could change that, but so far, all treaties have been too weak and fragile—not to mention lacking enforcement[15]—to urge states into the logic of common responsibility for the Earth. For this to happen, we need a deliberate, bold move towards trusteeship for the Earth.

---

10 Joseph Beale, 'The Jurisdiction of a Sovereign State' (1923) 36(3) *Harvard Law Review* 245.

11 Patricia Mische, 'National Sovereignty and Environmental Law', in Simone Bilderbeck (ed), *Biodiversity and International Law* (IUCN NL, Amsterdam 1992).

12 Rio Declaration on Environment and Development, (14 June 1992) UN DocA/CONF.151/26/1(1), Principle 2.

13 *Ibid*, Principle 7.

14 Klaus Bosselmann, 'Democracy, sovereignty and the challenge of the global commons' in Laura Westra, Janice Gray and Franz-Theo Gottwald (eds), *The Role of Integrity in the Governance of the Commons: Governance, Ecology, Law, Ethics* (Springer, 2017), 58.

15 UN Environment Programme, 'Dramatic Growth in Laws to Protect Environment, But Widespread Failure to Enforce, Finds Report' (2019), online: https://www.unenvironment.org/news-and-stories/press-release/dramatic-growth-laws-protect-environment-widespread-failure-enforce accessed 07 April 2020.

As a first step, we can ask ourselves who owns the Earth? Answering this question can lead us to some insights of who actually is in charge at present, to appreciate the critical role of legal concepts such as property and sovereignty in the context of global environmental protection and why a transnational approach based on Earth trusteeship is needed.

Who owns the Earth?

Who owns the Earth? For lawyers such a question is quite intriguing. We are used to capturing reality in legal terms, especially in legal property terms.

In a broad sentimental way, we can say all of us living today and whoever will come after us own the earth. And not just humans. All inhabitants of the planet 'own' the Earth in a sense that they need spaces to live in. But such an idea of ownership refers to a biological condition and does not tell us anything about power and control. Once we talk about power and control, the question arises what it means to legally own Earth.

For a start, only land can be owned in the legal sense, not water (including the oceans) or air (including the atmosphere). The Earth overall is 123 billion acres in size, of which 37 billion acres are land.[16] These 37 billion acres are currently shared by 7.3 billion people, so each of us theoretically owns five acres.[17] This is plenty of space per capita and should theoretically allow humanity to utilise available resources without overshooting the Earth's life-supporting capacity. In reality, there is a single person who legally owns about 6.6 billion acres, or one-sixth of the Earth's land surface. This person is Queen Elizabeth II, the Queen of 32 countries and head of a Commonwealth of 54 countries.[18] She owns, for example, the second-largest country on Earth, Australia, and also the third-largest country, Canada.

Legal ownership means control and power, but a lot depends on whether land is owned individually or collectively and whether ownership involves obligations of care and stewardship. In the case of Queen Elizabeth, she does not control the land herself, of course, but her countries do. Thanks to state sovereignty, Australia and Canada, for example, can do with their land whatever they like. They sure have done that extensively, and in recent times in the most exploitative way: Australia's coal mines[19] and Canada's oil sands[20] are responsible for a considerable chunk of carbons emitted into

[16] Mathis Wackernagel, What We Use and What We have: Ecological Footprint and Ecological Capacity (2002) online: https://edisciplinas.usp.br/pluginfile.php/49503/mod_resource/content/1/texto17.pdf

[17] *Ibid.*

[18] See Kevin Cahill, *Who Owns the World? The Hidden Facts Behind Land Ownership* (Mainstream Publisher, 2006).

[19] J Moss, 'When it comes to climate change, Australia's mining giants are an accessory to the crime' *The Conversation* (25 September 2009) online: https://theconversation.com/when-it-comes-to-climate-change-australias-mining-giants-are-an-accessory-to-the-crime-124077.

[20] Leslie Shiell and Suzanne Loney, 'Global Warming Damages and Canada's Oil Sands' (2007) 33(4) *Canadian Public Policy/Analyse de Politique* 419.

the global atmosphere, which incidentally, is not owned by anyone. The atmosphere, like the oceans, is *res nullius* (nobody's thing) and does not have any legal status that could be used to protect against interferences such as greenhouse gas emissions or, in the case of oceans, acidification, pollution, overfishing and biodiversity loss.[21]

Remember, legal ownership means power and control. As each of the world's 196 countries are 'owners' of their territories, they not only can do within their own territories whatever they like, they can also externalise any waste and pollution originating from their respective territories. This is either been done through commercial deals (eg, Europe's export of waste to poor countries in Africa or Asia).[22] Or it is done through discharges into areas outside national jurisdictions, ie, into the oceans (eg, plastic) and the atmosphere (eg, greenhouse gases). Both forms of discharge are, at present, perfectly legal. Apart from a few global treaties[23] and the legal doctrine of state responsibility[24]—both rather weak instruments—there is nothing that could legally prevent states from collectively destroying the Earth.

Countries do not intentionally destroy the Earth, of course, but they behave as if this is inevitable or, at least, just a distant risk. The reason for this ignorance is that governments continue to produce laws—domestically and internationally—that are essentially geared to secure 'their' property at the exclusion of all others. 'The other' comes in many forms: other states, other people (non-citizens, foreigners), other beings (animals and plants), other areas (global commons) and other times (future generations). Fundamentally, state sovereignty is about excluding 'the other' and cooperation between states is hampered by a counterproductive me–over–you attitude called national interest.

In this way, not just national laws, but the world's entire legal system was developed on the basis of protecting the individual ownership of states, corporations and people. In other words, national and international laws are largely about competing property rights. In today's culture of competition and rights, success is determined by ownership. You either own something in which case you are somebody or you own nothing in which case you are nobody.

[21] Friedrich Soltau, 'Common Concern of Mankind' in Kevin Gray, Richard Tarasofsky and Cinnamon Carlarne (eds), *The Oxford Handbook of International Climate Change Law* (Oxford University Press, 2016) 203.

[22] Mauro Anastasio, 'The EU countries using the rest of the world as a dumping ground', (13 February 2019) META from the European Environmental Bureau, online: https://meta.eeb.org/2019/02/13/revealed-the-eu-countries-using-the-rest-of-the-world-as-a-dumping-ground/.

[23] Examples of international treaties include the *Convention on Biological Diversity* 1992 (adopted 5 June 1992, entered into force 29 December 1993) (1992) 31 ILM 818; *Convention on Long-Range Transboundary Air Pollution* (adopted 13 November 1979, entered into force 16 March 1983) (1979) 18 ILM 1449; and *United Nations Framework Convention on Climate Change* (adopted 9 May 1992, entered into force 21 March 1994) (1992) UN Doc A/AC237/18, 31 ILM 848.

[24] See Bosselmann, *The Principle of Sustainability: Transforming Law and Governance* (n 5) 187–191.

What at a personal level may hardly be noticeable—most of us own, at least, 'something'—at a collective and global level appears as a massive problem: the richest 26 people own half of the world's assets[25] and the three richest people in the US—Jeff Bezos, Bill Gates and Warren Buffet—own as much wealth as the bottom half of the US population of 160 million.[26] The net worth of these three people alone is USD 286 billion which is higher than the combined annual Gross Domestic Product (GDP) of 47 countries.[27]

At global level, the combined GDP of the world's 11 richest countries—in descending order: United States, China, Japan, Germany, India, United Kingdom, France, Brazil, Italy, Canada and Korea[28]—is the same as the combined GDP of the remaining 185 countries. Small wonder that these 11, and only a further 15 or so other countries, are firmly in charge of everything that affects the lives of the world's entire population: what is being done about climate change, nuclear weapons, poverty, food security or the internet, including our personal data. Rich countries shape the international agenda and would never accept anything that could jeopardise their specific economic and strategic interests.

Yet, even such imbalances between the world's few rich and the many poor people cannot deny the reality of the situation that we are in. Ultimately, the lives and living standards of all people—rich or poor—depends on our ability to preserve the Earth's ecological systems. We are all in this together and only a common effort to take responsibility for Earth can save us. I believe that the law has a very important role to play here.

Reclaiming Earth: trusteeship of the global commons

There is an ever-growing movement of environmental lawyers that has found its expression in the advocacy of Earth jurisprudence, Earth law and ecological law.[29] Some recent developments give us a sense just how significant this legal movement has been.

---

25 Max Lawson et al., 'Public Good or Private Wealth?' (January 2019) Oxfam Briefing Paper, 28 online: https://oxfamilibrary.openrepository.com/bitstream/handle/10546/620599/bp-public-good-or-private-wealth-210119-en.pdf?utm_source=indepth accessed 7 April 2020.

26 Chuck Collins, 'The Wealth of America's Three Richest Families Grew by 6,000% since 1982' *The Guardian* (31 October 2018) online: https://www.theguardian.com/commentisfree/2018/oct/31/us–wealthiest–families–dynasties–governed–by–rich accessed 7 April 2020.

27 Wikipedia, *International Inequality* (2020) online: http://en.wikipedia.org/wiki/International_inequality accessed 7 April 2020.

28 Measured in USD: Knoema, *World GDP Ranking 2019|GDP by Country|Data and Charts* (29 January 2020) online: https://knoema.com/nwnfkne/world–gdp–ranking–2019–gdp–by–country–data–and–charts accessed 7 April 2020.

29 See Klaus Bosselmann and Prue Taylor (eds), *Ecological Approaches to Environmental Law* (Edward Elgar, 2017).

In 2016, some 100 professors of environmental law adopted a manifesto called 'From Environmental Law to Ecological Law' at the International Union for Conservation of Nature (IUCN) Academy of Environmental Law Colloquium in Oslo, Norway. The *Oslo Manifesto*[30] has since been endorsed by hundreds of environmental lawyers and law organisations from around the world and has led to the establishment of the Ecological Law and Governance Association (ELGA) in 2017.[31] ELGA is a global network of lawyers and environmental activists that coordinates initiatives for transforming law and governance.

One of these initiatives is the Earth Trusteeship Initiatives (ETI), established on 10 December 2018 in the Peace Palace in The Hague, Netherlands. This day marked the 70th anniversary of the adoption of the *Universal Declaration of Human Rights.*[32] With the support and endorsement of many human rights, environmental and professional organisations, the ETI launched the *Hague Principles for a Universal Declaration on Responsibilities for Human Rights and Earth Trusteeship.*[33]

The three 'Hague Principles' set out the framework for Earth trusteeship. All rights that human beings enjoy depend on responsibilities that we have for each other and, crucially, for the Earth. We cannot live in dignity and well-being without accepting fundamental duties for each other and for Earth. These are trusteeship duties. We must understand ourselves as 'People for Earth' or trustees of Earth.[34] As citizens of our respective countries, we must demand our governments to accept Earth trusteeship. State sovereignty implies obligations as trustees of human rights and the Earth.

In our current legal system, Earth has no meaning or status. Earth is taken for granted as if it does not need to be protected. On the other hand, we all know that critical planetary systems are at risk (the atmosphere, oceans, global biodiversity). We also know that protection efforts based on negotiations between states have not worked very well. A logical step forward is, therefore, to establish trusteeship obligations of states themselves, rather than relying on political compromises between states. The sovereign state is not so sovereign as to ruin its own territory, transboundary ecological systems, and Earth as a whole.

In the light of what we know about our age of human planetary dominance (the Anthropocene), we need to revisit the concept of state sovereignty

30 'Oslo Manifesto' (*ELGA*, June 2016), online: www.elga.world/oslo–manifesto/ accessed 7 April 2020.

31 'Our Misson, Our Vision' (*ELGA*, 2020), online: www.elga.world/ accessed 7 April 2020.

32 'Earth Trusteeship' (*Earth Trusteeship*, 2020) online: www.earthtrusteeship.world/ accessed 7 April 2020.

33 'The Hague Principles' (*Earth Trusteeship*, 2020) online: www.earthtrusteeship.world/the-hague-principles-for-a-universal-declaration-on-human-responsibilities-and-earth-trusteeship/ accessed 7 April 2020.

34 'About Us' (*People for Earth*, 2016) online: www.peopleforearth.kr/eng/default.asp accessed 7 April 2020.

inherited from an age when a global environmental crisis did not exist.[35] Now is the time to advance the concept of sovereignty as a concept of rights and responsibilities.[36] The rights of self-determination and non-intervention must be complemented by responsibilities for human rights and the Earth.[37] In my address to the UN General Assembly in April 2017, I said the following:

> The ethics of stewardship or guardianship for the community of life is one of the most foundational concepts in the history of humanity. It is inherent in the teachings of the world's religions and the traditions of indigenous peoples and is, an integral part of humanity's cultural heritage. Yet, our political and legal institutions have not taken Earth ethics to heart. The Earth as an integrated whole may be featuring in images, in science and in ethics, but does not feature in law. Earth and the areas outside national jurisdictions (the global commons) are considered as *res nullius*, a legal nullity without inherent rights. Not that Earth cares about such rights. It is we humans who must choose to care about them. If we keep ignoring them, then basically we are saying that the Earth system doesn't really matter. We take it for granted—like sunshine and rain—and of no relevance to the system of law that governs society and states. Given that the ethics of Earth stewardship are widely accepted today we should be ready for taking the next step: Earth trusteeship.
>
> Earth trusteeship is the essence of what Earth jurisprudence is advocating, but, more importantly, it has also been advocated in key international environmental documents. Earth trusteeship is the institutionalization of the duty to protect the integrity of ecological systems.
>
> This duty is expressed in no less than 25 international agreements—from the 1982 *World Charter for Nature* right through to the 2015 *Paris Climate Agreement*![38] To act on this duty 'states need to cooperate in the spirit of global partnership' as, for example, Principle 7 of the 1992 *Rio Declaration* says.[39]

The legal argument for Earth trusteeship can be firmly based on ethics common to all cultures and fundamental obligations of states expressed in many international agreements. The challenge ahead is to convince governments that the step to Earth trusteeship is not only necessary, but actually possible and not too difficult to take.

---

35 Nico Schrijver, 'The Dynamics of Sovereignty in a Changing World' in Konrad Ginther, Erik Denters and PJIM De Waart (eds) *Sustainable Development and Good Governance* (Kluwer Law International, 1995), 80–89.

36 Bosselmann, *The Principle of Sustainability: Transforming Law and Governance,* (n 5) 169.

37 Eyal Benvenisti, 'Sovereigns as Trustees of Humanity: On the Accountability of States to Foreign Stakeholders' (2013) 107(2) *American Journal of International Law* 295.

38 Rakhyun E Kim and Klaus Bosselmann, 'Operationalizing Sustainable Development: Ecological Integrity as a Grundnorm in International Law' (2015) 24(2) *Review of European, Comparative and International Environmental Law* 194, 194–208.

39 Klaus Bosselmann, 'The Next Step: Earth Trusteeship', (April 2017) Address to the United Nations General Assembly, 2–3 online: http://files.harmonywithnatureun.org/uploads/upload96.pdf.

An important part of meeting this challenge is the public debate around the global commons. As climate change has become the most pressing issue of our time—largely thanks to powerful protests of young people all over the world—a shift of thinking seems to be occurring. Rather than having to justify calls for action, people put governments on the back foot: lack of action can no longer be justified. More radical measures than negotiating climate deals are needed.

To think that global warming can be negotiated is like thinking rainfall and sunshine could be negotiated. The biogeochemical cycles of the atmosphere follow laws of nature, not laws of humans. It is therefore more realistic and promising to take the atmosphere into focus and recognise it in law! At present, the law treats the atmosphere as an open access resource without any safeguards, ie, a *res nullius.* This legal vacuum has worked to the advantage of property owners who have filled the vacuum by exercising their property rights. Any holder of property rights—you and me or the entire fossil fuel industry—can freely emit carbon dioxide into the atmosphere. Only negotiated deals and compromises would limit these emissions. It would be far more effective if property rights are limited by the atmosphere as a global commons. This would constitute a legal duty to protect the integrity of the atmosphere as a whole and reverse the logic of emissions: they are only protected by property rights in so far they do not compromise the integrity of the atmosphere.

Emissions would no longer be free, but subject to hefty fees and taxes. As trustees of the atmosphere, states and the international community of states would have a legal obligation to charge users of the atmosphere such as corporations, banks and consumers, and to progressively ban any greenhouse gas emissions. Just as the owner of a house controls who lives there and under what conditions.

From the perspective of citizens, this logic is compelling and could, for example, be supported by the well-established public trust doctrine. The public trust doctrine says that natural commons should be held in trust as assets to serve the public good.[40] It is the responsibility of the government, as trustee, to protect these assets from harm and ensure their use for the public and future generations. So nationally, the government would act as an environmental trustee, internationally, states would jointly act as trustees for the global commons such as the atmosphere.

Considering that only about 90 companies are responsible for two-thirds of carbons emitted into the atmosphere, a global trusteeship institution could quickly fix the problem of climate breakdown.[41] All it takes is the political will to do so!

---

[40] Burns H Weston and David Bollier, *Green Governance: Ecological Survival, Human Rights, and the Law of the Commons* (Cambridge University Press, 2013) 245–248.

[41] Robert Costanza, 'Claim the Sky!' (2015 6(1)) *Solutions* 21.

The idea of trusts of the global commons has been promoted by environmental lawyers such as Mary Wood[42] and Peter Sand,[43] and economists such as Peter Barnes[44] and Robert Costanza.[45] Trusteeship governance is also advocated by the general literature on the commons.[46]

Essentially, international law and the United Nations (UN) are ready to develop institutions of trusteeship governance. There is, for example, a tradition of UN institutions with a trusteeship mandate including the (now defunct) UN Trusteeship Council, the World Health Organization (WHO) with respect to public health and—somewhat ironically—the World Trade Organization (WTO) with respect to free trade.[47] A number of other UN or UN-related institutions with weaker trusteeship functions exist also.[48] Quite obviously, states have been capable of, expressively or implicitly, creating international trusteeship institutions. These developments—and in particular the existence of supranational organisations such as the European Union—demonstrate that sovereignty of states can be transferred to international levels.

The UN Trusteeship Council could quite easily be revived as an Environmental Trusteeship Council following proposals by the Global Governance Commission in 1995 which were supported by a number of states and particularly championed by the former UN Secretary General, the late Kofi Annan. A combination of environmental activism (the 'Greta effect') and new political alliances between motivated progressive states can make a crucial difference. Chances are that such combined effort will be very powerful as our global ecological, financial, political and democratic systems continue to disintegrate.

Trusteeship governance will not be initiated by the 'top', ie, the UN and its member states themselves, but rather by global civil society forces outside the system. To this end, we can build on many years of activism and proposals for institutional change. Nor can states be allowed to exclusively run and control

---

[42] Mary C Wood, 'Nature's Trust: A Legal, Political and Moral Frame for Global Warming' (2007) 34(3) *Environmental Affairs* 577; Mary C Wood, *Nature's Trust: Environmental Law for a New Ecological Age* (Carolina University Press, 2013).

[43] Peter H Sand, 'Sovereignty Bounded: Public Trusteeship for Common Pool Resources' (2004) 4(1) *Global Environmental Politics* 47; Peter H Sand, 'The Rise of Public Trusteeship in International Law' (2013) *Global Trust Working Paper Series* 04/2013, 21; Peter H Sand, 'The Concept of Public Trusteeship in the Transboundary Governance of Biodiversity' in Louis Kotzé and Thilo Marauhn, *Transboundary Governance of Biodiversity* (Brill, 2014).

[44] Peter Barnes, *Capitalism 2.0: Who Owns the Sky? Our Common Assets and the Future of Capitalism* (Island Press, 2001); Peter Barnes, *Capitalism 3.0: A Guide to Reclaiming the Commons* (Berret–Koehler Publishers, 2006).

[45] 'Claim the Sky' (*AVAASZ.org*, 12 May 2015) online: https://secure.avaaz.org/en/petition/Claim_the_Sky/?pv=58

[46] See, for example, David Bollier, *Think Like a Commoner: A Short Introduction to the Life of the Commons* (New Society Publishers, 2014); David Bollier and Burns H Weston, *Green Governance: Ecological Survival, Human Rights and the Law of the Commons* (Cambridge University Press, 2013); Silke Helfrich and Jörg Haas (eds), *The Commons: A New Narrative for Our Time* (Heinrich Böll Stiftung, 2009); Elinor Ostrom, *Governing the Commons: The Evolution of Institutions for Collective Action* (Cambridge University Press, 1990).

[47] Bosselmann, *Earth Governance: Trusteeship of the Global Commons* (n 1) 198–232.

[48] *Ibid*, 206.

global trusteeship institutions such as a World Environment Organization or a Global Atmospheric Trust. Rather, their governance ought to be jointly formed by representatives from global civil society, UN and states, each with an equal say in decision-making.

So far, governments have been very slow learners and, most alarmingly, they have been too close to corporate powers. The challenge for civil society is, therefore, to bring them back into a position that allows them to actually govern and help solving the crisis rather than just managing or even exacerbating it.

Sovereignty and trusteeship

It has been observed by many political analysts and activists that our democratic institutions have been hijacked by neoliberal economics. The unholy alliance between politics ('sovereignty') and private interests ('property') raises serious questions about the ability for the public to influence policy. Furthermore, as Barnes points out, '[n]ot even seated at democracy's table —not organised, not propertied, and not enfranchised—are future generations, ecosystems, and nonhuman species'.[49]

Neoliberalism has undoubtedly affected how environmental policy and law is conceived *within* states also. Primarily, they are characterised by what Mary Wood calls a 'discretionary frame'.[50] This means that governments have positioned themselves as holding discretionary powers to permit resource exploitation.[51] Domestic environmental commons may be 'government-owned' but this is not to say that they are managed on behalf of future generations, nonhuman species, or ordinary citizens.[52] To the contrary, domestic commons such as forests, water, and energy have been privatised and commercialised in most countries.

We can clearly see that 'governance' today is about a *quid pro quo* relationship between politicians and corporations.[53] The rewards include an unshaken guarantee of property rights, friendly regulators, subsidies, tax breaks and free use of the commons. What this ultimately means is that when issues such as environmental degradation arise, governments do not govern, rather create as little interruption to market forces as possible. In the words of Peter Barnes, 'we face a disheartening quandary here. Profit-maximising corporations dominate our economy. Their programming makes them enclose and diminish commonwealth. The only obvious counterweight is government, yet government

---

[49] Barnes (2006) (n 44), 38. See further, Naomi Klein, *On Fire: The (Burning) Case for a Green New Deal* (Simone Schuster, 2019); Naomi Klein, *The Shock Dcotrine: The Rise of Disaster Capitalism* (Henry Holt and Company, 2008); Tim Kuhner, *Capitalism v Democracy: Money in Politics and the Free Market Constitution* (Stanford University Press, 2014).

[50] Wood (2007) (n 46).

[51] *Ibid*, 592.

[52] Barnes (2006) (n 44), 43.

[53] *Ibid*, 37.

is dominated by these same corporations'.[54] The assumption that the state promotes 'the common good' is sadly false.[55]

On the other hand, the legitimacy of the state rests on its function to act for, and on behalf of, its citizens. This requires consent with the governed.[56] Governmental duties can therefore be understood as fiduciary obligations towards citizens.[57] Such fiduciary obligations are typically recognised in public law,[58] exist in common law and civil law although in varying forms and degrees,[59] and are also known in international law.[60] The fiduciary function of the state can also be described as a trusteeship function.[61]

How then can state sovereignty can be reconciled with trusteeship? *Prima facie* both seem to have different purposes, yet they are part of the same basic function of the state: to serve the citizens it depends on and is accountable to.

Furthermore, global commons governance brings sovereignty and trusteeship close together.[62] As has been noted, the traditional concept of sovereignty is less compelling today than it was in the past because of a 'glaring misfit between the scope of the sovereign's authority and the sphere of the affected stakeholders'[63] This 'glaring misfit' engenders inefficient, undemocratic and unjust outcomes for under or un-represented affected stakeholders.[64] Non-citizens, future generations and the natural environment all fall into such a category of 'affected stakeholders'. To overcome this misfit, states need to increasingly perform trusteeship functions.

Fiduciary duties of the state

The state gains its legitimacy exclusively from the people who created it. While the legality of a state depends on recognition by other states, once in

---

54 *Ibid*, 45.
55 *Ibid*.
56 Richard Ashcraft (ed), *John Locke: Critical Assessments* (Routledge, 1991) 524. According to Locke, '(G)overnment is not legitimate unless it is carried on with the consent of the governed'.
57 Evan Fox-Decent, *Sovereignty's Promise: The State as a Fiduciary* (Oxford University Press, 2012); Tamar Frankel, 'Fiduciary Law' (1983) 71(3) *California Law Review* 795.
58 Including constitutional law, administrative law, tax law, criminal law and environmental law.
59 For example, the United States, Canada, Australia and New Zealand recognise them with respect to indigenous peoples, ratepayers and (with the exception of New Zealand) in the form of public trusts, whereas continental European countries more fundamentally rely on public law to assume fiduciary relationships between individuals and governments.
60 Michael Blumm and Rachel Guthrie, 'Internationalizing the Public Trust Doctrine' (2012) 45 *University of California, Davis Law Review* 741; Henry H Perritt Jr, 'Structures and Standards for Political Trusteeships' (2004) 8(2) *UCLA Journal of International Law and Foreign Affairs* 385; Edith Brown Weiss, 'The Planetary Trust: Conservation and Intergenerational Equity' (1984) 11(4) *Ecology Law Quarterly* 495.
61 Paul Finn, 'The Forgotten "Trust": The People and the State' in Malcolm Cope (ed), *Equity: Issues and Trends* (The Federation Press, 1995) 131–151.
62 Stephen Stec, 'Humanitarian Limits to Sovereignty: Common Concern and Common Heritage Approaches to Natural Resources and Environment' (2010) 12(3) *International Community Law Review* 361, 384–385, 378–380.
63 Benvenisti (n 41), 301.
64 *Ibid*.

existence a state can only ever legitimise its continued existence through ongoing trust by its people. The core idea of the modern democratic state is that it acts through its people, by its people and for its people. This implies a fiduciary relationship between people and state and is arguably the only legitimate basis for political authority in the English civil war, American Revolution, and then again confirmed in the French Revolution.[65] It is echoed in constitutional documents such as the 1776 Pennsylvania *Declaration of Rights*: '[A]ll power being … derived from the people; therefore all officers of government, whether legislative or executive, are their trustees and servants, and at all times accountable to them'.[66] John Locke had famously asserted that legislative power is 'only a fiduciary power to act for certain ends' and that 'there remains still in the people a supreme power to remove or alter the legislative, when they find the legislative act contrary to the trust reposed in them'.[67]

Likewise, Immanuel Kant drew the moral basis of fiduciary obligations from the duty-bound relationship between parents and children.[68] Kant claimed that children have an innate and legal right to their parents' care. In a similar sense, he believed that state legitimacy was grounded in the existence of commonly shared values and interests, which we can refer to as a 'basic norm' (akin to Kelsen's *grundnorm*).[69] Apart from creating legal certainty, Kant's basic norm is exclusively concerned with achieving lasting peace. A strong argument can be made that, today, this basic norm includes sustainability and the protection of ecological integrity.[70] Further, it holds clear jurisprudential potential to protect the ecological integrity of Earth on the basis that no rational human, or nation state, could imagine a world where sustaining and protecting the planet is not a prior duty to any further activity, duty or right that those persons or states may hold.[71] This puts the state into the position as guardian or trustee of the natural environment.

That state sovereignty is fundamentally a trust relationship cannot be dismissed as a mere ideal. Trusts and the implicit fiduciary relationships can be traced back to Middle Eastern origins, Roman and Germanic law. They are also inherent in the teachings of the world's religions and are prevalent in non-Western cultures.[72] In fundamental terms, the trust relationship is

---

65 W Michael Reisman, 'Sovereignty and Human Rights in Contemporary International Law' (1990) 84(4) *American Journal of International* Law 867.

66 Evan Criddle and Evan Fox–Decent, 'A Fiduciary Theory of Jus Cogens' (2009) 34(2) *Yale Journal of International Law* 331; *Pennsylvania Constitution* 1776, Article IV.

67 Ashcroft, (n 56).

68 Criddle and Fox-Decent (n 66), 352.

69 Bosselmann, *The Principle of Sustainability: Transforming Law and Governance* (n 5) 94.

70 *Ibid.*

71 Mehmet Ruhi Demiray 'Natural Law Theory, Legal Positivism and the Normativity of Law' (2015) 20(8) *The European Legacy* 822.

72 Bosselmann, *The Principle of Sustainability: Transforming Law and Governance* (n5) 378–379.

also anchored in the *Universal Declaration of Human Rights.* Article 21(3) states that 'the will of the people shall be the basis of the authority of government'.[73]

Following Eyal Benvenisti, we can conceive of three normative arguments for state trusteeship. First, sovereignty should be viewed as a vehicle for the exercise of personal and collective self-determination.[74] Collective self-determination embodies the freedom of a group to pursue its interests, further its political status, and 'freely dispose of [its] natural wealth and resources'[75] or, of course, protect and preserve them. Second, sovereign states are agents of humanity as a whole as all human beings are holders of rights not because states granted them, but because they are entitlements of free born, equal human beings.[76] The legitimacy of a state ultimately depends on its ability to honour and respect human rights, hence the trusteeship function of the state with respect to humanity. Third, the right to own natural resources ('territorial sovereignty') is intrinsically linked with the responsibility to protect them. Any disjuncture would jeopardise the sustained use by citizens, hence the need for state trusteeship of the (borderless) natural environment.

In essence, the legitimacy of the state of the twenty-first century utterly rests on its ability to function as a trustee of human rights and the natural environment.

Conclusion

Earth governance is the expression of protecting the Earth and its ecological systems through politics and law. While the importance of protecting the natural environment has been well recognised, there are currently no legal obligations on states to protect the environment within or beyond national boundaries. The question of legal ownership of the Earth is crucial to understanding the power and control which states, companies and individuals exercise over natural resources. The paramountcy of property rights in legal systems means that owners can exploit these resources as they wish and exclude the interests of other affected stakeholders: other people, beings, areas and generations. Furthermore, the power accompanying ownership means that only a few very rich countries, companies and people set the entire international environmental agenda. The concept of Earth trusteeship has arisen in the environmental legal movement, which argues that states should adopt trusteeship obligations for the Earth's ecological systems. This would ensure stronger environmental protection compared to current

73 *Universal Declaration of Human Rights,* (adopted 10 December 1948 UNGA Res 217 A(III).
74 Benvenisti (n 34) 301.
75 *International Covenant on Civil and Political Rights,* (adopted 16 December 1966, entered into force 23 March 1976) (1966) 999 UNTS 171, Article 1.
76 Benvenisti (n 34) 305.

diluted compromises balancing the environment against economic growth and efficiency.

Earth trusteeship also requires a redefinition of the idea of state sovereignty where states not only have traditional rights of self-determination and non-intervention but also have responsibilities for human rights and the Earth. While initially appearing irreconcilable, Earth trusteeship is compatible with sovereignty as it forms part of the fiduciary duties owed by states to their citizens. The worldwide neoliberal economic system encouraging privatisation and mass exploitation undermines the legitimacy of a state through its failure to serve the best interests of its citizens. The global scale of climate change challenges the narrow Westphalian conception of sovereignty and demands a departure from the traditional rule that care for the environment ends at national boundaries. Protection of the Earth's ecological systems must be a domestic concern as much as an international concern. Ultimately, it is not states, but the well-being of Earth, which must determine the degree and quality of environmental protection. Such an Earth-centred viewpoint forces our political institutions into the logic of Earth trusteeship.

Disclosure statement

No potential conflict of interest was reported by the author(s).

Beyond Sustainability and the Anthropocene: Enhancing the Conservation Value of Ecosystems using Ecological Restoration!

Afshin Akhtar-Khavari

ABSTRACT
Environmental law is ontologically committed to competition. This is evidenced by its use of framing concepts like sustainability which assume that landscapes have always had the carrying capacity to regenerate on their own. The Anthropocene, if anything, points to the deep entanglements that exist in nature and for human beings. Whilst competition explains evolutionary trends, there is much evidence pointing to the idea that cooperation and symbiosis amongst living things is a much better indicator of long-term change in the natural environment. Deep entanglements are better supported through cooperation than competition. Drawing on ideas from scientific research on symbiosis, this paper argues that environmental law is missing deep ontological commitments to cooperation between human beings and the natural world. Restoration, approached not just as a technical rules-based response to damage and degradation, but as an activity requiring cooperation with the natural world would potentially better support flourishing socio-ecological landscapes.

Introduction

In one week, a country like Australia experienced ravaging fires burning through important parts of the country. As if that was not enough, some of these same regions also experienced floods, hail and also dust storms. Some of these parts of Australia had also been through severe drought for many years. Is this the Anthropocene? An epoch that stands for the idea that human beings are central to the significant alterations and changes in the natural world, such as for instance the climate systems that drove the weather variations and uncertainties for Australia.[1] As planet Earth pushes back against the impact of anthropogenic harm, scholars and others have

[1] See for example, Jeremy Davies, *The Birth of the Anthropocene* (University of California Press 2016).

been drawing on the concept of the Anthropocene to argue against the ongoing viability of established ideas and institutions, and have aimed at reorienting our thinking about the human-nature relationship.[2] Others have also moved on to the post-Anthropocene world, and our imagination and 'prefigurative politics'[3] has already started to play with concepts and finding names for it.[4] There is no shortage of new terms for big ideas, including for instance, the 'good Anthropocene',[5] the Ecozoic,[6] Chthulucene,[7] or the Symbiocene.[8] Alongside these we also have imaginative normative suggestions for pushing humanity to do things differently, such as 'Half-Earth',[9] and 'no-net-loss'.[10]

In many of these studies there is an effort to critique, to reimagine and idealise how human beings should live socio-ecologically. However, sustainability continues to be used globally as the normative institutional frame for environmental law developments.[11] Sustainability assumes that ecosystems have intact regenerative capacities, which is not necessarily going to be the case everywhere. This paper argues that restoration should be framed through ideas which can achieve net-gain, like flourishing socio-ecological landscapes, rather than sustainability. To do this however we require the ontologies of environmental law to shift, from competition amongst human beings, to cooperation directly involving the more-than-human-world. Using the literature on the science of symbiosis, this article will explore how cooperation can explain as much of what happens in the Anthropocene than competition. If disruption and change are the new normal, then human institutions have to take more seriously the ontologies that can facilitate a different trajectory in the Anthropocene. This paper concludes arguing that activities like restoration can achieve shorter-term technical solutions for

---

[2] Subcommission on Quarternary Stratigraphy, *Working Group on the 'Anthropocene': What is the Anthropocene? – Current Definition and Status* (23 February 2016) <http:/quaternary.stratigraphy.org/workinggroups/Anthropocene/>.

[3] John Law and John Urry, 'Enacting the Social' (2004) 33 *Economy and Society* 390.

[4] See for example, Albrecht's discussion of the idea of the Symbiocene in Glenn A Albrecht, *Earth Emotions: New Words for a New World* (Cornell University Press 2019); Ivan Vargas Roncancio et al, 'From the Anthropocene to Mutual Thriving: An Agenda for Higher Education in the Ecozoic' (2019) 11 *Sustainability* 3312.

[5] Elena Bennett et al, 'Bright Spots: Seeds of a Good Anthropocene' (2016) 14(8) *Frontiers in Ecology and the Environment* 441; Manuel Arias-Maldonado, 'Towards a Good Anthropocene?' in Manuel Arias-Maldonado and Zev Trachtenberg (eds), *Rethinking the Environment for the Anthropocene* (Routledge 2019).

[6] See Vargas Roncancio et al (n 4).

[7] Donna J Haraway, *Staying with the Trouble: Making Kin in the Chthulucene* (Duke University Press 2016).

[8] Albrecht (n 4).

[9] Edward O Wilson, *Half-Earth: Our Planet's Fight for Life* (Liveright Publishing Corporation 2016).

[10] See J B Ruhl, 'Currencies and the Commodification of Environmental Law' (2001) 53 *Stanford Law Review* 607; James Salzman and J B Ruhl, '"No Net Loss" – Instrument Choice in Wetlands Protection' in Jody Freeman and Charles D Kolstad (eds), *Moving to Markets in Environmental Regulation: Lessons from Twenty Years of Experience* (Oxford Scholarship Online 2006); Martine Maron et al, 'The Many Meanings of No Net Loss in Environmental Policy' (2018) 1 *Nature Sustainability* 19.

[11] The word 'institution' describes the broader function that the law can play in shaping and giving reason for the actions of individuals and organisations. See Kenneth M Ehrenberg, *The Functions of Law* (Oxford University Press 2016).

harm, and rebuild and make us aware of new ontologies for the Anthropocene.

Damage, degradation and destruction in environmental law

The Anthropocene is generally seen as closing off the Holocene Epoch, which was a period supportive of human civilisation because the Earth is seen as having had a stable environment during it.[12] The geological origins of the concept of the Anthropocene indicate that it is agnostic about whether we will have increased destruction, degradation and damage of ecosystems and habitats. There is much data however that suggests that this is now the case,[13] and the idea of planetary boundaries uses nine different parameters, for instance, to measure and ascertain the point at which anthropogenic harm can be problematic. The planetary boundaries work is designed as a framework to understand how much the natural environment can assimilate waste and harm, and remain resilient.[14] The data from published papers suggest that we have already crossed several important thresholds, particularly in relation to climate systems.[15] Ecosystems have always been able to assimilate waste and harm, whilst remaining resilient at the same time. The planetary boundaries framework is used for predicting when the assimilative capacity of ecosystems can fail or get overwhelmed.

At the landscape and more local level, the functional capacity of ecosystems are also threatened, and systemic degradation and destruction continue because of anthropogenic harms that come from the movements of invasive species (leading to homogenisation), habitat fragmentation and clearing, climate change, and the modification of biogeochemical cycles. The scale of such harms is now so significant that they have affected how well ecosystems can regenerate on their own.[16] Whilst in specific cases it will be hard to know whether an ecosystem is more or less resilient, and able to regenerate on its own, it is at least easy to notice degradation and destruction. In most scenarios restoration activities and inputs are mandated at the point when we have crossed a threshold or seen actual degradation and destruction rather than when a landscape is not regenerating effectively or flourishing.

International regimes in the past have been built on the assumption that assimilating harm and damage did not in the long term affect the regenerative

[12] Chris Wilson, Time, 'Obituary: Remembering the Holocene Epoch' (29 August 2016) <https://time.com/4471327/holocene-epoch-end-anthropocene/>.

[13] L Montanarella, R Scholes and A Brainich (eds), Intergovernmental Science-Policy Platform on Biodiversity and Ecosystem Services, *The IPBES Assessment Report on Land Degradation and Restoration* (2019) <https://ipbes.net/assessment-reports/ldr>.

[14] J Rockström et al, 'Planetary Boundaries: Exploring the Safe Operating Space for Humanity' (2009) 14(2) *Ecology and Society* 32.

[15] *Ibid*; Will Steffen et al, 'Planetary Boundaries: Guiding Human Development on a Changing Planet' (2015) 347(6223) *Science* 1259855.

[16] For a thorough discussion of these issues, see Montanarella, Scholes and Brainich (n 13).

capacity of the natural environment. For instance, the 1972 *Ocean Dumping* regime was built on the assumption that the ocean had an 'infinite ability to assimilate waste'.[17] The sustainability framework itself is also built on the assumption of 'stationarity',[18] or the ability of natural systems to regenerate.[19] It assumes that competition is the norm but that the complexity of the relationships at the local level have to be measured, managed and fairly administered in favour of everyone, including the natural environment. Whilst sustainability measures aim to protect and preserve the natural environment, they presume that there is not accumulated harm that needs to be managed.[20] Also, sustainability (given its value for human beings) is a local phenomenon, whereas the accumulation of harm also happens at the planetary scale. We use protection and preservation as concepts to manage the competitive pressures on the environment from our local activities. Whilst these concepts help, environmental law rarely aims at something equivalent to a 'net gain',[21] or cumulative value,[22] that adds to the functional capacity of ecosystems. As a result of its paradigm driven focus on protection and preservation, a significant portion of environmental law has been centred on human activities that use and consume the natural world. This takes us to the heart of some current challenges with environmental law—damage, degradation and destruction of ecosystems do not just happen overnight, but our systems do not seem particularly well equipped for avoiding or reducing them because we assume resilience, stability and a capacity in the natural world to always regenerate itself. The assumption of stability and regenerative capacities of nature behind sustainability encourage competition amongst humans for nature, and protection and preservation paradigms do not do much to cushion the fallouts.

The 2018 report of the Intergovernmental Science-Policy Platform on Biodiversity and Ecosystem Services (IPBES) on *Land Degradation and Restoration* (*IPBES Land Degradation* report) identified land degradation as a 'pervasive, systemic phenomenon' which 'occurs in all parts of the terrestrial

---

[17] See James Harrison, *Saving the Oceans Through Law: The International Legal Framework for the Protection of the Marine Environment* (Oxford University Press 2017) ch 5.

[18] Melinda Harm Benson and Robin Kundis Craig, *The End of Sustainability* (University Press of Kansas 2017).

[19] See Anastasia Telesetsky, An Cliquet and Afshin Akhtar-Khavari, *Ecological Restoration and International Environmental Law* (Routledge 2016 (hard copy) and 2019 (soft copy)) ch 2; Afshin Akhtar-Khavari and Benjamin Richardson, *Ecological Restoration Law: Concepts and Case Studies* (Routledge 2019).

[20] See Rebecca Nelson, 'Regulating Cumulative Impacts in Groundwater Systems: Global Lessons from the Australian Experience' in Cameron Holley and Darren Sinclair (eds), *Reforming Water Law and Governance* (Springer 2018).

[21] J W Bull and S Brownlie, 'The Transition From No Net Loss to a Net Gain of Biodiversity is Far From Trivial' (2017) 51(1) *Oryx: The International Journal of Conservation* 53; J B Ruhl and James E Salzman, 'Gaming the Past: The Theory and Practice of Historic Baselines in the Administrative State' (2011) 64(1) *Vanderbilt Law Review* 1.

[22] See Principle 7 of Society for Ecological Restoration International Science and Policy Working Group, *International Principles & Standards for the Practice of Ecological Restoration* (2nd edn 2019) <http://ser.org/page/SERStandards>.

world and can take many forms'.[23] It identified land degradation as 'costing more than 10 per cent of the annual global gross product in loss of biodiversity and ecosystem services'.[24] However, the report also defines land degradation as 'the many human-caused processes that drive the decline or loss in biodiversity, ecosystem function or ecosystem services in any terrestrial and associated aquatic ecosystems'.[25] This definition recognises the dynamic nature of damage and degradation requiring ongoing and active responses, rather than an approach which reacts to harm afterwards. Notwithstanding, the *IPBES Land Degradation* report in chapter 8—which deals with potential policy responses—does not reach far enough in defining land degradation as an ongoing activity. It asks for responses after the event rather than whilst harm is accumulating. The IPBES conceptual framework which framed the work in the *IPBES Land Degradation* report recognises that 'nature can contribute to people's lives', its policy responses appear procedural or administrative rather than working from a new vision of nature.[26]

The *IPBES Land Degradation* report is an example of a broader argument, that we need to constantly add to or build on the regenerative capacity of ecosystems rather than presume it. There is nothing new in the suggestions that environmental law is entrenched in a deeply anthropocentric, fragmented mindset, and local social priorities, rather than being situated in holistic and global agendas, and focused on ongoing harm that impacts on the regenerative capacity and ecological integrity of the environment. Generally speaking, environmental law appears to remain uncommitted or unaligned with any particular vision of nature, except that the natural world has to remain viable and able to absorb the impact that human beings have on it. This limits how the natural world is able to assert itself and flourish. Further, the stability and regenerative potential of ecosystems is no longer something we can presume given the scale of the choices that human beings have been in relation to anthropogenic harm in the Anthropocene.

To overcome some of these challenges environmental law across different jurisdictions has started to develop techniques and concepts that enable ongoing management. Concepts like adaptive management,[27] regeneration,[28] complexity,[29] ecological character,[30] and others have helped to give meaning

---

[23] Montanarella, Scholes and Brainich (n 13).
[24] *Ibid*.
[25] *Ibid*, XXVIII.
[26] For a description of the IPBES conceptual framework, see Intergovernmental Science-Policy Platform on Biodiversity and Ecosystem Services, *Conceptual Framework: Rationale for a Conceptual Framework for the Platform* <www.ipbes.net/conceptual-framework>.
[27] For example, R Gregory, D Ohlson and J Arvai, 'Deconstructing Adaptive Management: Criteria for Applications to Environmental Management' (2006) 16(6) *Ecological Applications* 2411.
[28] For example, Herbert Girardet, *Creating Regenerative Cities* (Routledge 2015).
[29] David G Green et al, *Complexity in Landscape Ecology* (Springer 2006).
[30] For a general discussion of ecological character and its displacement, see the original study of W L Brown Jr and E O Wilson, 'Character Displacement' (1956) 5 *Systems Zoology* 49. The concept is used

to the iterative, ongoing, and adaptive relationships and interactions that human beings can have with the natural environment so as to ensure that we do not break down the resilience of systems at the local or global scale. Nelson's work on cumulative impacts of activities and decisions on the environment recognises that ongoing degradation is significant for the carrying capacity of ecosystems and landscapes.[31] Another work by Bull and Maron has involved asking what net anthropogenic contributions are being made 'towards global species diversity for all taxa?'.[32] Lawyers and policy makers are also increasingly working with concepts that measure ongoing impacts on the environment so that governance initiatives, like environmental impacts assessment, are not just foregrounded at the start of an activity. For instance, international law has started to require ongoing impact assessments to ensure that activities do not harm the environment in ways that were not predetermined.[33] Offset arrangements are instituted by various legal systems that aim to replace the equivalence of what is being harmed in another area and ensure that the overall impacts from activities are kept neutral. Whilst these measures serve a purpose they also reduce problems down to technique and praxis, rather than shape the way we think about the world and ontologies that sustain our approaches and solution.

Symbiosis and flourishing socio-ecological landscapes

Concepts like ecosystem services,[34] and nature's contribution to people,[35] appear to have replaced commitments to ethically and philosophically oriented disposition found in 'deep ecology'.[36] An increasing body of critical and imaginative environmental humanities scholarship is starting to shape methodologies for new environmental laws.[37] In this section the paper will begin the process of mapping briefly an alternative to sustainability.

---

to manage wetlands of international significance, through the 1971 *Ramsar Convention on Wetlands of International Importance*. See for example, Jenny Davis and Margaret Brock, 'Detecting Unacceptable Change in the Ecological Character of Ramsar Wetlands' (2008) 9(1) *Ecological Management and Restoration* 26.

31 Rebecca Nelson, 'Breaking Backs and Boiling Frogs: Warnings from a Dialogue Between Federal Water Law and Environmental Law' (2019) 42(4) *University of New South Wales Law Journal* 1179.

32 J W Bull and M Maron, 'How Humans Drive Speciation as well as Extinction' (2016) *Proceedings of the Royal Society B: Biological Sciences* 20160600.

33 For example, see Jorge E Viñuales, 'The Contribution of the International Court of Justice to the Development of International Environmental Law: A Contemporary Assessment' (2008) 32 *Fordham International Law Journal* 232.

34 For example, see J B Ruhl and James Salzman, 'Ecosystem Services and the Public Trust Doctrine: Working Change From Within' (2006) 15 *Environmental Law Journal* 223.

35 This concept is in the foundation conceptual framework developed by the IPBES. See, Intergovernmental Science-Policy Platform on Biodiversity and Ecosystem Services (n 26).

36 For example, see Peter Burdon (ed), *Exploring Wild Law: The Philosophy of Earth Jurisprudence* (Wakefield Press 2011).

37 For example, see Andreas Philippopoulous-Mihalopoulos and Victoria Brooks (eds), *Research Methods in Environmental Law* (Edward Elgar 2017).

In the book *Times of Crisis*, Michel Serres has argued that economic crisis are like earthquakes caused by what he calls 'societal tectonic plates'.[38] One of the major themes in this book, which is also central to some of his other books like *The Natural Contract*,[39] and also *Biogea*,[40] is that planet Earth and the environment have to be more active as key players in political, legal and cultural discourses. His concept of the 'natural contract' requires that we re-examine some basic assumptions that continue to drive human institutions. Serres puts forward the idea of the 'natural contract' to incubate a different possibility to what we know as the 'social contract', an idea that has framed much of modern liberal democratic ideas of the State.[41]

In this project he argues that concepts like the 'environment' explain the human environment rather than the natural or more-than-human world. If the idea of the social contract enabled human flourishing, then perhaps the 'natural contract' can be seen as framing socio-ecological flourishings. The idea of something 'flourishing' has traditionally been used to explain self-actualisation or fulfilled human lives, but there is no reason why it cannot be co-opted for a broader purpose. The idea that socio-ecological or entangled lives can also flourish and develop rather than just those of individuals, and then only human lives, is an idea that can provoke much thought. The word flourishing has its origins in Aristotelian ethics,[42] and the word 'eudaimonia' has received a lot of scholarly attention, as it has been the cornerstone of ethics particularly in relation to understanding what it means to do well and to live fulfilled lives.[43]

Significant studies however have emerged in the past few decades that discuss how entangled human beings are with everything else around us.[44] This requires that we also think about the 'flourishing' of human beings in a different light. The idea that the world is made up of individuals, atoms, singularities and objects continues to be dominant, yet this focus appears to enable only partial explanations of the nature of reality. Margulis, whose influence on the science of symbiosis is unquestionable, has argued that evolution and biological changes come from acquiring 'symbiots'.[45] Whilst some discussions of the Anthropocene sometimes positions the human being as an autonomous entity acting upon the Earth, others talk about the socio-

---

[38] Michel Serres, *Times of Crisis* (Bloomsbury 2014).

[39] Michel Serres, *The Natural Contract* (University of Michigan Press 1995).

[40] Michel Serres, *Biogea* (University of Minnesota Press 2012).

[41] Jean-Jacques Rousseau, *The Social Contract and Discourses* (CreateSpace Independent Publishing Platform 2017)

[42] For example, see Hope May, *Aristotle's Ethics: Moral Development and Human Nature* (Bloomsbury 2011).

[43] For an example of a recent study, see M J Newby, *Eduaimonia: Happiness is Not Enough* (Metador 2011).

[44] For example, see Haraway (n 7). Also see, Karen Barad, *Meeting the Universe Halfway: Quantum Physics and the Entanglement of Matter and Meaning* (Duke University Press 2007).

[45] Lynn Margulis, 'Symbiogenesis and Symbionticism' in Lynn Margulis and Rene Fester (eds), *Symbiosis as a Source of Evolutionary Innovation: Speciation and Morphogenesis* (University of Massachusetts Amherst 1991) 11.

ecological, or the deep ways in which human bein.gs are enmeshed and integrated into nature.[46] When the focus is on individuals and atoms, priority is placed on values like competition, causalities, survival of the fittest, autonomy, and agency. Even the idea of the Anthropocene itself is linked to the composite nature of human beings, as co-constituted or symbionts ourselves, rather than as essences of some kind, and free from influences from other living things. That is, the unique stratigraphic signals or markers that we are responsible for are not uniquely ours given how deeply entangled we are with nature.[47]

Our entangled world is organised and influenced not by individuals or autonomous agents acting on one another, but creations and objects that are thinly or thickly co-constituted at the local and also the global level. Whilst ideas like the socio-ecological[48] push boundaries in terms of recognising that human beings and the natural world are not separate from one another, there are thin and thick versions of what this means and how we (and non-human organisms) are co-constituted with material and non-human living things. To explore flourishings, we need to have discussions of what entanglement means for dealing with both the human and non-human social and temporal dimensions of life. Flourishing ecosystems require that human beings recognise the thin and thick nature of how entangled we are in nature and what this tells us about the ways in which we are constituted in the harm, damage and degradation of nature. As such flourishing lives can only be conceived as being embedded in 'flourishing' socio-ecological landscapes. There are others who have made a range of arguments about the deep emotional connections that human beings have with nature and which are critical for what is otherwise a fulfilled human life. For example, the idea of biophilia that Erich Fromm conceived of in the 1960s has had traction,[49] and most recently Glenn Albrecht wrote the book *Earth Emotions* discussing amongst others the deep distress and psychological harm that comes from how we engage and function within the natural world.[50]

The symbiotic, or persistent and mutually beneficial, relationships between living organisms is a useful model for understanding how very different living organisms can exist and flourish together, but also create something that did

[46] See Nicholas Hold and Sy Taffel (eds), *Ecological Entanglements in the Anthropocene* (Lexington Books, 2016).

[47] Lynn Margulis makes a similar argument about how 'animal and plant fossils are … compositite products of coevolved microbial communities … That they bear genus and species names, as do fossil stromatolites, does not make them unities'. See Margulis (n 45) 10.

[48] For discussion of this concept, see Simron Jit Singh et al, *Long Term Socio-Ecological Research* (Springer 2012).

[49] Erich Fromm, *The Heart of Man: Its Genius for Good and Evil* (American Mental Health Foundation Books 1964).

[50] Albrecht (n 4).

not pre-exist their relationships.[51] Symbiosis can helpfully model the nature of the complexities and relationships that can support flourishing socio-ecological landscapes. The idea of mutualism in ecology has received a degree of attention because it provides an alternative narrative to the antagonistic, conflictual or competitive nature of how living things exist around each other.[52] It is a 'pervasive habit amongst living organisms', but it needs to be distinguished from simple acts of mutual aid.[53] For instance animals and birds dispersing seeds are not necessarily in a deep symbiotic and persistent mutually beneficial relationships. The difference between being thinly and deeply entangled is important for understanding why certain beneficial relationships in nature are impacted by anthropogenic harm.[54] There are a range of concepts like mutualism, protocooperation, facilitation and others which explain the narrow and thin physical and observable ways in which the individual, atom, or agent benefit from being entangled with others. It is not productive to try and separate these terms but the idea of symbiosis does point us to a different explanation of mutualism that is structurally significant, and explains relationships that cannot exist without the entanglements.

Symbiosis explains the 'persistent mutually beneficial associations',[55] or 'protracted physical association' that exist in much of nature.[56] For instance, the eukaryote would not have emerged from the prokaryote without its symbiotic relationship with the mitochondria. Also, over 90% of land plants are in symbiotic relationships with the *mycorrhizal* fungi that allow trees a greater opportunity to absorb and distribute nutrients, while the fungi draw on the sugar from the plants. The science of symbiosis is replete with studies that discuss the idea of mutual interdependencies, to the extent that the explanations for certain kinds of behaviours depend on these existing constitutive relationships. The benefits that partners gain in symbiotic relationships can be 'functionally distinct' or may 'vary with circumstance' but the importance of symbiosis has been explained in terms of how cooperation shapes the evolution of living things more than competition has done.[57] This does not suggest that symbiosis only explains cooperative behaviour, and in fact antagonist relationships also exist in symbiotically organised systems.[58] Symbiotic relationships however create new 'ecological opportunities' for living things

[51] This definition is derived from Angela E Douglas, *The Symbiotic Habit* (Princeton University Press 2010).
[52] For example, see Douglas H Boucher, *The Biology of Mutualism: Ecology and Evolution* (Oxford University Press 1985). See also, Judith L Bronstein (ed), *Mutualism* (Oxford University Press 2015).
[53] See Bronstein (n 52) ch 1.
[54] For this discussion, see Douglas (n 51) ch 5.
[55] *Ibid*, ch 1 and 6.
[56] Margulis (n 45).
[57] Douglas (n 51) 12–13. See also, Jan Sapp, 'Living Together: Symbiosis and Cytoplasmic Inheritance' in Lynn Margulis and Rene Fester (eds), *Symbiosis as a Source of Evolutionary Innovation: Speciation and Morphogenesis* (University of Massachusetts Amherst 1991).
[58] Douglas (n 51) pt 5.3.

which can trigger 'diversification of the symbiotic organisms'.[59] For instance, the diversification and spread of terrestrial plants is deeply connected to the availability of nutrients through the symbiotic relationship that they have with *mycorrhizal* fungi.[60]

Discussions of symbiosis are important not just because it is so prevalent in nature, and also in terms of the make-up and health of human beings, but because of what it has to teach us about entanglements. Symbiosis also reveals how much more susceptible the environment is not just from the focus we put on the health and viability of individual organisms or ecosystems, but more critically for the alternative vulnerabilities that come from being entangled in the material world. For instance, habitat fragmentation can reduce the viability of trees that rely on a diversity of birds, rather than just one kind, for seed dispersal.[61] Whilst in this instance the symbiotic relationship is not even deep, and what scientists would call 'nonspecific' in the sense that many birds can do the job, the potential impact of the loss of the tree may only get noticed over time. Also, the cascading effects of the loss of bird diversity is an important feature that comes to light by studying and prioritising their entanglement with other lives in the forest.

Lastly, and perhaps more critically, symbiosis is about enabling conflicts to get resolved, not because partners are looking to win, but because they depend on long-term or persistent reciprocal and mutually beneficial and cooperative relationship for survival.[62] Working towards establishing symbiotic relationships can cost living things, but benefits can also come from evolving, thriving and learning to manage the conflicts in symbiotic relationships. For instance, some of the flowers of the *Ficus* tree, collected in what is known as its *syconium* get used by female wasps for laying their eggs. The wasps pollinate the flowers but the *Ficus* also allows some of its flowers to be used for wasp production.

The idea of symbiosis has the potential to reorient how we think about the world, beyond focusing us just on the potential of cooperation to achieve new goals. In symbiosis, the world is always in the process of becoming.[63] Whilst protection and preservation of the environment are critical, those concepts do not necessarily require that individuals constantly listen for the opportunity to give back to nature. Evolutionary processes and milestones take time. The

---

[59] *Ibid*, 126 and ch 5.

[60] Luc Simon et al, 'Origin and Diversification of Endomycorrhizal Fungi and Coincidence with Vascular Land Plants' (1993) 363 *Nature* 67. See also, K A Pirozynski and D W Malloch, 'The Origin of Land Plants: A Matter of Mycotropism' (1975) 6 *BioSystems* 153.

[61] For example, see the 2003 study by Cordeiro and Howe that showed that a tree in Africa recorded significant drops in seed dispersal in fragmented forests because of the drop in the diversity of birds available to assist with the symbiotic activity. N J Cordeiro and H F Howe, 'Forest Fragmentation Severs Mutualism between Seed Dispersers and an Endemic African Tree' (2003) 100 *Proceedings of the National Academy of Sciences USA* 14052.

[62] See discussion of the idea of conflict and conflict resolution in symbiosis in Douglas (n 51) ch 3.

[63] Martin Heidegger, *Being and Time* (Martino Fine Books 2019).

productive potential and force of symbiotic relationships come from struggles, as aptly summarised by Clancy:

> Long periods of harmonious co-existence may be the evolutionary precursor for true symbiotic relationships. Billions of years ago, another ancient cyanobacteria was engulfed and 'domesticated' by an ancestor of plants. It shed most of the genes it needed for an independent existence and became what we now know as the chloroplast. In return for a safe environment, these chloroplasts performed photosynthesis for their hosts, fuelling a new form of life that eventually spread over much of the Earth. It's like this same kind of division of labor was a seed for the development of multi-cellular organisms. Here, evolution is not a weapons race, but a peace treaty among interdependent nations.[64]

Conclusion: restorative inputs and cooperation

We commonly look at degraded, destroyed and damaged landscapes and ask how they need to be repaired and who should bear the cost for it. Alternatively, we use the concept of protected areas to maintain the quality of their ecological characteristics, such as for instance in relation to Ramsar wetlands.[65] Human input is required to bring some life back into the ecosystem in damaged landscapes, and in protected areas we seek to assess the extent to which we exclude ourselves from that environment in the hope that our activities will not degrade it. In protected areas however we cannot control the broader and more pernicious impact that the damage and degradation of Earth systems can have on the environment and protected areas more generally (for example through climate change). In degraded landscapes we have rarely considered what ongoing and cumulative inputs could have contributed to in terms of the potential net gain in the functional capacity of those ecosystem. Whilst in relation to protected areas ongoing management could be viewed as inputs into the system, the number of Ramsar wetlands that have lost their ecological character over the years is significant and rising.[66]

Sustainability is about managing competition for the long-term. In this context damage and degradation are dealt with using technical measures that will fix problems. For instance, in Queensland, Australia the rehabilitation and remediation of mine sites are responses to damage and degradation.[67] There are also a wide variety of restoration responses similar to those in Queensland for activities that cause damage and

[64] Kelly Clancy, Nautilus, 'Survival of the Friendliest: It's Time to Give the Violent Metaphors of Evolution a Break' (23 March 2017) <http://nautil.us/issue/46/balance/survival-of-the-friendliest>; Albrecht (n 4) ch 4.

[65] *Convention on Wetlands of International Importance especially as Waterfowl Habitat* (Adopted 2 February 1971, Entered into force 21 December 1975) 996 UNTS 245.

[66] M J R Dixon et al, 'Tracking Global Change in Ecosystem Area: The Wetland Extent Trends Index' (2016) 193 *Biological Conservation* 27.

[67] The following two pieces of legislation regulate mines in Queensland: *Mineral Resources Act 1989* (Qld) and *Environmental Protection Act 1994* (Qld).

degradation.[68] Conceptually, there are also innovative ideas, like net-gain, no-net-loss, half-Earth,[69] and a host of others that set abstract limits and conditions on activities so we can measure our performance against them. For instance, in 2016 Bull and Maron developed the idea of 'net anthropogenic contributions towards global species diversity for all taxa' to describe how we can contribute to flourishing socio-ecological landscapes.[70] Whilst these are all well-argued and interesting ideas, they need to go beyond technical solutions and reorient the ontological frames that we operate through to avoid other significant challenges for the future.

This creates a challenge for environmental law. It needs to move beyond just technically managing human beings and instead create social institutions which will reorient ontologies towards more cooperative relationships between human beings and the natural world. The hard work for environmental law therefore is not that it has to create more meaningful rules to manage competitions amongst human beings. Rather, the challenge that environmental law has to face is to enable cooperative acts and initiatives that can build new ontologically significant social and cultural institutions. For instance, there is much literature and discussion already examining the significance of ecological restoration, not just for the recovery of an ecosystem, but in terms of shaping how human beings then continue to think about and relate to the natural environment after having done the work.[71] The importance of ecological restoration is then not measured in terms of the outcomes but the change in terms of how people will come to view the value of the natural environment.

Following these discussions, it seems sensible to propose that we need to be on the lookout for activities, adventures, and possibilities that can enable more cooperative rather than competitive relationships. The idea of *restorative inputs* would be an example of something like this, where human beings would be actively thinking about their impact on the natural environment. At every turn, decisions would have to consider the natural environment in the context of its restorative conditions. That is, flourishing socio-ecological landscapes require more human inputs into the natural environment. This is not the same for instance as the 'polluter pays' principles or 'offsets' that delegate and shift the onus of responsibilities to others, but rather requires that we completely reorient what we do to develop new ways of thinking about inputs into the natural environment. Principle 8 of the second

---

[68] In this regard, offsets are important initiatives and the United States Wetlands Mitigation and also the Conservation Banks are good examples.

[69] Wilson (n 9).

[70] Bull and Maron (n 32).

[71] William R Jordan, *The Sunflower Forest: Ecological Restoration and the New Communion with Nature* (University of California Press 2003). This book is increasingly recognised as one of the first monograph length discussions of the significance and benefit of restoration for changing the human-nature relationship.

Primer of the International Society for Ecological Restoration discusses the idea that ecological restoration can be viewed as 'part of a continuum of restorative activities'.[72] In this principle the Primer also suggests for instance that rehabilitation or remediation could be activities that are important along this continuum of activities for bringing back native ecosystems. Restorative inputs could therefore take many forms and shapes and its significance would be in terms of facilitating deeper engagement with the impacts and influences that we have on one another and, more importantly, nature. Ontological change is not easy and resort to disruptive technologies and ideas are needed to help us shift from competitive to cooperative relationships that can enable a different evolutionary socio-ecological platform.

Disclosure statement

No potential conflict of interest was reported by the author(s).

[72] See Principle 8 of Society for Ecological Restoration International Science and Policy Working Group (n 22).

Earth system law for the Anthropocene: rethinking environmental law alongside the Earth system metaphor

Louis J. Kotzé

ABSTRACT

Despite its noble intentions and some victories, environmental law has been and continues to be complicit in driving the processes and paradigms that give rise to the Anthropocene. Environmental law is also unable to respond to the regulatory challenges that arise from the Anthropocene's complex Earth system. We need a new legal paradigm that is better fit for purpose in the Anthropocene called *Earth system law*. A key reason for environmental law's failures and an obstacle preventing its transformation, is its reluctance to embrace and respond to the notion of the Earth system. My hypothesis is that the Earth system metaphor should be key in rethinking environmental law with the ultimate view to constructing Earth system law for the Anthropocene. The primary purpose of this paper is to explore what the Earth system metaphor entails and what it might imply for environmental law's transformation to Earth system law.

I. Introduction

State-of-the-art research increasingly reveals the many gaps in our social regulatory institutions for governing global scale challenges,[1] in particular global sustainability challenges arising from the Earth system.[2] It seems highly likely that 'addressing problems of global change will require a step change in research on fundamental questions of governance, economic systems,

---

[1] 'Social regulatory institutions' for the purpose of the present analysis broadly includes all 'norms, expectations, rules, and organizations through which societies figure out what to do and organize themselves to do it'. William Clark, Paul Crutzen and Hans Schellnhuber 'Science for Global Sustainability: Towards a new Paradigm' in Hans Schellnhuber et al (eds), *Earth System Analysis for Sustainability* (MIT Press 2004) 21.

[2] See, for example, Frank Biermann, '"Earth System Governance" as a Crosscutting Theme of Global Change Research' (2007) 17 *Global Environmental Change* 326.

and the assumptions, beliefs, and values underlying human behavior'.[3] The rapidly deteriorating state of the Earth system has now become starkly evident through the lens of the Anthropocene.[4] The Anthropocene, perhaps more so than any other contemporary trope, clearly reveals the urgent need for wholescale social transformation and a step change in and of our social regulatory institutions if they are to remain relevant, useful and effective in their pursuit of global sustainability.[5] In fact, the imagery of the Anthropocene as 'rupture' in Earth's recent history signifies a 'rapid transition to a new geological epoch'.[6] This underlines the prevailing view that

> major societal or systemic shifts take place through the creation of new orders of governance entailing new modes of knowledge and technologies of power by which the individual is constituted. There is already much to indicate that such a point has now been reached with the perception of a planetary crisis.[7]

As a consequence,

> Political, social, and economic systems will need to dramatically change… Doing nothing will increasingly not be an option as the global systems we depend on for air to breathe, water to drink, and food to eat shift in response to our actions. Law will not be exempt from these changes. Pressures to adapt to the Anthropocene, or to mitigate the changes producing the Anthropocene, will in turn put substantial pressures on the legal system, which will have to change in response.[8]

Law is a prominent and critically important social regulatory institution as it is central to our political, economic, religious and cultural systems. In a broad sense, law includes 'the systematic regulation of the life of a community by standards treated as binding the members of the community and its institutions'.[9] To this end, 'law is a purposeful vehicle for shaping behavior to achieve desired ends';[10] it has been, still is, and will likely always be, a foundational element of the social system that operates to ensure ordered co-existence wherever humans are present. Yet, although humans tend to revert to law in search of regulatory solutions, order, peace, justice and harmony,

---

[3] William Reid et al, 'Earth System Science for Global Sustainability: Grand Challenges' (2010) 330 *Science* 916, 917.

[4] Will Steffen et al, 'Stratigraphic and Earth System Approaches to Defining the Anthropocene' (2016) 4 *Earth's Future* 324, 337.

[5] I use 'sustainability' here in the sense of its being a goal to strive towards (similar to achieving justice, democracy, freedom and peace), and not as a state of being or a specific condition that must be achieved, maintained or improved. See Clark, Crutzen and Schellnhuber (n 1) 17.

[6] Clive Hamilton, 'The Anthropocene as Rupture' (2016) 3(2) *The Anthropocene Review* 93, 100.

[7] Gerard Delanty and Aurea Mota, 'Governing the Anthropocene: Agency, Governance, Knowledge' (2017) 20(1) *European Journal of Social Theory* 9, 24.

[8] Eric Biber, 'Law in the Anthropocene Epoch' (2017) 106(1) *The Georgetown Law Journal* 1, 4.

[9] Timothy Endicott, *Law and Language* (Stanford Encyclopedia of Philosophy, 2016) 5, online: https://ora.ox.ac.uk/objects/uuid:971283aa-d36f-4ce9-831d-e52c58e8609f.

[10] Gillian Hadfield and Barry Weingast, 'What is Law? A Coordination Model of the Characteristics of a Legal Order' (2012) 4(2) *Journal of Legal Analysis* 471, 473.

law as a means to these ends is ultimately imperfect and does not always achieve these ends.

While this is true for law generally, it is specifically true for environmental law and its pursuit of global sustainability.[11] Recent research clearly reveals environmental law's perceived regulatory gaps, its structural complicity in creating the conditions that drive the Anthropocene (such as its neoliberal ontology and anthropocentric support of some privileged human subjects); its inability to halt, reverse and remedy socio-ecological damage and resultant injustices (as the lacklustre global climate change regime aptly suggests); and its lack of regulatory ambition in relation to addressing global sustainability (evidenced in particular by its lack of binding, higher order ecological norms).[12] Particularly relevant for present purposes, the architecture of environmental law, including its core assumptions, orientation, operation and objectives, are not commensurate with the most recent understanding of the many regulatory challenges that arise from within a deeply complex and interlinked Earth system in the context of the Anthropocene.[13]

Numerous scholars agree that when it comes to reforming environmental law in the light of a possible new geological epoch, the Anthropocene requires far more than merely tinkering at the margins.[14] We do not only require reforms currently driven by noncommittal global political processes involving high rhetoric and little definitive action that are squarely focused on generating more, or slightly improved, environmental laws. Such an unambitious approach remains firmly entrenched in the comfortable and accommodative, but deeply deceiving, confines of Holocene stability.[15]

We need a new legal paradigm that is better fit for purpose in the unstable Anthropocene. As a minimum, such a new paradigm must depart from ecological dynamism and fully embrace the Earth system's key characteristics such as interconnectedness, unpredictability, instability and complexity,

---

[11] I limit my focus in this paper to *environmental* law in a generic sense (also not confined to one specific jurisdiction). I do so for the sake of brevity, but more importantly because environmental law, as the traditional body of law seeking to achieve sustainability, arguably presents the most likely candidate to start with when thinking about the contours of Earth system law. In doing so, however, I fully recognise that law in a general sense, and law's specific sub-divisions such as private law, property law, corporate law and so forth, will necessarily also be relevant for thinking about Earth system law for the Anthropocene. See, for example, Biber (n 8).

[12] Duncan French and Louis Kotzé, '"Towards a Global Pact for the Environment": International Environmental Law's Factual, Technical and (Unmentionable) Normative Gaps' (2019) 28 *Review of European, Comparative and International Environmental Law* 25; Louis Kotzé, 'International Environmental Law's Lack of Normative Ambition: An Opportunity for the Global Pact for the Environment?' (2019) 16 *Journal for European Environmental and Planning Law* 213; Louis Kotzé, 'International Environmental Law and the Anthropocene's Energy Dilemma' (2019) 36 *Environmental and Planning Law Journal* 437.

[13] Antonio Cardesa-Salzmann and Endrius Cocciolo, 'Global Governance, Sustainability and the Earth System: Critical Reflections on the Role of Global Law' (2019) 8(3) *Transnational Environmental Law* 437.

[14] See the diverse views in Louis Kotzé (ed), *Environmental Law and Governance for the Anthropocene* (Hart 2017).

[15] John Dryzek, 'Institutions for the Anthropocene: Governance in a changing Earth System' (2016) 46(4) *British Journal of Political Science* 937, 938.

instead of taking Holocene stability for granted. It must also discard its singular focus on the 'environment' as its regulatory object, and instead focus on the much more broadly conceived *Earth system* and everything that goes with that impulse in the context of the Anthropocene. Several terms have been suggested for such a new legal paradigm, including 'Earth-centred law', 'Anthropocene environmental law', and 'planetary boundaries law'.[16] While all of these have merit in their own right, my principal hypothesis in this contribution is that the Earth system metaphor should be key in rethinking environmental law in the Anthropocene. Such a systems perspective that is fully anchored in the Anthropocene's planetary context, is most accurately captured by the term *Earth system law*.

I will endeavour to show that, at its core, Earth system law lies at the interface of Earth system science on the one hand (which is a 'holistic super-discipline that tries to embrace all processes in nature and society as one interlinked system'[17]), and environmental law and its associated scholarship on the other hand (which is a key part of 'organised human responses to earth system transformation').[18] At a normative regulatory level, I ultimately envision Earth system law to be a new legal paradigm that must better respond to the type of planetary system challenges that the dynamic and complex Earth system presents, while at once offering solutions aimed at increasing Earth system resilience.[19] At the level of scientific enquiry, I envision Earth system law to offer a framework alongside which it should be possible to critique the current deficiencies of environmental law in the Anthropocene; to serve as an umbrella concept or framework that enables a creative re-imagination of environmental law for the Anthropocene; to open up the hitherto 'closed' epistemologies of Earth system science for environmental lawyers while at once revealing the juridical aspects of Earth system governance for Earth system scientists, and in so doing to serve as a coherent interdisciplinary epistemological bridge between law and other sciences; to more clearly reveal, in a systemised way, the regulatory implications of the Earth system metaphor for law generally and for environmental law specifically; and to ultimately

[16] Klaus Bosselmann, 'Shifting the Legal Paradigm: Earth-centered Law and Governance' in Paulo Magalhães et al (eds), *The Safe Operating Space Treaty: A New Approach to Managing our Use of the Earth System* (Cambridge Scholars Publishing 2016) 64–82; *Maria Alexandra Sousa* Aragão, 'Legal Tools to Operationalize Anthropocene Environmental Law' in Paulo Magalhães et al (eds) *The Safe Operating Space Treaty: A New Approach to Managing our Use of the Earth System* (Cambridge Scholars Publishing 2016) 83–103; Guillaume Chapron et al, 'Bolster Legal Boundaries to Stay Within Planetary Boundaries' (2017) 1 *Nature Ecology and Evolution* 1.

[17] Eva Lövbrand, Johannes Stripple and Bo Wiman, 'Earth System Governmentality Reflections on Science in the Anthropocene' (2009) 19 *Global Environmental Change* 7, 7.

[18] Biermann (n 2), 328.

[19] Carl Folke, Stephen Carpenter, Brian Walker, Marten Scheffer, Terry Chapin and Johan Rockström, 'Resilience Thinking Integrating Resilience, Adaptability and Transformability' (2010) 15(4) *Ecology and Society* 1.

serve as a new crosscutting theme of scientific enquiry for scholars working in the area of sustainability.

As a contribution to the debate on rethinking environmental law for the purpose of the Anthropocene, this paper builds on two earlier publications. In the first publication, I have explored with Rakhyun Kim the juridical dimensions of Earth system governance, and we made out a broad case in support of developing Earth system law.[20] In the second publication, while explicitly acknowledging there might be others, I have elaborated three considerations that environmental law will need to embrace in the course of its transformation to Earth system law (ie, inclusivity, interdependencies and complexity).[21] Putting the cart before the horses, as they did in a sense, neither of these papers fully explained what the Earth system metaphor actually entails and what it could mean for environmental law's transformation to Earth system law. While such epistemic gaps do little to help us develop a fully theorised framework for Earth system law, they are not unique to law, but also arise in the related domain of global governance where commentators have noted the following: 'rather than accepting the Earth System metaphor as a taken-for-granted starting point for future global environmental change research, we invite more scholars to critically reflect upon which political spaces it renders thinkable and governable'.[22] For environmental law to remain and to become an even more relevant regulatory institution in the Anthropocene, environmental lawyers will equally have to start critically reflecting on the usefulness and implications of the Earth system metaphor for environmental law.

In an effort to address the epistemic gaps sketched above, and to critically reflect upon which legal spaces the Earth system metaphor 'renders thinkable and governable', I endeavour in this paper to interrogate the implications of the Earth system metaphor for environmental law. The discussion commences in Part 2 by first unpacking the meaning of the term 'Earth system', specifically as it is used in Earth system science literature. The discussion then offers a concise description of the evolution of the Earth system metaphor and how it became embedded within the contemporary Earth system science research agenda. Despite some evidence of its gradual infiltration into the social science domain, notably through the Earth system governance scientific agenda,[23] I argue in Part 3 that the Earth system metaphor has not yet been fully embraced by environmental law and environmental lawyers, but that it should be because of Earth system law's promise and

---

[20] Louis Kotzé and Rakhyun Kim, 'Earth System Law: The Juridical Dimensions of Earth System Governance' (2019) 1 *Earth System Governance* 1.

[21] Louis Kotzé, 'Earth System Law for the Anthropocene' (2019) 11 *Sustainability* 1.

[22] Eva Lövbrand, Johannes Stripple and Bo Wiman, 'Earth System Governmentality Reflections on Science in the Anthropocene' (2009) 19 *Global Environmental Change* 7, 8.

[23] See, for a general overview, 'About the Project' (*Earth Systems Governance*, 2020) online: https://www.earthsystemgovernance.org/about-the-project/.

potential to address the Earth system's complex regulatory challenges. On the basis of the assumption that the Anthropocene trope foregrounds the Earth system as a dynamic, complex, unpredictable and interconnected regulatory object, Part 4 then explores some of the possible implications of the Earth system metaphor and the opportunities it presents for rethinking environmental law, including several considerations that could be considered when contemplating the development of Earth system law for the Anthropocene.

II. The Earth system metaphor

In order to identify, understand and describe the regulatory implications of the Earth system metaphor for environmental law, it is useful to first try and understand what the Earth system means. Earth system scientists see the Earth system as,

> [A] single, planetary-level complex system, with a multitude of interacting biotic and abiotic components, [which has] evolved over 4.54 billion years and which has existed in well-defined, planetary-level states with transitions between them … The Earth System is driven primarily by solar radiation and is influenced by other extrinsic factors, including changes in orbital parameters and occasional bolide strikes, as well as by its own internal dynamics in which the biosphere [which includes humans] is a critical component.[24]

While some specifics vary between different descriptions, the Earth system includes a number of components and associated processes.[25] These include: (i) the 'physical world' consisting of the geosphere (including the lithosphere which is the rigid outer shell of the planet), the hydrosphere (the combined mass of water on Earth), the cryosphere (consisting of all frozen parts on Earth) and the atmosphere; (ii) the 'biological world' including the biosphere (those parts containing life); and (iii) the 'mental world' of the anthroposphere (also called the technosphere), which includes all those parts made and/or modified by humans.[26] These components do not exist and operate in isolation. In fact, they are characterised by an evolutionary continuum: ie, the biological world emerged from the physical world, and the mental world later emerged from the biological world.[27] It is useful to point out already here that environmental law as a human artefact is especially present in the biological and mental worlds, as it is a key part of the 'deeper

[24] Steffen et al (n 4), 325.

[25] Peter Cox and Neboja Nakicenovic, 'Assessing and Simulating the Altered Functioning of the Earth System in the Anthropocene' in Schellnhuber et al (n 1), 342.

[26] Peter Haff, 'Humans and Technology in the Anthropocene: Six Rules' (2014) 1 *The Anthropocene Review* 126; Bronislaw Szerszynski, 'Viewing the Technosphere in an Interplanetary Light' (2017) 4(2) *The Anthropocene Review* 92.

[27] Wolfgang Lucht and Rajendra Pachauri, 'The Mental Component of the Earth System' in Schellnhuber et al (n 1), 342.

human characteristics that capture our core values and how we view our relationship to the rest of the Earth System'.[28]

In addition to these components and processes, the characteristics of the Earth *system* are of paramount importance.[29] A general and broad concept that could be applied in numerous contexts (for example, a political system, economic system, social system and so forth):

> A system is an entity that maintains its existence and functions as a whole through the interaction of its parts ... this group of interacting, interrelated or interdependent parts that form a complex and unified whole must have a specific purpose, and in order for the system to optimally carry out its purpose all parts must be present. Thus, the system attempts to maintain its stability through feedback. The interrelationships among the variables are connected by a cause and effect feedback loop, and consequently the status of one or more variables, affects the status of the other variables. Yet, the properties attributable to the system as a whole are not those of the individual components that make up the system.[30]

There are several key considerations flowing from this description of a system.[31] First, a system (the Earth's included) is greater than the sum of its component parts which, by definition, implies that the combined system is somehow 'better than you would expect from the individual parts, because the way they combine adds a different quality'.[32] Put differently, something that is made up of many individual parts that are causally connected and that all interact in tandem, functions more optimally than if these parts were to operate unrelatedly and in isolation. The Earth system is therefore not only the biosphere (often understood as the 'natural environment'), which continues to be the predominant concern of environmental law as we shall see below, but all three interdependent and interrelated Earth system 'worlds' that co-exist.

Second, causality is central to a system and is specifically evident in a system's feedbacks. 'Feedback' in this context refers to a chain of cause-and-effect relations that forms a closed loop, which in turn means that 'information about the past or present state of part of a system can influence its

---

[28] Will Steffen et al, 'The Emergence and Evolution of Earth System Science' (2020) 1 *Nature* 54, 61.

[29] Although Earth system science was not the first to introduce systems-thinking to the global sustainability debate. Long before the emergence of Earth systems science, systems thinking was already central to some disciplines such as ecology and biology sciences (eg ecosystems management). But what Earth system science did manage to do was to develop a perspective of the entire Earth being a system as a whole; ie, 'The Earth itself *is* a system'. Will Steffen et al (eds), *Global Change and the Earth System: A Planet Under Pressure* (Springer 2004) 3.

[30] Orit Assaraf and Nir Orion, 'Development of Systems Thinking Skills in the Context of Earth System Education' (2005) 42(5) *Journal of Research in Science Teaching* 518, 519–20.

[31] See, for an overview, Naotatsu Shikazono, *Introduction to Earth and Planetary System Science: New View of Earth, Planets and Humans* (Springer 2012).

[32] 'Definition of 'more/greater than the sum of its parts'' (*Collins*, 2020) online: https://www.collinsdictionary.com/dictionary/english/more-greater-than-the-sum-of-its-parts.

present or future state'.[33] Thus, any outputs of a system are not merely 'lost' outputs. They continuously flow back as inputs into that same system in a closed circuit or loop:

> [S]ystems are characterized by strong interactions between the different components. They interact and sometimes one component counteracts the other. Due to the strong coupling between these elements, a failure in one or more elements can lead to cascading failures which may have catastrophic consequences on the functioning of the system as a whole.[34]

For the purpose of the Earth system, where one variable (such as ozone content or soil moisture) is affected, others (such as atmospheric temperature) will therefore also be affected.

Third, because a system is complex, unstable and unpredictable by design, it continuously pursues stability or equilibrium; often over very long periods of time. The Earth system's many closed causal loops are non-linear which, in turn, leads to a degree of causality that becomes all but impossible to untangle. In addition to such intertwined causality, the non-linear closed causal loops of the Earth system could either be positive, which amplifies change to the system and make it more unstable; or negative, which dampen change to the system and tends to make it more stable and to bring it back into a state of equilibrium.[35] It is the combination of, and interplay between, the positive and negative feedback loops that provide the Earth system its self-regulatory characteristic and that consequently enables it to bounce back and to maintain stability/equilibrium. To this end it could be said that the Earth system continuously pursues stability while seeking to maintain conditions that are conducive to life on Earth. Yet, such stability/equilibrium is not 'immutable', as Lenton says.[36] Where positive feedback loops hit the Earth system too hard, it might be unable to bounce back to its original state and may even be propelled into an alternative state. Geological forces such as volcanoes and earthquakes, and now *humans*, as the Anthropocene suggests, are capable of interfering with Earth's self-regulation and its equilibrium and stability. This is so because human-induced positive feedback loop impacts amplify Earth system change to such an extent, that the system may be unable to recover and return to a state of equilibrium.

By way of summary, the Earth system consists of all interacting physical, chemical, and biological global-scale cycles and energy fluxes which collectively provide the conditions necessary to enable and sustain life on Earth. It is a materially closed system consisting of interlinked physical, chemical and biological processes that cycle materials and energy in non-linear,

[33] Timothy Lenton, *Earth System Science: A Very Short Introduction* (Oxford University Press 2016) 5.
[34] Steven Lierman, 'Law as a Complex Adaptive System: The Importance of Convergence in a Multi-layered Legal Order' (2014) 21(4) *Maastricht Journal of European and Comparative Law* 611, 612.
[35] Lenton (n 33), 6–7.
[36] *Ibid*, 7.

complex and dynamic ways within the system; all living organisms are active participants in (not simply passive respondents to) this system and *vis-à-vis* the range of other non-living Earth system components;[37] and the time scales of global change are highly variable (eg human time versus geological time).[38]

The Earth system metaphor departs from such an understanding of the Earth system, and has since become a popular scientific framing and contemporary analytical framework in the domain of Earth system science to describe, understand and respond to the complex interactions between Earth system components and processes, including exploring potential pathways to address Earth system vulnerability and to ensure resilience.[39] Impossible to map in any detail here, the emergence and historical evolution of the Earth system metaphor as the key foundation of Earth system science, has recently been described by Steffen and colleagues.[40] By way of a simplified summary, the idea of the Earth being a complex integrated system was already suggested as far back as the 1700s by scientists such as Von Humboldt, and in the early 1900s by Vernadsky with the publication of his book *The Biosphere*.[41] In the early 1970s, Lovelock introduced the (not altogether uncontroversial)[42] term *Gaia*, which describes Earth as a single living organism and tightly coupled feedback system,[43] consisting of 'the biosphere and all of those parts of the Earth with which it actively interacts to form the hypothetical new entity with properties that could not be predicted from the sum of its parts'.[44] In terms of the Gaia hypothesis, planetary processes are not reserved exclusively for the non-human domain; 'life itself is an active and necessary player in planetary dynamics'[45] to the extent that life shapes the system. Or in the words of Latour, 'far from being a Galilean body stripped of any other movements than those of billiard balls, the Earth has now taken back all the characteristics of a full-fledged *actor*'.[46] At around the same time, the 1972 Apollo 17 image of Earth (or the 'Blue Marble'), presented the

---

[37] Steffen et al (n 29), 7.

[38] Bronislaw Szerszynski, 'The Anthropocene Monument: On Relating Geological and Human Time' (2016) 20(1) *European Journal of Social Theory* 111.

[39] Eva Lövbrand, Johannes Stripple and Bo Wiman, 'Earth System Governmentality Reflections on Science in the Anthropocene' (2009) 19 *Global Environmental Change* 7.

[40] Steffen et al (n 28). See, also Ola Uhrqvist, 'One Model to Fit All? The Pursuit of Integrated Earth System Models in GAIM and AIMES' (2015) 40(2) *Historische Sozialforschung* 271.

[41] Steffen et al (n 4), 325.

[42] See, for instance, Alex Kleidon, 'Testing the Effects of Life on Earth's Functioning: How Gaian is the Earth System?' (2002) 52 *Climatic Change* 383.

[43] Timothy Lenton, Ken Caldeira and Eörs Szathmáry, 'What does History Teach us about the Major Transitions and Role of Disturbances in the Evolution of Life and of the Earth System?' in Schellnhuber et al (n 1), 29.

[44] James Lovelock and Lynn Margulis, 'Atmospheric Homeostasis by and for the Biosphere: The Gaia Hypothesis' (1974) XXVI *Tellus* 2–10 at 3. See, also James Lovelock, 'Gaia as Seen Through the Atmosphere' (1972) 6 *Atmospheric Environment* 579.

[45] Steffen et al (n 29), 3.

[46] Bruno Latour, 'Agency at the Time of the Anthropocene' (2014) 45(1) *New Literary History* 1, 3.

first image of Earth as an entire entity, which offered humans a visual *planetary* perspective of Earth. In 1999, Schellnhuber, a pioneer of Earth system science, predicted that humanity is about to embark on a 'second "Copernican" revolution', which 'will enable us to look back on our planet to perceive one single, complex, dissipative, dynamic entity, far from thermodynamic equilibrium—the "Earth system"'.[47] At the global policy level, the United Nations (UN) choose the slogan 'Only one Earth' as the leitmotif for its first major global Conference on the Human Environment that was held in Stockholm in 1972. In doing so, the UN endorsed the view, if only symbolically, that 'a single, united population inhabiting a single planet needs to govern its own future'.[48] In sum, more fully confronting the intellectual, scientific and regulatory challenges posed by systems-thinking, the Earth system metaphor was conceptualised by physicists, geologists and climatologists 'thinking about the history of our planet';[49] by the realisation that environmental change is occurring globally and it is necessary to respond to such global change; the regulatory challenges emanating from the notion of 'full Earth';[50] and by Earth system science's significant advances in computer modelling, remote sensing, global observation systems, and global datasets.[51]

In essence, the foregoing evolution of the Earth system metaphor has occurred as a response to the deficiencies (scientific, regulatory and otherwise) resulting from a traditional linear, one dimensional and segmented approach to understanding and responding to, what were perceived to be discreet, unrelated, localised 'environmental' problems that only occur in specific and disconnected geographic locations. These 'environmental' problems were seen to arise in a state of relative Holocene stability, which consequently posed minimal challenges to the type of simple, top-down, unconnected, mostly state-driven, command-and-control regulatory institutions (especially apparent in environmental law), that were aimed at tackling negative externalities of transactions instead of also addressing structural issues underlying those human processes that cause socio-ecological damage of the entire Earth system.[52] Within the context of Holocene stability:

> [P]olitical and economic institutions could often take for granted the presence of the non-human world and the ecological systems in which human societies are embedded … [and] institutional success came most straightforwardly in the form of rules or informal arrangements to control access, rather than in

---

[47] Hans Schellnhuber, '"Earth System Analysis" and the Second Copernican Revolution' (1999) 402 *Nature* C19, C20.
[48] Uhrqvist (n 40), 273.
[49] Timothy Lenton, *Earth System Science: A Very Short Introduction* (Oxford University Press 2016) 12.
[50] Uhrqvist (n 40), 272.
[51] International Biosphere-Geosphere Programme 'Global Change and the Earth System: A Planet Under Pressure' 11 April 2011 *IGPB Science Series No. 4*, 1, 5.
[52] Jorge Viñuales, 'The Organisation of the Anthropocene in Our Hands?' (2018) 1(1) *International Legal Theory and Practice* 1, 2.

> adaptation to ecological dynamism of the sort that could be expected were stable Holocene conditions to change.[53]

This reductionist approach, and our social regulatory institutions' full embrace of Holocene stability, has not served us well:

> although humanity has been capable of transforming the Earth through a deluge of entangled but uncoordinated actions, it was evidently intellectually unprepared to do so or to cope with the consequences at the level of whole-systems wisdom. Nobody had a grand plan for planetary refurbishment.[54]

In stark contrast to this reductionist approach, the significantly more all-embracing Earth system metaphor instead shifts its holistic focus to the planetary scale. In doing so, it extends Earth system science's enquiry into new areas seeking to understand complex and dynamic human and non-human relationships, complex self-organising systems, irreversible impacts of interacting stresses, multiple scales of organisation, and the various actors and their agendas that influence Earth system change.[55] In the words of Hamilton:

> The concept of the Earth System encompassed and transcended previous objects of study such as "the landscape", "ecosystems" and "the environment"; it is the Earth taken as a whole in a constant state of movement driven by interconnected cycles and forces, from the planet's core to the atmosphere and out to the moon, and powered by the flow of energy from the Sun. It is a single, dynamic, integrated system, and not a collection of ecosystems.[56]

Such a view is now supported by the main findings of the International Geosphere-Biosphere Programme, namely that the Earth is a system that life itself helps to control; global change is real and happening and significantly transcends localised 'environmental' concerns such as water, soil, air pollution or biodiversity loss; humans have become a force of nature and we now drive multiple, interacting effects that cascade through the Earth system in complex ways; and Earth system dynamics are characterised by critical thresholds and abrupt changes that are unpredictable, which means that the Earth is currently operating in a no-analogue state.[57]

The brief summary above suggests that the Earth system metaphor and its associated Earth system science agenda offer an inclusive epistemic platform to more fully engage in research spanning numerous disciplines that could

---

53 Dryzek (n 15), 938.

54 Clark, Crutzen and Schellnhuber (n 1), 8.

55 Sustainability science has emerged as 'a response to the substantial but limited understanding of nature-society interactions gained in recent decades through work in the environmental sciences that factors in human impacts, and work in social and development studies that factors in environmental influences'. Jill Jäger, 'Sustainability Science' in Eckart Ehlers and Thomas Krafft (eds), *Earth System Science in the Anthropocene: Emerging Issues and Problems* (Springer 2006) 20.

56 Hamilton (n 6), 94.

57 International Biosphere-Geosphere Programme "Global Change and the Earth System: A Planet Under Pressure" 11 April 2011 *IGPB Science Series No. 4*, 1, 2–3.

respond to the complex challenges of Earth system change by enabling 'a powerful new science capable of effectively integrating a wide array of disciplines towards understanding our home planet in all its complexity'.[58] Part 3 below will explore the current place and contribution of environmental law in this 'powerful new science', while Part 4 will reflect on some implications of the Earth system metaphor and the opportunities it presents for transforming environmental law into Earth system law.

III. Environmental law and the Earth system metaphor

Environmental law is part of the social science domain. Although social scientists increasingly recognise the significance of humans as a driving force of Earth system changes, the relevance of the Earth system metaphor for many years largely remained confined to the Earth system science domain, with few deliberate attempts at translating its relevance and implications for the social sciences.[59] Research by pioneers such as Schellnhuber, however, gradually began showing the need to more fully integrate human dynamics into an Earth system framework, including the social aspects of these dynamics, while foregrounding the very real risk that 'global change may not unfold as a linear change in Earth-System functioning but, rather, that human pressures could trigger rapid, irreversible shifts of the system into states that would be catastrophic for human well-being'.[60]

Since the early 2000s, the Earth system metaphor has been further popularised in the social sciences domain by the introduction of the Anthropocene,[61] and later, by the associated imagery of the planetary boundaries which reveals the deeply linked social and ecological aspects of the Earth system.[62] It has since become virtually impossible to speak about the Earth system without also invoking the notion of the Anthropocene.[63] On the one hand, the Anthropocene serves as the new name of the specific period in which the Earth system now finds itself in the geological time scale by 'classifying', as Biermann says, this new state.[64] On the other hand, the

[58] Steffen et al (n 28), 57.

[59] Eckart Ehlers and Thomas Krafft, 'Managing Global Change: Earth System Science in the Anthropocene' in Ehlers and Krafft (n 55), 5–12.

[60] Steffen et al (n 28), 57.

[61] Paul Crutzen and Eugene Stoermer, 'The "Anthropocene"' (2000) 41 *IGBP Newsletter* 17–18; Uhrqvist (n 40), 292.

[62] Johan Rockström et al., *A safe operating space for humanity*, (2009) 461 *Nature* 472; Will Steffen et al., *Planetary boundaries: Guiding human development on a changing planet*, (2015) 347(6223) *Science* 1259855.

[63] The Anthropocene has become 'a central and yet ambiguous system of thought for Earth System Science that both challenges and reproduces the Enlightenment promise of human self-realisation, autonomy and control'. Eva Lövbrand, Stripple and Wiman (n 22), 8. See, also Mark Maslin and Simon Lewis, 'Anthropocene: Earth System, Geological, Philosophical and Political Paradigm Shifts' (2015) 2(2) *The Anthropocene Review* 108.

[64] Frank Biermann, *Earth System Governance: World Politics in the Anthropocene* (MIT Press 2014) 4.

Anthropocene trope has also succeeded (despite critique),[65] to further illuminate the centrality of humans as a key component of the Earth system. In doing so, the Anthropocene trope clearly reveals the significant power of humans to upset Earth system equilibrium:[66] similar to volcanoes, erosion, earthquakes and natural selection, humans have now assumed the power to change other components and processes of the Earth system.[67] We are not external to 'nature', but instead a central part of an interlinked Earth system that we also influence through our primal urges, cultures and beliefs, our efforts to survive and to dominate, and our intrinsic desire to master other vulnerable humans and non-humans.

In the course of two decades, the Anthropocene has come to signify much more than an objective condition of planetary change; it has now become 'an interpretative category by which contemporary societies reflect upon themselves and upon life itself and reimagine their space and time. The Anthropocene as a cultural model is not then a politically neutral concept, but contains strong normative elements'.[68] In other words, the Anthropocene trope has effectively transcended its initial designation as a new geological epoch:

> The Anthropocene ranks among the most ambitious scientific programmes of the past 15 or 20 years … and it is tempting to treat it as a new metanarrative for the twenty-first century. It is effectively an all-encompassing framework that seeks to make sense of the 'earth-system' as a whole: it delineates the planet's natural history and turns it into a new geological period, it specifies the particular influence of human action on the emergence of that epoch, and it accounts for the relationships between the 'scientific' and the 'political' implications of these transformations.[69]

In light of the fact that the Anthropocene is now variously applied as an epistemological lens in search of new ways to better understand the place of humans in, and our impacts on, the Earth system,[70] how have the social sciences generally, and environmental law specifically, responded to the

---

65 Andreas Malm and Alf Hornborg, 'The Geology of Mankind? A Critique of the Anthropocene Narrative' (2014) 1(1) *The Anthropocene Review* 62.

66 Although, importantly, the Anthropocene's human (*Anthropos*) should not and cannot be universalised because 'different societies around the world have contributed differently and unequally to pressures on the Earth System and will have varied capabilities to alter future trajectories'. Will Steffen et al, 'Trajectories of the Earth System in the Anthropocene' (2018) 115(33) *Proceedings of the National Academy of Sciences* 8252, 8252.

67 One study usefully divides the human domination trajectory into four phases: (i) discovery of fire and use of fire tools, and the expanding reach of ancient cultures; (ii) domestication of animals, increased transportation and spread of colonialism; (iii) industrialisation and increased lifestyle expectations; and (vi) advanced industrialisation and globalisation. Billie Turner and Susannah McCandless, 'How Humankind Came to Rival Nature: A Brief History of the Human-Environment Condition and the Lessons Learned' in Schellnhuber et al (n 1), 227–43.

68 Delanty and Mota (n 7), 24.

69 Daniel Chernilo, 'The Question of the Human in the Anthropocene Debate' (2017) 20 *European Journal of Social Theory* 44, 45.

70 Whitney Autin, 'Multiple Dichotomies of the Anthropocene' (2016) 3(3) *The Anthropocene Review* 218–30.

Anthropocene's Earth system perspective and the many scientific and regulatory challenges that such a perspective raise?

Possibly inaugurating an important and timely 'cognitive shift',[71] the holistic vision of the Earth system as seen through the lens of the Anthropocene trope has now become a central concern, regulatory object and objective, perspective of, and guiding narrative in, a range of human efforts to think about, design and implement ways to survive an unstable and unpredictable human-dominated geological epoch.[72] Traditionally, such thinking has almost exclusively occurred in (and continue to predominate) the natural science domain, as the foregoing discussion suggested. While many social scientists (especially lawyers) are notoriously disciplinary-bound,[73] the natural sciences are also partly to blame for social science's reticence to more fully embrace, and orientate itself, around the Earth system metaphor: because of a 'mismatch between formalised methods and fuzzy social realities', the 'proponents of an integrated earth system analysis often relegate governance research to an auxiliary, advisory, and essentially non-scientific status'.[74] It was only with the establishment of the International Human Dimensions Programme on Global Environmental Change in 1996, that a comprehensive scientific platform was provided to facilitate social science research into the human drivers of Earth system change and its social implications for human health and well-being.[75]

Consequent on such initiatives, the burgeoning field of 'Earth system governance' that has been pioneered by Biermann around 2007,[76] is perhaps the clearest example of the Earth system metaphor's attempts to infiltrate the social sciences, and serves as a stark contrast to environmental law and its lawyers' continued ambivalence towards, and reluctance to fully embrace, the Earth system perspective. Yet, at the same time, the burgeoning Earth system governance programme also offers hope for environmental law's possible eventual future embrace of the Earth system perspective, as we shall see below. Biermann defines Earth system governance as:

> [T]he sum of the formal and informal rule systems and actor-networks at all levels of human society that are set up in order to influence the coevolution

---

71 Jeremy Schmidt, 'The Moral Geography of the Earth System' 2019(44) *Transactions of the Institute of British Geographers* 721–734 at 722.

72 See, on the impact and future scientific potential of the Anthropocene trope, Frank Biermann and Eva Lövbrand (eds), *Anthropocene Encounters: New Directions in Green Political Thinking* (Cambridge University Press, 2019).

73 Viñuales does not find this surprising: 'law and legal studies have been considered—and institutionally organised—as a separate subject for centuries. Lawyers are partly responsible. We spend far too much time speaking to each other, and our conceptions of interdisciplinarity have remained fairly simplistic'. Viñuales (n 52), 7.

74 Biermann (n 2), 328.

75 Oran Young, Leslie King and Heike Schroeder (eds), *Institutions and Environmental Change: Principal Findings, Applications, and Research Frontiers* (MIT Press 2008).

76 For a general overview, see Biermann (n 64).

> of human and natural systems in a way that secures the sustainable development of human society—that is, a development that meets the needs of present generations without compromising the ability of future generations to meet their own needs.[77]

Situated as it is at the interface of Earth system science and governance theory, the Earth System Governance network is guided by this broad understanding of Earth system governance. Its research agenda collectively attempts to identify, understand, explain and find solutions to problems that arise from all

> organised human responses to earth system transformation, in particular the institutions and agents that cause global environmental change and the institutions, at all levels, that are created to steer human development in a way that secures a "safe" co-evolution with natural processes.[78]

The challenge of Earth system governance is to respond to the:

> [S]erious mismatch between the research and recommendations of earth system analysts and the actions of political decision makers, who still operate within the parameters of a nation-state system inherited from the twentieth century. Policymakers in the twentieth century gained much experience in managing confined ecosystems, such as river basins, forests, or lakes. *In the twenty-first century, they are faced with one of the largest governance challenges humankind has ever had to deal with; protecting the entire earth system*, including most of its subsystems, and building stable institutions that guarantee a safe transition process and a coevolution of natural and social systems at planetary scale.[79]

Not exclusively reserved for political scientists, the Earth System Governance network and its research agenda also cover law and legal science generally and environmental law specifically. This much is clear from the closely intertwined relationship between law and governance at a general level,[80] and specifically from the network's focus on 'formal and informal rule systems' and 'organised human responses', as we saw above. The network further includes several (environmental) lawyers within its ranks,[81] and its research covers issues such as inequality, democracy and power, and justice and allocation that are directly relevant for environmental law and thus require inputs from environmental lawyers.[82]

In recognition of law's centrality to, and growing importance in, the network and it research, a special Task Force on Earth System Law was

---

77 Biermann (n 2), 329.
78 *Ibid*, 328.
79 Biermann (n 64), 9. Emphasis added.
80 Louis Kotzé, *Global Environmental Governance: Law and Regulation for the 21st Century* (Edward Elgar 2012).
81 See, 'People' (*Earth System Governance*, 2020) online: https://www.earthsystemgovernance.org/people/lead-faculty/.
82 Sarah Burch et al, 'New Directions in Earth System Governance Research' (2019) 1 *Earth System Governance* 1.

connected.[92] These interlinkages, in turn, highlight 'the need to include human activity and the social sciences in understanding the future of the Earth system'.[93] While the Earth system metaphor usefully links the domains of those natural and social sciences that focus on achieving global sustainability, law in general, and environmental law specifically, have played only a peripheral part in contributing to Earth system-oriented solutions. Environmental lawyers must urgently take up the challenge to embrace the Earth system metaphor in order to fully capitalise on its regulatory and scientific potential and advantages. This is so because environmental law, in a re-imagined guise, will remain a critically important part of the suit of regulatory responses that must address Earth system change, especially to the extent that it has considerable potential to facilitate prevention, mitigation, adaptation and resilience to such change.[94] To this end, the Earth system metaphor offers a fresh impetus and useful contemporary framework for lawyers to critically assess whether environmental law, in its present form and state, is still fit for purpose in the Anthropocene epoch. Where this is not the case, the Earth system metaphor provides guidance that it derives from Earth system science as to what needs to change, how it should change, and the extent of the reforms that would be required of environmental law.

For this to happen, environmental law will have to immerse itself more fully in the growing interdisciplinary Earth system science effort on which it should draw. Environmental lawyers could capitalise on existing interdisciplinary knowledge and experience by, first, trying to understand what the Earth system means in general terms and for environmental law specifically. The 'holistic super-discipline'[95] that is Earth system science, already offers comprehensive natural science-based insights into what the Earth system is, how humans and other forces impact this system, and the type, range and depth of possible challenges that arise from these impacts that will have to be addressed. Second, these insights must then be translated into the social world of environmental law, informed as such an exercise could be by the Earth system governance experience. After all, the social science domain of Earth system governance, which has fully embraced the Earth system metaphor, has already made significant headway into identifying, understanding and designing possible governance-based responses to the regulatory issues that Earth system challenges create.

The (admittedly ambitious) end goal of any transformations that such an interdisciplinary re-imagination might entail includes, *inter alia*, enabling a

---

92 Alf Hornborg, 'Conceptualizing Socioecological Systems' in Alf Hornborg and Carole Crumley (eds), *The World System and the Earth System: Global Socioenvironmental Change and Sustainability Since the Neolithic* (Routledge, 2006) 1, 2.

93 Diana Liverman and Rosa Cuesta, 'Human Interactions with the Earth System: People and Pixels Revisited' (2008) 33 *Earth Surface Processes and Landforms* 1458, 1459.

94 Kotzé and Kim (n 20); Kotzé (n 21).

95 Lövbrand, Stripple and Wiman (n 22), 7.

new version of environmental law to: rectify as far as possible past and present Earth system destruction; to prevent and/or minimise future harm; to comprehensively address all aspects of human and non-human socio-ecological injustices for present and future generations; to discard environmental law's false assumptions of Holocene stability and predictability by instead embracing, for example, instability, unpredictability and complexity as core assumptions; and to maintain and restore the integrity of Earth's life support system as a precondition for global sustainability.[96]

2. Relearning alongside systems thinking

Another objective of the foregoing interdisciplinary transformations would be for environmental law to reorganise itself around systems thinking. The resultant body of Earth system law should enable us to see the bigger picture and to comprehensively and more effectively respond to the regulatory challenges of the Earth system. Fully embracing a systems approach would allow Earth system law to respond not only to 'environmental' issues, but also to a far broader range of reciprocally interlinked challenges of the entire Earth system.

The main challenge in this respect would not be to transform the nature or essence of law as such. Law (and its specialised regimes such as environmental law), after all, is a system: the 'legal system [is] a source of rules for regulating other social systems'.[97] Law is even seen to be a complex adaptive system (as we shall also see further below) in the sense that it, among others, fully embraces and even depends on legal pluralism:

> law is no longer solely constructed at the national level. The notion of legal pluralism indicates that the national and subnational levels coexist with legal systems being developed at the European and the international level. These legal systems interact, influence and counteract each other.[98]

And in the environmental law domain specifically, Kim and Mackey convincingly argue that 'international environmental law is a complex system where treaties and institutions self-organize and exhibit emergent properties'.[99]

I suspect the main challenge then is fairly straightforward (but no less daunting): if environmental law already exhibits systems qualities, we would 'merely' need environmental lawyers to recognise these qualities and to design, develop, apply, enforce and revise environmental law for the purpose of governing the Earth system around systems thinking. The step

---

[96] Rakhyun Kim, 'Transnational Sustainability Law: Wither International Environmental Law?' (2016) 46(6) *Environmental Policy and Law* 405.

[97] JB Ruhl, 'Law's Complexity: A Primer' (2008) 24(4) *Georgia State University Law Review* 885, 897.

[98] Lierman (n 34), 612.

[99] Rakhyun Kim and Brendan Mackey, 'International Environmental Law as a Complex Adaptive System' (2014) 4 *International Environmental Agreements: Politics, Law and Economics* 5, 5.

change that would be required is to more fully identify, understand, further develop and apply the systems characteristics of environmental law; an exercise that could occur within the remit of Earth system law and its research agenda, the latter which has already been elaborated elsewhere.[100] In short, environmental lawyers will have to *relearn* by going back to the basics. Relearning will ask of us to first and foremost reappreciate those aspects that make environmental law a system and that enable environmental law to interact with and respond to other systems, such as the Earth system. As Ruhl muses with reference to law more generally:

> The legal system. It rolls easily off the tongues of lawyers like a single word-the-legalsystem-as if we all know what it means. But what is the legal system? How does it behave? What are its boundaries? What is its input and output? How will it look in one year? In ten years? How should we use it to make change in some other aspect of social life?[101]

Relating these questions to environmental law specifically, I would argue that many environmental lawyers, myself included, do not yet fully appreciate the system qualities of environmental law and the potential of environmental law to further develop these qualities and to better cohere with and respond to the system qualities of what it seeks to regulate. Many environmental lawyers are not always predisposed to think in terms of systems; that is to say, not all of us depart from and always embrace systems-oriented ontologies, effectively shutting out as this does, the ability to characterise environmental law, and perhaps more critically, the *regulatory object* of environmental law, in terms of deeply intertwined systems.[102] We have neither been trained to do so, nor does our discipline, its science and practice necessarily demand it. We see this in the neatly compartmentalised textbooks we write, the issue-specific courses we teach and study, and in the way we apply environmental law. For example, environmental law is presented as distinctly un-systemised and compartmentalised: (i) geographically (international, regional, national and local law); (ii) according to subject area and regulatory object that are often treated as distinct and unrelated areas (oceans governance, biodiversity conservation, air pollution etc); (iii) in terms of the narrow spectrum of its prevailing normativity (binding norms seem to be preferred over non-binding norms); (iv) in terms of its temporal dimensions (environmental law mostly focuses on the past and present and not also on the future despite its high rhetoric of 'future generations');[103] (v) in terms of

---

[100] Kotzé and Kim (n 20), 8–10.

[101] Ruhl (n 97), 885.

[102] This is, however, not a phenomenon that is unique to law and to lawyers. See, among others, Julie Libarkin and Josepha Kurdziel, 'Ontology and the Teaching of Earth System Science' 2006 54(3) *Journal of Geoscience Education* 408–413; Assaraf and Orion (n 30), 520–3.

[103] See, eg, the 1987 Report of the World Commission on Environment and Development: Our Common Future.

environmental law's one dimensional preoccupation with addressing obvious externalities that manifest clearly and that can be proven, instead of also the past, present and future systemic drivers of these externalities and their possible unclear speculative effects that have not yet materialised; and (vi) in terms of environmental law's almost exclusive reliance on the state as its source of legitimacy, authority and executing agent instead of also embracing other non-state actors and sources of authority. And in terms of the application of environmental law, the closest environmental lawyers arguably come to systems thinking is to contemplate the causality of actions and their legal consequences (for example, in terms of the law of delict or tort law a causal nexus between conduct (operating a mine close to a wetland) and damage (pollution of that wetland) must be proven).

How then do we get from *there* to *here*? The Earth system metaphor's full embrace of systems thinking could help environmental law and its lawyers to relearn and to go back to the basics of understanding the systems qualities of environmental law. To this end, the Earth system metaphor offers an opportunity 'to perceive the big picture, to ask and answer the genuine systems questions, and to identify the prime pathways toward global sustainability in strategy [*sic*] space (that is, the sum of likely decision outcomes available to all relevant actors)'.[104] This is because,

> Earth System Science focuses on the connections between the myriad processes that happen on, above, and below the Earth's surface. The fundamental connections between biological organisms, including people, large scale plate tectonic processes, atmospheric and oceanic interactions, and other spheres of the Earth are important for understanding whole Earth phenomena. This systems view, that no single process happens in isolation, works well for understanding the big picture.[105]

From a practical point of view, the Earth system metaphor and its associated rationalities make 'the planet knowable as the "Earth System" and, thus, manageable or governable in the sense that they allow for integrated or even seamless models in which it is possible to make strategic calculations of the effects of different policies'.[106] In other words, seeing the Earth as a system, 'affects expectations on what kinds of knowledge decision-makers need in order to be able to act responsibly and legitimately'.[107] Viewing the Earth as a system enables us to better appreciate that environmental law's problems are not only 'environmental'; they are deeply interlinked, multi-scalar and temporal social, economic, health and political issues, and they are caused by non-human and human forces. Earth system changes are therefore not

[104] Hans Schellnhuber *et al*, 'Earth System Analysis for Sustainability' (2005) 47(8) *Environment* 10, 14.
[105] Julie Libarkin and Josepha Kurdziel, 'Ontology and the Teaching of Earth System Science' 2006 54(3) *Journal of Geoscience Education* 408,412.
[106] Uhrqvist (n 40), 275.
[107] *Ibid.*

the sum of what is perceived to be a reductionist approach to environmental law's major concerns, namely: climate change, air pollution, water pollution, land degradation, deforestation, ocean acidification, plastic pollution etc. These 'environmental' problems are only a small part of the much larger Earth system context:

> Traditional notions of environmental policy, pollution control and nature conservation no longer capture current global developments that transform the biogeophysical cycles and processes of our planet. New perspectives and research are needed to understand the complex relation between global transformations of social and natural systems, including accelerating economic integration, globalization in all its forms, internationalization of policy processes, and the multi-scale consequences of ecological transformation.[108]

This might imply that 'we need to go beyond "environmental" law, in its present understanding as the law tackling negative externalities, and focus on how law more generally organises the transactions or processes that prompted the Anthropocene'.[109] By way of example, amending environmental law to periodically increase penalties for a coal power plant situated on the banks of a river that it pollutes will always remain important as a method of deterrence. In addition, however, an Earth system approach would require holistic reforms that aim to tackle not only the negative externalities of such pollution, but also the structural processes underlying the causes of that pollution including, for example, economic and consumption drivers that encourage development of coal power stations, spatial planning laws that allow such facilities to be built in sensitive areas, international relations and trade laws regulating the export of electricity to another country, investment laws that must ideally encourage the expansion of renewable energy plants, and labour and social security laws allowing cheap migrant labourers to temporarily work for minimum wages in the coal mines that feed the power plant. In this view, the specific localised 'environmental' problem becomes a global Earth system problem that requires a holistic response from an Earth system-oriented body of law.

3. Complex adaptive law for a complex adaptive Earth system

The imagery of the Anthropocene suggests we live in unprecedented times of unpredictable and extreme socio-ecological upheaval (at least in terms of the human experience).[110] In stark contrast to the Holocene's relative stasis, harmony and predictability (or simplicity), the one issue that does seem to

---

[108] Frank Biermann et al, 'Earth System Governance: A Research Framework' (2010) 10 *International Environmental Agreements: Politics, Law and Economics* 277, 279.
[109] Viñuales (n 52), 9–10.
[110] Hamilton (n 6).

be certain in this unchartered epoch is that *complexity* will now become the norm rather than the exception. In other words, inherent as it is to the type of systems thinking described above, the context of complexity is now a central premise for understanding and responding to Earth system transformations. What does complexity mean in this context?

The notion of complexity derives from complexity theory and general system theory. Complexity theorists seem to distinguish between algorithmic complexity prevalent in mathematics and information technology; deterministic complexity which focuses on chaos and catastrophe theory; and aggregate complexity which involves 'how individual elements work in concert to create systems with complex behaviour'.[111] These are not necessarily unrelated, as they all share a common trait; namely they are concerned with how the 'nature of a system may be characterized with reference to its constituent parts in a non-reductionist manner'.[112] Of these three divisions, it is aggregate complexity that would probably be most directly relevant for Earth system science because it focuses on holism and synergies resulting from the interaction of system components and on the relationships between these. While complex systems, such as the Earth's, are often characterised by notions such as circularity, dynamism, uncertainty, non-reductionism, non-linearity, interconnectivity, functional interdependency, and unpredictability, these characteristics are not necessarily undesirable. As Ruhl says,

> 'the environment [by which he means the Earth system] operates in a state of highly complicated, organized disorder. Indeed, scientists are beginning to understand that the disorder—the chaos that is inherent in the environment —is its means of sustainability.[113]

Because Earth system characteristics such as complexity are not only analytical but also potentially normative,[114] concerns related to ways in which to understand and respond to such complexity will necessarily extend to regulatory institutions such as environmental law. As a response to the need to embrace complexity, the Earth system metaphor usefully introduces the context of complexity into regulatory and scientific debates and practices. Perhaps mainly as a result of its ontological design and its pursuit of certainty, normative hierarchy, order, structure, and tightly managed structured outcomes, as well as its organisation around distinct and centralised sources of (mostly public) power, environmental law does not respond well to complexity. Environmental law is instead a 'nonadaptive heap of prescriptive and

[111] See, for example, Steven Manson, 'Simplifying Complexity: A Review of Complexity Theory' (2001) 32 *Geoforum* 405, 405.

[112] Steven Manson, 'Simplifying Complexity: A Review of Complexity Theory' (2001) 32 *Geoforum* 405, 406.

[113] JB Ruhl, 'Thinking of Environmental Law as a Complex Adaptive System: How to Clean up the Environment by Making a Mess of Environmental Law' (1997) 34(4) *Houston Law Review* 933, 935.

[114] Biermann (n 2), 330.

proscriptive commandments'[115] that aim to offer certainty, stability, predictability and simplicity in a complex world. For environmental law to accommodate and to respond to Earth system complexity, it will have to discard assumptions of Holocene simplicity and ecological equilibrium upon which it is built and from where it proceeds in order to regulate. Environmental law must instead fully embrace Earth system complexity in order to remain relevant, effective and fit-for-purpose in the Anthropocene. If it fails to do so, environmental law runs the risk of losing its regulatory value because it will remain premised on false assumptions that are not commensurate with a complex Earth system.[116]

To this end, we might have to consider the 'dynamical forces within the legal system' we devise to manage our impacts on the Earth system, in order for environmental law to itself become a 'complex adaptive system'[117] that adapts and responds to the complex adaptative Earth system.[118] Complex adaptive systems are complex in that they are 'diverse and made up of multiple interconnected elements, and adaptive in that they have the capacity to learn from experience and adapt to the changing environment'.[119] They are further characterised by generic properties such as dispersed interaction, the absence of a global controller, cross-cutting hierarchical organisation, continual adaptation, perpetual novelty, and non-equilibrium dynamics.[120]

Measured against such a description, environmental law is unable to fully respond to the complex adaptive Earth system:

> [O]ur present framework of environmental law is designed as if its subject matter is dictated by uniformitarianism rather than a set of dynamic, adaptive systems. Complex adaptive systems, because of their highly collectivized, non-linear, dynamic behavior, defy prediction through classical reductionist method, or any other known method for that matter. Yet we have not designed our environmental law system with this underlying property in mind. Rather, it is mired in a reductionist, linear, predictivist mentality ignorant of underlying complex system behaviors.[121]

The challenges that complexity raises for environmental law are obviously mind-boggling; not least because such challenges will require us to rethink environmental law's 'technological' aspects such as those relating to predictability. In the process of complexifying environmental law, we will also need to maintain environmental law's core legal nature as a standard of value that performs an axiological function, and its function as a cultural practice that

115 Ruhl (n 113), 941.
116 Kim and Mackey (n 99), 6.
117 Ruhl (n 113), 938.
118 Kim and Mackey (n 99).
119 Lierman (n 34), 629.
120 Kim and Mackey (n 96), 9.
121 Ruhl (n 113), 940.

performs a group identification function. But if environmental law does succeed in taking its cue from complexity theory and systems thinking and to embrace and to respond to Earth system complexity, next generation environmental law will look very different from what we currently have. For example, the future global climate law regime will possibly have to be far more ambitious and comprehensive in order to cater for uncertainty and to respond to extreme levels of climate harm and disruption that are not exclusively caused by climate-related processes; it must have more explicit reciprocal connections with, and deliberate measures to facilitate, interactions between other related international, regional and national law regimes; it must enable a broader scope of state and non-state actors collectively to engage in cooperative global climate governance that is not territorially bounded and jurisdictionally circumscribed; and it must be more flexible and adaptive in relation to achieving its ultimate objective of global sustainability.[122] To this end, an Earth system-oriented global climate law might have to consider and address, all at once, many other issues that are related to global climate change such as stratospheric ozone depletion, loss of biosphere integrity and ocean acidification, to name but a few. For this purpose, an Earth system-oriented legal response to global climate change, which is one of the nine interrelated planetary boundaries, could be achieved by holistically considering the myriad aspects regulated by the laws pertaining to all nine boundaries.[123] Another option lies in the newly emerging field of transnational climate law, which is an example of environmental law's tentative attempts to embrace complexity in terms of various governance levels and types of norms that could be utilised:

> Because climate change involves global systems with complex local linkages, the governance regime mixes the local and the global. National governments have taken action unilaterally and have been joined by non-state actors, which include subnational governments, corporations, and non-governmental organizations (NGOs). Subnational governments have also entered into cooperation agreements with each other and with foreign nations. Thus, climate change law has broken through the traditional boundaries of international law, requiring a shift to the new paradigm of transnational law.[124]

I would suggest that going forward, the emerging debates on transnational environmental law, which have been explored in detail elsewhere,[125] could be instructive to the extent that they illuminate the type of issues that must

[122] See, for example, Tim Stephens, 'Wishful Thinking? The Governance of Climate Change-related Disasters in the Anthropocene' in Rosemary Lyster and Robert Verchick (eds) *Research Handbook on Climate Disaster Law: Barriers and Opportunities* (Edward Elgar 2018) 31–45.

[123] See for a general discussion Duncan French and Louis Kotzé (eds), *Research Handbook on Law, Governance and Planetary Boundaries* (Edward Elgar forthcoming).

[124] Thijs Etty et al, 'Transnational Climate Law' (2018) 7(2) *Transnational Environmental Law* 191, 191.

[125] Heyvaert (n 87).

be considered in pursuit of mapping the outlines of complex adaptive Earth system law.

4. Bringing humans back into the Earth system

To the extent that the Earth system metaphor illuminates how deeply intertwined the biosphere and geosphere are,[126] it dissolves Cartesian dualisms and epistemologies of mastery by reconnecting humans with a hitherto externalised, submissive and compliant 'nature' somewhere out there, that can be 'managed' by Promethean humans.[127] The Earth system metaphor therefore fully embraces the idea of interconnectivity; the Anthropocene's emphasis of humans as part of the Earth system; and the associated awareness of the profound role and power of humans in transforming the Earth system alongside a realisation that how we use this awareness will shape the Earth's future and the future of *all* life, not only our own.[128] In the course of its rejection of Cartesian dualisms and human mastery, the Anthropocene abandons the idea that the Earth 'somehow provides a stable ground on which the social or human world is constructed'.[129] It instead exposes the extraordinary degrees of Earth system harm that has historically been caused, is currently being caused, and will be caused in future by humans.[130] As Dryzek says:

> The Anthropocene ... does not just amplify existing ecological concerns: it changes their content by putting humans at the centre of causal processes in the Earth system. In highlighting the vulnerability of the character of the system on which we depend to human action, it also confirms that this system is not something out there demanding limited and occasional attention. Rather, human-induced instability means this system is a key player in how human history will unfold.[131]

Such a perspective consequently shows that the Earth system is vulnerable and that humans are also vulnerable as a result of our own doing, and because we are merely a small, but influential, part of the vulnerable Earth system.[132] We are neither as invincible as we think we are, nor are the social rules we design to maintain deliberate patterns of advantage for a few, able to maintain such selective privilege *ad infinitum*. The Anthropocene instead exposes the fraud and deception by which a highly selective group of privileged, consumptive

[126] Although Earth system scientists acknowledge that Earth system science sometimes continues to find 'the incorporation of humans into the Earth system a challenging task'. Diana Liverman and Rosa Cuesta, 'Human Interactions with the Earth System: People and Pixels Revisited' (2008) 33 *Earth Surface Processes and Landforms* 1458, 1458.

[127] Sam Adelman, 'Epistemologies of Mastery' in Anna Grear and Louis Kotzé (eds), *Research Handbook on Human Rights and the Environment* (Edward Elgar 2015) 9–27.

[128] Clark, Crutzen and Schellnhuber (n 1), 2.

[129] Delanty and Mota (n 7), 29.

[130] Biermann (n 2), 330.

[131] Dryzek (n 15), 940.

[132] Louis Kotzé, 'The Anthropocene, Earth System Vulnerability and Socio-ecological Injustice in an Age of Human Rights' (2019) 10(1) *Journal of Human Rights and the Environment* 62.

and exploitative humans have been masking their co-responsibility for Earth system destruction; a destruction that has and continues to be facilitated by environmental law, as some critical legal scholars point out.[133] In fact, as a privileging human construct that benefits some privileged humans, anthropocentric (international environmental) law and its associated constructs and paradigms, such as property law, colonialism, slavery, state sovereignty and even human rights, have been complicit in causing the Anthropocene and its predatory forms of exploitation of a vulnerable Earth system.[134]

As a counternarrative, the Anthropocene's imagery of a vulnerable Earth system increasingly 'prompts new calls for thought and action that can imagine different relationships between geologic time, the cultural logics of capital and accumulation, and the ontological realities of our species-being'.[135] These new 'calls for thought and action' are also deeply *ethical*, as Burdon suggests:

> [T]here has never been a time when human history and the history of the Earth were so intertwined. Attempts to grapple with this insight cannot be resolved through scientific questioning alone and ought to give rise to an appreciation of the uniqueness and integrity of each component of the Earth system (humans included) and the world as a relational whole.[136]

The implications of such a realisation and the need for new imaginations could shake environmental law to its core. In addition to becoming systems-oriented as described above, environmental law will arguably have to be more sensitive and responsive to *Earth system vulnerability*. Earth system vulnerability is an all-embracing notion that potentially includes the human and non-human elements of the Earth system, by explicitly emphasising the fact that human vulnerability is ontologically intertwined with non-human vulnerability.[137] Earth system law will accordingly have to recognise and fully cater for Earth system vulnerability in its fullest sense. One way to do so is to discard assumptions of human mastery that anthropocentric environmental law still underwrites, and to cease benefiting only a selective privileged few humans (generally seen to reside in the global North) at the expense of those humans and their exploitable resources in the global South.[138]

---

133 Anna Grear, 'Deconstructing Anthropos: A Critical Legal Reflection on "Anthropocentric" Law and Anthropocene "Humanity"' (2015) 26(3) *Law and Critique* 225–49.

134 Kotzé (n 12).

135 Donna Houston, 'Crisis Is Where We Live: Environmental Justice for the Anthropocene' (2013) 10(3) *Globalizations* 439, 440.

136 Peter Burdon, 'Rethinking Global Ethics in the Anthropocene' in Peter Burdon, Klaus Bosselmann and Kirsten Engel (eds), *The Crisis in Global Ethics and the Future of Global Governance: Fulfilling the Promise of the Earth Charter* (Edward Elgar, 2019) 92, 95–96.

137 Anna Grear, 'The Vulnerable Living Order: Human Rights and the Environment in a Critical and Philosophical Perspective' (2011) (2)(1) *Journal of Human Rights and the Environment* 23, 42.

138 Shawkat Alam, Sumudu Atapattu, Carmen Gonzalez and Jona Razzaque (eds), *International Environmental Law and the Global South* (Cambridge University Press 2015).

Earth system law must therefore be far more focused on protecting non-humans, not because such an endeavour would benefit humans, but because Earth system law must adhere to an ethical obligation to address Earth system vulnerability in its widest sense by extending juridical care to law's non-traditional subjects. Such an approach should depart from the view that 'humans are dependent not only on one another but [also] on a series of trans-human systems, and this interdependence is a source of resilience—and vulnerability'.[139] We already see encouraging signs of what is possible in this context emerging around the globe in the form of rights of nature in countries such as India, Bolivia, Ecuador, Colombia, and New Zealand.[140] Mostly stemming from indigenous laws and cosmovisions, and their altogether more embracing ontologies of care, such alternative framings offer valuable examples of how Earth system law could discard the human as its main concern while at once being more sensitive to the vulnerability concerns of the entire living order, indeed of the entire Earth system. Earth system law that embraces vulnerability concerns, and specifically the concerns of non-humans, could offer possible pathways to counter the destructive power of (some privileged) humans, while at once addressing the extraordinary degree of Earth system harm that has been done, the intensifying harm that continues to be done to the Earth system, and the harm that, unless halted now, will undoubtedly continue in future. In doing so, Earth system law could bring humans back into the Earth system, as it were, by facilitating a new understanding of relational space/place and 'co-becoming in a relational world' that is based on the premise that 'not only are all beings—human, animal, plant, process, thing or affect—vital and sapient with their own knowledge and law, but their very being is constituted through relationships that are constantly re-generated'.[141]

V. Conclusion

The Earth system metaphor challenges us to discard what we think we know about environmental law's role in addressing the many regulatory challenges emanating from a complex Earth system in the Anthropocene. To this end, the Earth system metaphor suggests we need a new legal paradigm for the Anthropocene. This new legal paradigm need not necessarily become a distinct new field of law; although it could over time. For now, Earth system

[139] Angela Harris, 'Vulnerability and Power in the Age of the Anthropocene' (2014) 6 *Washington and Lee Journal of Energy, Climate, and the Environment* 98, 126.

[140] Louis Kotzé and Paola Villavicencio Calzadilla, 'Somewhere between Rhetoric and Reality: Environmental Constitutionalism and the Rights of Nature in Ecuador' (2017) 6(3) *Transnational Environmental Law* 401; Paola Villavicencio Calzadilla and Louis Kotzé, 'Living in Harmony with Nature? A Critical Appraisal of the Rights of Mother Earth in Bolivia' (2018) 7(3) *Transnational Environmental Law* 397.

[141] Bawaka Country et al, 'Co-becoming Bawaka: Towards a Relational Understanding of Place/Space' (2016) 40(4) *Progress in Human Geography* 455,456.

law could 'merely' represent a *framework for rethinking environmental law for the purpose of the Anthropocene*. Or as Affolder says with reference to transnational climate law, Earth system law could become a 'visual field' enabling environmental lawyers to identify, understand and explore, with some measure of 'determined attentiveness', the implications of the Earth system metaphor for environmental law.[142] In this respect, I agree that we might not always need a new distinct field of law for every regulatory challenge that arises (such as climate adaptation law, rain forest destruction law, or social media law). In some instances it might be possible, and even preferable, that 'legal institutions simply work away at the problem through unrelated, self-contained fields'.[143] For present purposes, therefore, I can only assume that the last word has not been said about whether Earth system law should or should not become a distinct new field of law.

What is much clearer, is that the development of such a new legal paradigm will require considerably creative out-of-the-box thinking alongside the imagery of the Earth system metaphor sketched out above. And this will not be a straight-forward process. After all, 'little is more difficult than learning to think differently. Yet, it is hard even to define the principal problems without upsetting longstanding traditions, beliefs, attitudes and the often unspoken assumptions on which we build our lives'.[144] Are we willing, and will we ultimately be able, to upset our traditions, beliefs, and attitudes when it comes to thinking about a different type of legal paradigm that is better fit for purpose in the Anthropocene? I have endeavoured here to describe why I think the Earth system metaphor could be relevant for, and valuable in, guiding the transformation of reductionist Holocene environmental law into a more fully systems-oriented legal paradigm for the Anthropocene that is commensurate with a complex Earth system and its myriad regulatory and existential challenges. While only time will tell, the ideas offered here could hopefully present a small, tentative step towards challenging some of our steadfast beliefs and assumptions related to the hitherto contribution of environmental law in governing Earth system challenges. In doing so, these ideas might ultimately prompt us to imagine Earth system law for the Anthropocene.

Acknowledgement

My sincere thanks to Frank Biermann, Jorge Viñuales, Harro van Asselt, Rakhyun Kim, Cameron Holley, Tim Stephens, and the anonymous reviewers for their helpful views on an earlier draft. All views and errors are my own.

[142] Natasha Affolder, "Transnational Climate Law" in Peer Zumbansen (ed), *Oxford Handbook of Transnational Law* (Oxford University Press forthcoming).

[143] JB Ruhl and James Salzman, 'Climate Change meets the Law of the Horse' (2013) 62(5) *Duke Law Journal* 975.

[144] Crispin Tickell, 'Societal Responses to the Anthropocene' (2011) 369 *Philosophical Transaction of the Royal Society* 926, 926.

Disclosure statement

No potential conflict of interest was reported by the author(s).

Funding

This paper was supported by the author's South African National Research Foundation project under grant agreement UID: 118746 and it was completed in April 2020.

(Transnational) law for the Anthropocene: revisiting Jessup's move from 'what?' to 'how?'

Laura Mai

ABSTRACT

In the Anthropocene, legal thinking is challenged to re-envision the 'human' position vis-à-vis the 'natural' 'environment'. To map this challenge, this paper draws on three theoretical perspectives: social-ecological resilience thinking, social systems theory and post-humanism. The paper then explores how Jessup's perspective on transnational law could be applied to further develop legal thinking in the Anthropocene. It proposes that legal scholarship and practice would benefit from revisiting Jessup's move from 'what?' to 'how?': Rather than thinking about *what* (transnational) law might, or might not, be, legal researchers and practitioners are now tasked to understand *how* law can be mobilised as a tool to navigate our relationship with the planet. The paper concludes that Jessup's practical, progressive and pragmatic approach provides a useful starting point for developing legal forms, strategies and technologies to navigate Anthropocene realities.

1. Introduction

Scientific analyses suggest that never before in the history of our planet have humans so fundamentally interfered with the Earth System.[1] Greenhouse gas emissions, chemical pollution, land-use change, freshwater use, atmospheric aerosol loading, changes in biochemical cycles, biodiversity loss and ozone depletion have evolved as key drivers of planetary change.[2] In 2000, Dutch atmospheric chemist Paul Crutzen and his colleague Eugene Stoermer suggested the term 'Anthropocene' as the name for a new geological epoch to acknowledge the central role that humans

---

[1] The Earth System is defined as 'the suite of interacting physical, chemical, and biological global-scale cycles (often called biogeochemical cycles) and energy fluxes which provide the conditions necessary for life on the planet'. It is conceptualised as a materially closed system with the sun as its external energy source; humans are understood to be part of it (Will Steffen and others, *Global Change and the Earth System: A Planet under Pressure* (Springer 2004) 7).

[2] For an early assessment see Johan Rockström and others, 'A Safe Operating Space for Humanity' (2009) 461 *Nature* 472.

now play in shaping the Earth System.[3] While the process of formally recognising the Anthropocene as a new era in the history of our planet is on-going,[4] scientific models predict that in contrast to the relatively stable conditions of the Holocene, the last post-glacial period which allowed humans to flourish, the Anthropocene will be characterised by increased instability and unpredictability.[5]

Conceptualising critical thresholds in the Earth System as 'planetary boundaries', research suggests that we must stay within these boundaries to prevent the onset of less accommodating living-conditions.[6] Taking the climate crisis as an example, models indicate that we have already crossed the relevant planetary threshold.[7] In fact, recent analyses suggest that the cumulative impacts of anthropogenic greenhouse gas emissions and biosphere degradation have put the planet on track to move into a 'hothouse' state—a condition of irreversible heating-up.[8] Scientists warn that if this scenario were to materialise, the impacts would 'likely be massive, sometimes abrupt, and undoubtedly disruptive', leading to societal declines and collapses, migrations and resettlements, as well as cultural change.[9] These prospects open up, with great urgency, analytical questions regarding how to 'govern' how, and to what extent, human activities impact the planet; and they lay bare normative issues regarding which values should guide these governance

[3] See Paul J Crutzen and Eugene F Stoermer, 'The "Anthropocene"' (2000) 41 *IGBP Global Change Newsletter* 17; see also Paul J Crutzen, 'Geology of Mankind' (2002) 415 *Nature* 23. The argument was further developed in Will Steffen, Paul J Crutzen and John R McNeil, 'The Anthropocene: Are Humans now Overwhelming the Great Forces of Nature?' (2007) 36 *Ambio* 614 (giving a concise overview of the history of the Anthropocene, from its onset at the beginning of the Industrial Revolution until the beginning of the 21st century); Will Steffen and others, 'The Anthropocene: Conceptual and Historical Perspectives' (2011) 369 *Philosophical Transactions of the Royal Society* 842 (arguing for the formal recognition of the Anthropocene as a geological epoch in Earth history). There has been disagreement about when the Anthropocene should be considered to have started, see eg, Simon L Lewis and Mark A Maslin, 'Defining the Anthropocene' (2015) 519 *Nature* 171; Jan Zalasiewicz and others, 'When Did the Anthropocene Begin? A Mid-twentieth Century Boundary Level Is Stratigraphically Optimal' (2015) 383 *Quaternary International* 196.

[4] For an overview of arguments supporting the formal recognition of the Anthropocene as a new epoch in planetary history see Jan Zalasiewicz and others, 'Making the Case for a Formal Anthropocene Epoch: An Analysis of Ongoing Critiques' (2017) 50 *Newsletters on Stratigraphy* 205. On 21 May 2019 the Anthropocene Working Group, charged with investigating whether the Anthropocene is to be added to the Geological Time Scale, released results of a binding vote clarifying what evidence is to be collected to mark the existence of the Anthropocene, see Subcommision on Quaternary Stratigraphy, 'Working Group on the "Anthropocene"' <http://quaternary.stratigraphy.org/working-groups/anthropocene/> (accessed 25 May 2020).

[5] For a recent analysis see Will Steffen and others, 'Trajectories of the Earth System in the Anthropocene' (2018) 115 *Proceedings of the National Academy of Sciences of the United States of America* 8252.

[6] The concept of 'planetary boundaries' was initially developed by Rockström and colleagues, see Johan Rockström and others, 'Planetary Boundaries: Exploring the Safe Operating Space for Humanity' (2009) 14 *Ecology and Society*; see also Rockström and others (n 2). The concept has been revised and applied in subsequent research, see eg, Will Steffen and others, 'Planetary Boundaries: Guiding Human Development on a Changing Planet' (2015) 347 *Science* 1259855; see also Steffen and others (n 5).

[7] Rockström and others (n 2) 472 (figure 1).

[8] Steffen and others (n 5), suggesting that in addition to climate change, biodiversity loss and the nitrogen cycle have already transgressed safe thresholds.

[9] *Ibid*, 8256–7.

processes.[10] Law, as a 'technology of social organisation'[11]—or, as 'socio-institutional constructs through which we attempt to mediate the human-environment interface'[12]—is deeply implicated in efforts to navigate the Anthropocene.

This paper reflects on the role of transnational law in the Anthropocene. Specifically, it explores how Philip Jessup's perspective on transnational law[13] may be mobilised to further develop legal thinking in the Anthropocene. While Jessup was fundamentally concerned with border-crossing human and institutional relationships that intensified during the twentieth century, this paper adds a further dimension to Jessup's 'problem matrix'—that of the bio-geochemical planetary system. To develop a deeper understanding of the shifts that are affecting the dynamics between humans, societies and the Earth today, the paper draws on three theoretical perspectives—social-ecological resilience thinking, social systems theory and post-humanism. The central questions which this paper seeks to address are: How are we, as humans, to understand our position *vis-à-vis* the 'natural' 'environment' when we play a central role in shaping that 'environment'? What does this re-positioning mean for law? And specifically, in what ways can Jessup's perspective on transnational law be mobilised to help navigate the 'human'-'environment' relationship under Anthropocene conditions?

The paper is structured as follows: The next section gives an overview of legal scholarship that has reflected on law in the Anthropocene. Section 3 introduces three theoretical perspectives on the 'human'-'environment' relationship and sets out what challenges that relationship poses for legal thinking in the Anthropocene. Section 4 connects these findings with Jessup's perspective on transnational law, highlighting in what ways Jessup's practical, progressive and pragmatic approach might be useful to further develop legal thinking under Anthropocene conditions. Section 5 concludes.

2. State of play: scholarship on law in the Anthropocene

Over the last decade, legal scholarship has engaged with the question of what the Anthropocene might mean for law. The literature highlights that the Anthropocene calls into question conceptual, doctrinal, methodological and normative orthodoxies that have characterised legal research and practice. However, far from forming a coherent field, the 'law in the Anthropocene'

[10] Frank Biermann, 'The Anthropocene: A Governance Perspective' (2014) *The Anthropocene Review* 57, 59.
[11] Jorge E Viñuales, 'The Organisation of the Anthropocene: In Our Hands?' (2018) 1 *International Legal Theory and Practice* 1, 2.
[12] Louis J Kotzé, 'Rethinking Global Environmental Law and Governance in the Anthropocene' (2014) 32 *Journal of Energy & Natural Resources Law* 121, 124.
[13] Philip C Jessup, *Transnational Law* (Yale University Press 1956).

literature hosts a variety of approaches, each carrying their own theoretical assumptions and pursuing specific research priorities. This section briefly reviews key contributions of this literature. In so doing, it identifies three strands of research: (i) scholarship which investigates the nature and role of international environmental law, including related and emerging fields such as transnational environmental law, global environmental law and earth system law; (ii) scholarship which explores how law more generally might have to change to deal with Anthropocene conditions; and (iii) scholarship that focuses on the activity of engaging with law in the Anthropocene, both in terms of legal research and practice.

2.1. The Anthropocene, international environmental law, and related and emerging fields

International environmental law is generally seen as having failed to adequately respond to the Anthropocene.[14] Specifically, international environmental law has been criticised for taking a siloed approach to dealing with environmental problems, rather than recognising that, in fact, environmental issue areas are inter-related.[15] Arguably, an international legal architecture which does not take a holistic approach that accounts for these dependencies cannot successfully navigate Anthropocene conditions. Further, scholars point out that international environmental law must move beyond its state-centric paradigm to account for interactions of various actors across multiple levels.[16] For some this implies embracing the idea of global environmental law;[17] others have engaged with the concept of transnational environmental law.[18] While global and transnational environmental law scholars acknowledge that their respective fields of research are connected by a shared interest in legal arrangements that seek to respond to environmental risks which

[14] For concise but comprehensive overviews see eg, Tim Stephens, 'Reimagining International Environmental Law in the Anthropocene' in Louis J Kotzé (ed), *Environmental Law and Governance for the Anthropocene* (Hart 2017).

[15] See eg, Kotzé (n 12) 147–9. This argument builds on literature which examined the fragmentation of international (environmental) law, including by looking at interactions and gaps between specific international treaty regimes; see eg, Meinhard Doelle, 'Linking the Kyoto Protocol and Other Multilateral Environmental Agreements: From Fragmentation to Integration?' (2004) 14 *Journal of Environmental Law and Practice* 75; Harro van Asselt, Federico Sindico and Michael A Mehling, 'Global Climate Change and the Fragmentation of International Law' (2008) 30 *Law and Policy* 423; Cinnamon P Carlarne, 'Good Climate Governance: Only a Fragmented System of International Law Away?' (2008) 30 *Law and Policy* 450; Harro van Asselt, 'Managing the Fragmentation of International Environmental Law: Forests at the Intersection of the Climate and Biodiversity Regimes' (2012) 44 *New York University Journal of International Law and Politics* 1205.

[16] See eg, Kotzé (n 12) 144–7.

[17] See eg, Ellen Hey, 'Global Environmental Law' (2008) 19 *Finnish Yearbook of International Law* 5; Tseming Yang and Robert V Percival, 'The Emergence of Global Environmental Law' (2009) 36 *Ecology Law Quarterly* 615; Tseming Yang, 'The Emerging Practice of Global Environmental Law' (2012) 1 *Transnational Environmental Law* 5; Louis J Kotzé, *Global Environmental Governance: Law and Regulation for the 21st Century* (Edward Elgar 2012) 281–92.

[18] Literature on transnational environmental law in the Anthropocene is discussed in Section 4 below.

transcend domestic and international law perspectives,[19] differences exist. For instance, it has been suggested that global law concerns the 'external "global" edge of the transnational domain'.[20]

Besides unfolding discourses on global and transnational environmental law, scholars have identified the need for a normative shift away from the 'palliative' narrative of sustainable development, which is seen to mask a 'growth-without-limits' logic,[21] towards a truly ecocentric approach of environmental law.[22] Suggested solutions include establishing a *grundnorm*, for example, a commitment or principle of ecological integrity that would guide international environmental law towards meeting the demands of the Anthropocene.[23] Such a norm could be enshrined in a global environmental constitution or be embedded in the context of constitutional norms.[24] Recent advances suggest the possibility of moving towards a new paradigm of environmental law scholarship—'Earth System Law' or '*Lex Anthropocenae*'—which would comprehensively deal with the 'juridical aspects' of governing the Earth System across jurisdictions and environmental issue areas, thereby 'seeking to improve the ability of the law to respond to complex socio-ecological challenges'.[25]

---

[19] See the discussion of transnational law in Kati Kulovesi, Michael Mehling and Elisa Morgera, 'Global Environmental Law: Context and Theory, Challenge and Promise' (2019) 8 *Transnational Environmental Law* 405, 407–10. See also Veerle Heyvaert and Thijs Etty, 'Introducing Transnational Environmental Law' (2012) 1 *Transnational Environmental Law* 1, 3.

[20] Neil Walker, *Intimations of Global Law* (Cambridge University Press 2015) 18.

[21] Louis Kotzé, 'A Global Environmental Constitution for the Anthropocene?' (2019) 8 *Transnational Environmental Law* 11, 17.

[22] See Louis J Kotzé and Duncan French, 'The Anthropocentric Ontology of International Environmental Law and the Sustainable Development Goals: Towards an Ecocentric Rule of Law in the Anthropocene' (2018) 7 *Global Journal of Comparative Law* 4; see already Prue Taylor, *An Ecological Approach to International Law: Responding to the Challenges of Climate Change* (Routledge 1998).

[23] See Klaus Bosselmann, 'The Imperative of Ecological Integrity: Conceptualising a Fundamental Legal Norm for a New "World System" in the Anthropocene' in Louis J Kotzé (ed), *Environmental Law and Governance for the Anthropocene* (Hart 2017); Rak E Kim and Klaus Bosselmann, 'International Environmental Law in the Anthropocene: Towards a Purposive System of Multilateral Environmental Agreements' (2013) 2 *Transnational Environmental Law* 285.

[24] See generally Louis J Kotzé, *Global Environmental Constitutionalism in the Anthropocene* (Hart 2016); see also Louis J Kotzé and Wendy Muzangaza, 'Constitutional International Environmental Law for the Anthropocene?' (2018) 27 *Review of European, Comparative and International Environmental Law* 278 (the paper assesses whether 'higher-order' environmental norms, either as customary international law or *ius cogens*, exist); see specifically also Kotzé (n 21) and Louis Kotzé and Duncan French, 'A critique of the Global Pact for the Environment: A Stillborn Initiative or the Foundation for *Lex Anthropocenae*?' (2018) 18 *International Environmental Agreements* 811 (both papers discuss whether the Global Pact for the Environment has the potential to establish a set of global constitutional norms which answer to Anthropocene demands); see already Dan Bodansky, 'Is there an International Environmental Constitution?' (2009) 16 *Indiana Journal of Global Legal Studies* 565 (taking a sceptical stance as to whether the idea of constitutionalism can substantively contribute to addressing environmental problems).

[25] Louis J Kotzé and Rakhyun E Kim, 'Earth System Law: The Juridical Dimensions of Earth System Governance' (2019) 1 *Earth System Governance* 1, 1–2; see also Louis J Kotzé, 'Reflections on the Future of Environmental Law Scholarship and Methodology in the Anthropocene' in Ole W Pedersen (ed), *Perspectives on Environmental Law Scholarship: Essays on Purpose, Shape and Direction* (Cambridge University Press 2018). An initiative advancing this research project is the Earth System Governance Task Force

2.2. The Anthropocene and law beyond environmental law

A second strand of the law in the Anthropocene literature suggests that one must look beyond international environmental law to understand the nature and role of law in the new planetary epoch. According to this view, environmental law functions primarily as a regulative adjustment mechanism that deals with the externalities of activities which harm the planet, rather than with the underlying causes of these harms. It is thus argued that to effectively respond to Anthropocene conditions, legal scholarship must examine 'how law more generally organises transactions or processes that prompted the Anthropocene'.[26] This would require developing an understanding of how foundational doctrinal concepts —such as 'causality', 'subject', 'obligation', 'property', 'responsibility/liability', 'legal personality', 'corporation', 'constitution' and 'sovereignty'—might have to be adjusted.[27] Relevant research endeavours are beginning to be carried out at the international[28] and the national level.[29]

2.3. Legal methodology and practice in the Anthropocene

Finally, the law in the Anthropocene literature has reflected on how engaging with law, both in terms of research and practice, will change in the new planetary epoch. Specifically, various scholars have highlighted the need for legal researchers to work across, and integrate insights from, both the social and natural sciences[30] as well as the humanities.[31] Others argue for a 'return to the basics of the discipline of environmental law', highlighting the need for new 'vocabulary', theoretical perspectives and methodologies.[32] Yet again, others posit that a critical engagement with the Anthropocene narrative is needed to uncover how law is implicated in sustaining inter- and intra-species hierarchies.[33] Finally, scholars have examined how Anthropocene conditions affect legal practice, in particular the role of the courts and

on Earth System Law <www.earthsystemgovernance.org/research/taskforce-on-earth-system-law/> (accessed 22 October 2019).

26 Viñuales (n 11) 9–12.

27 *Ibid.*

28 See eg, Davor Vidas and others, 'International Law for the Anthropocene? Shifting Perspectives in the Regulation of the Oceans, Environment and Genetic Resources' (2015) 9 *Anthropocene* 1, 2–5.

29 For an examination of the US context see Eric Biber, 'Law in the Anthropocene Epoch' (2017) 106 *Georgetown Law Journal* 1, 40–60.

30 See eg, Tim Stephens, 'What Is the Point of International Environmental Law Scholarship in the Anthropocene?' in Ole W Pedersen (ed), *Perspectives on Environmental Law Scholarship: Essays on Purpose, Shape and Direction* (Cambridge University Press 2018) 135–7; Kotzé, 'Reflections on the Future of Environmental Law Scholarship and Methodology in the Anthropocene' (n 25) 151–6.

31 See eg, Saskia Vermeylen, 'Materiality and the Ontological Turn in the Anthropocene: Establishing a Dialogue between Law, Anthropology and Eco-Philosophy' in Louis J Kotzé (ed), *Environmental Law and Governance for the Anthropocene* (Hart 2017).

32 Andreas Philippopoulos-Mihalopoulos, 'Critical Environmental Law in the Anthropocene' in Louis J Kotzé (ed), *Environmental Law and Governance for the Anthropocene* (Hart 2017).

33 See eg, Anna Grear, 'Deconstructing *Anthropos*: A Critical Legal Reflection on "Anthropocentric" Law and Anthropocene "Humanity"' (2015) 26 *Law Critique* 225.

practices of adjudication, pointing out that Anthropocene realities give rise to novel questions and constellations that require judicial attention.[34]

This brief overview of the various strands of literature on law in the Anthropocene highlights that questions about law in the new planetary epoch remain unsettled. It is evident that the Anthropocene prompts legal scholarship to engage in 'deeper epistemological and ontological inquiries into regulatory interventions that dictate human behaviour on Earth'.[35] Against this backdrop, the aim of this paper is to explore how a return to Jessup's understanding of transnational law might be useful for legal research and practice in order to navigate Anthropocene realities. Before turning to Jessup in Section 4, the next section reviews three strands of literature that may inspire legal scholarship in this endeavour.

3. Looking across disciplines: three theoretical perspectives on 'human'-'environment' interactions

This section introduces three theoretical perspectives which have sought to shed light on the 'human'-'environment' interface, namely socio-ecological resilience thinking, social system theory and post-humanism. In considering the three literatures the guiding question is: how does each perspective situate 'humans' and/or society *vis-à-vis* the 'natural' 'environment'? At the outset, it is important to highlight that the three chosen literatures are not operating on consistent premises. On the contrary, each perspective carries its own disciplinary baggage and pursues a distinct research agenda. In combination, however, the three literatures offer a valuable starting point for reflecting on the social, natural and artificial dimensions of the Anthropocene and what challenges these dimensions pose for legal thinking. By combining insights from ecology, the social sciences and the humanities, this section also demonstrates how cross-disciplinary approaches bring fresh perspectives to legal thinking that can help making sense of planetary developments.

3.1. Social-ecological resilience thinking

Drawing on systems dynamics and human ecology, social-ecological resilience thinking acknowledges that social and ecological spheres are 'linked'

---

[34] Lynda Collins, 'Judging the Anthropocene: Transformative Adjudication in the Anthropocene Epoch' in Louis J Kotzé (ed), *Environmental Law and Governance for the Anthropocene* (Hart 2017); specifically on the role of courts in the climate change context see eg: Emily Barritt and Boitumelo Sediti, 'The Symbolic Value of *Leghari v Federation of Pakistan:* Climate Change Adjudication in the Global South' (2019) 30 *King's Law Journal* 203; Geetanjali Ganguly, Joana Setzer and Veerle Heyvaert, 'If at First You Don't Succeed: Suing Corporations for Climate Change' (2018) 38 *Oxford Journal of Legal Studies* 841; Elizabeth Fisher, Eloise Scotford and Emily Barritt, 'The Legally Disruptive Nature of Climate Change' (2017) 80 *Modern Law Review* 173.

[35] Kotzé, 'Reflections on the Future of Environmental Law Scholarship and Methodology in the Anthropocene' (n 25) 149.

and that the 'delineation between social and natural systems is artificial and arbitrary'.[36] In so doing, it conceptualises social and ecological systems as open systems which impact each other via flows of inputs, outputs and feedback mechanisms. In this context, ecological systems are understood as 'self-regulating communities of organisms interacting with one another and with their environment'.[37] Social systems are not specifically defined but are understood to comprise 'property rights, land and resource tenure systems, world views, knowledge about the environment and ethics'.[38] Together, social and ecological systems are seen to function as coupled sub-systems of integrated social-ecological systems. An example helps to illustrate:

> A suburb and a nearby wetland are both part of the same system. The government agency that is managing the wetland, the developers who would like to drain it ... and the scientists who believe it provides valuable ecosystem services are all part of the system ... Change the system in one place (eg, drain the wetland, or change the legislation that protects it, or change the attitudes of the developers or change the information flows from the scientists) and you will inevitably see feedback responses elsewhere in this social-ecological system.[39]

While the above example illustrates how social and ecological systems may interact at local levels, social-ecological systems thinking is also relevant on regional and planetary scales. Specifically, social-ecological system thinking highlights that '[s]ocieties are not only interconnected globally through political, economic, and technical systems, but also through the Earth's biophysical life-support systems'.[40] By making explicit that humans are deeply implicated in planetary processes, social-ecological systems thinking is foundational for understanding the Anthropocene. It advances theory by expressly recognising that humans and the ecosphere are dependent on, and linked to, each other. Further, it highlights that interactions and dependencies between humans and the ecosphere are complex, follow non-linear trajectories and are characterised by high-levels of uncertainty.[41] However, the social-ecological resilience literature takes society as a given; it does not further unpack the concept of 'social system', and it does not explain how exactly society relates to the 'natural' 'environment'.

---

[36] Fikret Berkes and Carl Folke, 'Linking Social and Ecological Systems for Resilience and Sustainability' in Fikret Berkes and Carl Folke (eds), *Linking Social and Ecological Systems: Management Practices and Social Mechanisms for Building Resilience* (Cambridge University Press 1998) 4.

[37] Fikret Berkes, Johan Colding and Carl Folke, 'Introduction' in Fikret Berkes, Johan Colding and Carl Folke (eds), *Navigating Social-Ecological Systems: Building Resilience for Complexity and Change* (Cambridge University Press 2003) 3.

[38] *Ibid*, 2–3; Berkes and Folke (n 36) 4.

[39] Brian Walker and David Salt, *Resilience Thinking: Sustaining Ecosystems and People in a Changing World* (Island Press 2006) 32–4.

[40] Carl Folke and others, 'Reconnecting to the Biosphere' (2011) 40 *Ambio* 719, 720.

[41] For an introduction to non-linearity in social-ecological systems see eg, Walker and Salt (n 39) chap 2; for an overview of the implications of complex interactions in social-ecological systems see eg, Jianguo Liu and others, 'Complexity of Coupled Human and Natural Systems' (2007) 317 *Science* 1513.

3.2. Social systems and ecological communication

To this end, Luhmann's systems theory offers some insight into how social systems, including law, relate to their ecological contexts. According to Luhmann, society consists of operationally closed, self-referential (or 'autopoietic') communication systems which function according to a particular binary code and rely on programmes to operationalise these codes. The legal system, for example, functions according to the code lawful/unlawful[42] and uses laws, regulations, contracts and other normative devices as programmes to operationalise this code.[43] According to Luhmann, social systems sit within 'eco-complexes'.[44] Hence, contrary to social-ecological resilience theory, Luhmann does not conceptualise the ecosphere as consisting of ecosystems because, in his view, ecosystems do not differentiate between 'system' and 'environment', meaning that they do not have a system boundary. According to Luhmann, the absence of a system boundary denies the possibility of a system in the first place.[45] In other words: Luhmann argues that while social systems consist of communication, the eco-complex consists of 'natural facts', such as 'islands, oceans and technologies, etc, but also of human beings, ie, concrete individuals and their conscious processes'.[46] Thus, in Luhmann's view, natural facts 'all belong to the environment of the social system of society'.[47]

The second key feature which for our purposes differentiates Luhmann's systems theory from social-ecological resilience thinking is his rejection of the idea that direct interactions exist between social systems and the eco-complex. This is consistent with his understanding of social systems as operationally closed, self-referential systems which constantly maintain a system boundary by differentiating themselves from their environment on the basis of coding operations. As such, Luhmann's social systems are not conceptualised as parts of a whole (as is the case for the social and ecological sub-systems that make up social-ecological systems), but as the 'difference between system and environment'.[48] Instead of direct interactions between social systems and the eco-context, Luhmann argues that social systems may be 'irritated' by changes in the eco-complex, meaning that changes may 'trigger resonance' in the coding operations of the social system:

---

[42] Niklas Luhmann, 'Law as a Social System' (1989) 83 *Northwestern University Law Review* 136, 140.

[43] Niklas Luhmann, 'Operational Closure and Structural Coupling: The Differentiation of the Legal System' (1991) 13 *Cardozo Law Review* 1419, 1428–9 and 1434. On legal codes and programmes specifically see Niklas Luhmann, *Das Recht der Gesellschaft* (Suhrkamp 1995) chap 4.

[44] Niklas Luhmann, *Soziale Systeme: Grundriß einer Allgemeinen Theorie* (Suhrkamp, 17th edn 2018) 55, fn 52.

[45] On 'boundary maintenance' as system maintenance see *ibid*, 35.

[46] Niklas Luhmann, 'Ecological Communication: Coping with the Unknown' (1993) 6 *Systems Practice* 527, 531.

[47] *Ibid*, 532.

[48] Luhmann (n 44) 22; see also Niklas Luhmann, *Ecological Communication* (John Bednarz tr, Polity Press 1989) 6–7.

> physical, chemical or biological facts create no social resonance as long as they are not the subject of communication … Society is an environmentally sensitive (open) but operatively closed system. Its sole mode of observation is communication. It is limited to communicating meaningfully and regulating this communication through communication … The environment of the social system cannot communicate with society … The environment can make itself noticed only by means of communicative irritations or disturbances … .[49]

For Luhmann, the difficulty in addressing environmental problems is that they create too little as well as too much resonance within society. On the one hand, at the boundary between the social system and the eco-complex, changes in the system environment create too little resonance, because only when environmental changes pass through the 'double-filter of coding and programming' do they acquire 'internal relevance' for operationally closed social systems.[50] However, once changes have acquired such relevance, they are processed by the system and have the capacity to trigger far-reaching effects in other systems: 'function systems are differentiated, coded and programmed for functionally specific high output', they 'constantly scour their socially internal environment for impulses and pick up what is offered to them'.[51] As such, 'turbulences' occurring in one social system are likely to be quickly transferred to other systems.[52]

Luhmann makes clear that environmental changes are not easily internalised by functionally differentiated social systems, including law. For example, Luhmann points out that function systems develop their own 'future/past perspectives', their own 'temporal horizons and temporal urgency', which may not align with the 'temporality of the process in the ecological or even social environment of the system'.[53] Luhmann concludes that the 'legal solution of environmental problems remains as abstract as it is inconsequential' and highlights the need for legal innovation: 'A legal categorization of precepts for environmental concern can only be worked into the law, if at all, with other concepts … ecological communication deforms classical structures of the legal system … on more than just the level of the content of norms'.[54]

[49] Luhmann, *Ecological Communication* (n 48) 28–9.
[50] *Ibid*, 116.
[51] *Ibid*, 118.
[52] *Ibid*, 117.
[53] *Ibid*, 57; see also Benjamin J Richardson, 'Doing Time – The Temporalities of Environmental Law' in Louis J Kotzé (ed), *Environmental Law and Governance for the Anthropocene* (Hart 2017) 56: 'The lack of symmetry between human and natural time-scales, caused by factors such as economic and technological changes, is widening as human cultural evolution dramatically accelerates our trajectory away from nature's temporal rhythms'.
[54] Luhmann, *Ecological Communication* (n 48) 74–5.

3.3. Post-humanism

While Luhmann's theory of social systems is helpful to understand how 'interactions' (or rather, 'irritations' and system-internal response mechanisms) between social systems, including law, and the ecological context come about, it does not enquire deeper into the nature of the physical aspects of human existence. This is where post-humanism, introduced here as a third theoretical perspective, proves helpful. Post-humanism highlights that in the Anthropocene it is no longer possible to divide the world 'into a box marked "Nature" and into one marked "Human"'.[55] Rather, 'humans' are seen to be intricately intertwined with 'nature', forming new assemblages that defy clear cut distinctions along established ontological lines. As Harraway notes

> Critters interpenetrate one another, loop around and through one another, eat each other, get indigestion, and partially digest and partially assimilate one another, and thereby establish sympoietic arrangements that are otherwise known as cells, organisms, and ecological assemblages.[56]

Adding another dimension—technology—Braidotti argues that by 'becoming-earth', the process through which we are 'reconfiguring the relationship to our complex habitat, which we used to call "nature"',[57] we have created 'a nature-culture continuum which is technologically mediated and globally enforced'.[58] Braidotti's 'philosophy of becomings rests on the idea that matter, including the specific slice of matter that is human embodiment, is intelligent and self-organizing … [ie] not dialectically opposed to culture, not to technological mediation, but continuous with them'.[59] In Braidotti's view, a new understanding of subjectivity is required which recognises humans as 'environmentally bound and territorially based', 'embodied entities [which] feed upon, incorporate and transform their (natural, social, human or technological) environment constantly'.[60]

This new understanding of subjectivity poses significant challenges for legal thinking. As the law in the Anthropocene literature points out, legal discourse has been characterised by distinctly anthropocentric perspectives.[61]

---

[55] Clive Hamilton, 'Human Destiny in the Anthropocene' in Clive Hamilton, Christophe Bonneuil and François Gemenne (eds), *The Anthropocene and the Global Environmental Crisis* (Routledge 2015) 34.

[56] Donna J Harraway, *Staying with the Trouble: Making Kin in the Chthulucene* (Duke University Press 2016) 59. Harraway prefers the term 'Chthulucene' to 'Anthropocene', see at 55: 'the Chthulucene is made up of ongoing multispecies stories and practices of becoming-with in times that remain at stake, in precarious times, in which the world is not finished and the sky has not fallen – yet … Unlike the dominant dramas of Anthropocene … discourse, human beings are not the only important actors in the Chthulucene, with all other beings able simply to react'.

[57] Rosi Braidotti, *The Posthuman* (Polity Press 2013) 81.

[58] *Ibid*, 82.

[59] *Ibid*, 35.

[60] *Ibid*, 139.

[61] See eg, Kotzé and French (n 22).

One only need to think about the concept of 'human rights' or the belief that 'humans' can 'regulate' the 'environment' though targeted 'interventions', as if the planet was an object that could be shaped and moulded according to our needs. Indeed, some now argue that with current climatic developments, the Earth, understood as the territory on which we live, is emerging as an agent with the capacity to act politically.[62] These reflections open up questions about how law may deal with new actors and new forms of agency which blur the line between the 'environment' and 'humans'. Further, it points to the need to reconsider the normative foundations of law, specifically regarding interactions among species, and between species and the natural (planetary) and artificial (technological) components of their habitats.

In summary, the three literatures introduced in this section highlight that the signposts which used to guide legal thinking in the Holocene are not adequate to navigate Anthropocene realities. Specifically, social-ecological resilience thinking and social systems theory indicate that shifts in spatial–temporal dynamics will require law to move beyond its state-centric paradigm, become more flexible and develop the ability to adopt a future-oriented, forward-thinking approach to mirror planetary developments as they unfold. Further, the emergence of new forms of subjectivity and agency, comprising composites of human-natural-technological elements, requires law to rethink its anthropocentric foundations and find ways to overcome the entrenched ontological divide between 'humans' and 'nature'. This will also require law to engage with its normative foundations which touch on ethical questions and are likely to be politically contested.

4. Revisiting Jessup's move from 'what?' to 'how?': (transnational) law for the Anthropocene

Having shown what challenges the Anthropocene poses for legal thinking, this section explores how Jessup's approach to transnational law may provide a useful framework for envisioning new legal forms, technologies and strategies to equip law for dealing with Anthropocene realities. It argues that it is Jessup's practical, progressive and pragmatic approach to legal theory and practice that makes his perspective particularly well suited for this task. The first part of this section explores Jessup's move from

[62] Bruno Latour, *Down to Earth: Politics in the New Climatic Regime* (Polity 2018) 112, note 12; see also Bruno Latour, 'Agency at the Time of the Anthropocene' (2014) 45 *New Literary History* 1, arguing that the 'Earth has taken back all the characteristics of a fully-fledged *actor* ... an agent of what I have proposed to call our common *geostory*' (3). Latour further explains: '[t]hrough a complete reversal of Western philosophy's most cherished trope, human societies have resigned themselves to playing the role of the dumb object, while nature has unexpectedly taken on that of the active subject! Such is the frightening meaning of "global warming": through a surprising inversion of background and foreground, it is *human* history that has become frozen and *natural* history that is taken on a frenetic pace' (11–12).

'what?' to 'how?'; the second part seeks to demonstrate how that move might contribute to advancing legal thinking in the Anthropocene.

4.1. The move from 'what?' to 'how?'

Jessup's approach to transnational law builds on three key elements: (i) taking practicalities as a starting point—looking at real-world situations; (ii) demanding progressive thinking—acknowledging the need for legal innovation; and (iii) embracing pragmatism—working with open-textured concepts.

First, Jessup views transnational law as a problem-solving device that guides real-life situations and is applied and invoked by a range of actors, including diplomats, business people, citizens, international agencies and courts around the world.[63] Specifically, Jessup's perspective is rooted in an awareness that existing categorisations of law—international and national, public and private—may not match neatly onto real-world situations and, in fact, may prove insufficient for addressing them. In his own words, Jessup envisages transnational law as a 'larger storehouse of rules' that one can draw on should established categories prove insufficient.[64]

Second, Jessup's approach towards transnational law is distinctly progressive. He recognises that legal thinking is constantly developing to deal with the emergence of new situations and problem constellations. Jessup warns that legal thinking should not 'become frozen' as this would 'hamper progress toward the ever needed new solutions of problems whether old or new'.[65] As such, Jessup is open to, and in fact he is demanding, legal innovation. As Zumbansen notes, 'Jessup offered the compelling observation that lawyers needed to find a way of expanding their legal conceptual and doctrinal repertoire in order to effectively address the growing variety of border-crossing human and institutional relations around the world'.[66]

Third, besides being practically-minded and progressive in orientation, Jessup's approach to transnational law is thoroughly pragmatic to the extent that, for the sake of flexibility, he refuses to define the very concept that he is arguing for. On a close reading of the text, one finds that Jessup does not define exactly what he means by transnational law. Of course, his formulation that transnational law comprises 'all law which regulates actions or events that transcend national frontiers' including public and private international law as well as 'other rules which do not wholly fit into such standard

[63] Jessup (n 13) 3–4 (giving various examples of contexts in which transnational situations may arise).
[64] *Ibid*, 15.
[65] *Ibid*, 7.
[66] Peer Zumbansen, 'Introduction: Transnational Law, with and beyond Jessup' in Zumbansen (ed), *The Many Lives of Transnational Law: Critical Engagements with Jessup's Bold Proposal* (Cambridge University Press 2020) 5.

categories'[67] is widely known. However, Jessup makes clear that he wishes to avoid defining transnational law in more detail,[68] stating that 'there is no law forbidding a scholar to choose his [or her] own definition – or requiring him [or her] to formulate one, for that matter'.[69] One technique which Jessup employs to achieve definitional flexibility is reliance on 'catch-all categories'. For example, when surveying actors that may be implicated in transnational situations, Jessup lists 'individuals, corporations, states, organizations of states, or *other groups*' as relevant entities.[70] Similarly, as shown above, when explaining which laws make up the body of transnational law, Jessup includes a reference to 'other rules' as a catch-all category.

Jessup's refusal to define transnational law is the final, and perhaps the decisive, step in his move from 'what?' to 'how?' Instead of pondering what transnational law might, or might not, be,[71] Jessup takes as his starting point the question *how* transnational law has to be understood to provide solutions to real-world problems.

4.2. Towards transnational law for the Anthropocene

Over the last 60 years transnational law has demonstrated its flexibility in addressing border-crossing problems, most notably by challenging, and complementing, state-centred and place-based understandings of law.[72] However, adding the planetary dimension of the Anthropocene to Jessup's understanding of real-world problems, which he first and foremost understands as 'human problems',[73] requires us to think beyond the spatial dimensions of the law. As argued above, the Anthropocene shifts not only spatial but also temporal dimensions; it demands flexible and future-oriented approaches to navigating planetary realities; it brings to the fore new forms of agency and subjectivity that do not easily fit with law's anthropocentric foundations; it challenges legal thinking to find ways to overcome the entrenched ontological divide between 'humans' and 'nature'; and it requires law to engage with its normative foundations. While pioneers have already started to engage with some of these questions,[74] our understanding and imagination of legal

[67] Jessup (n 13) 2 [emphasis added].
[68] *Ibid*, 7.
[69] *Ibid*, 9.
[70] *Ibid*, 3.
[71] See eg, Roger Cotterell, 'What is Transnational Law?' 37 *Law and Social Inquiry* 500, suggesting that 'conceptualizing transnational law' and 'mapping' it as 'a new legal field' might help 'both juristic practice and sociolegal scholarship'.
[72] See eg, the contributions included in Gunter Handl, Joachim and Peer Zumbansen (eds), *Beyond Territoriality: Transnational Legal Authority in an Age of Globalization* (Brill 2012).
[73] Jessup (n 13), see specifically the heading of his first chapter 'The Universality of the *Human* Problems' [emphasis added] and at 3: '*human* relationships transcending the limits of the various states' [emphasis added].
[74] See specifically Andreas Philippopoulos-Mihalopoulos, 'Towards a Critical Environmental Law' in Andreas Philippopoulos-Mihalopoulos (ed), *Law and Ecology: New Environmental Foundations*

forms, strategies and technologies for the Anthropocene remains incomplete and fragmented.[75]

Taking seriously calls to engage with, and integrate, insights across disciplines, this paper argues that Jessup's perspective on transnational law could provide a framework for legal scholars to apply a technique which Braidotti, philosopher and feminist theorist, refers to as 'defamiliarization'—the process by which one takes a 'critical distance from dominant visions of the subject' (in our case (transnational) law) to overcome 'familiar habits of thought and representation' and 'pave the way for creative alternatives'.[76] Viewed from this perspective, transnational law has the potential to function—once again—as a testing ground and creative space;[77] this time in the context of the new planetary epoch. Jessup laid out valuable starting points for this endeavour, including: taking real-world situations as the starting point for conceptual and theoretical projects; working with open-ended concepts; defying the urge of using rigid definitions; and having the courage to challenge mainstream views.

Further, in light of changing planetary realities, Jessup's thinking requires us to re-envision the very concept of transnational law. In the Anthropocene, taking seriously the move from 'what?' to 'how?' means overcoming the conception of transnational law as a specific category of laws, namely as one that captures norms which (a) cut across jurisdictional boundaries, (b) are generated by non-state actors,[78] and (c) are held together by the fact that they address specific issue areas, such as environmental degradation (resulting in 'transnational environmental law'), human rights protection (resulting in 'transnational human rights law') or business practices (resulting in 'transnational commercial law').[79] In other words, now may be the time to leave behind

(Routledge 2011) (arguing for the move towards 'Critical Environmental Law' that repositions law—theoretically, methodologically and conceptually—'after the collapse of the boundaries between the natural/human/artificial'). See also the literature on Wild Law, which proposes that positive legal frameworks should reflect human beings as part of the geological and biological components of the Earth Community, see eg, the contributions in Peter Burdon (ed), *Exploring Wild Law: The Philosophy of Earth Jurisprudence* (Wakefield Press 2011). See also Christopher D Stone, 'Should Trees Have Standing?—Toward Legal Rights for Natural Objects' (1972) 45 *Southern California Law Review* 450.

[75] See Section 2.

[76] Braidotti (n 57) 88–9.

[77] See Zumbansen (n 66) 43 ('transnational law is here understood, above all, as a legal methodology through which we engage existing legal frameworks and principles against the background of newly emerging and evolving actors, norms and processes. Transnational law, then, should be seen as a critical methodological space and laboratory'); see also Peer Zumbansen, 'Transnational Law, Evolving' in Jan M Smits (ed), *Encyclopedia of Comparative Law* (Edward Elgar 2006) 899 ('transnational law continues to evolve as a thought experiment in legal methodology and legal theory').

[78] See eg, Kotzé and Kim (n 25) 7 (describing transnational law as 'a non-state-centric system of law that does not solely depend on sovereignty or the state and its authority for its legitimacy. Both state and non-state actors take part in transnational legal processes to make and obey law').

[79] With regard to transnational environmental law see eg, Jolene Lin, 'The Emergence of Transnational Environmental Law in the Anthropocene' in Louis J Kotzé (ed), *Environmental Law and Governance for the Anthropocene* (Hart 2017) 330 (describing transnational environmental law as 'all environmental law norms that apply to transboundary activities or that have effects in more than one jurisdiction … the concept of [transnational environmental law] recognises that important environmental regulation takes place outside formal treaty regimes'). For a recent and comprehensive discussion of the genealogy

a domain- and actor-specific conception of transnational law which primarily focuses on 'private' actors and which carves out specific transnational legal domains. To address Anthropocene realities, a legal approach that integrates perspectives across actors (human-natural-technological), scales (planetary-regional-national-local, non-spatial) and issue areas is needed.

5. Conclusion

Drawing on three theoretical perspectives, this paper has sought to demonstrate in what ways Anthropocene realities challenge legal thinking. Engaging with literatures from ecology, sociology and the humanities, the paper demonstrated how transdisciplinary perspectives can help legal scholarship to better understand, and meaningfully engage with, the concept of the Anthropocene. In so doing, the paper identified a number of key challenges that legal thinking will have to confront in the new planetary epoch, including changes in spatial–temporal dynamics, emerging forms of agency and subjectivity, and the need for law to re-consider its normative foundations. The paper proposed that one avenue of addressing these challenges, is to revisit Jessup's approach to transnational law. It argued that Jessup's practical, progressive and pragmatic approach to addressing real-world problems provides a framework that shifts the focus from asking 'what is transnational law?' to enquiring *how* transnational law has to be understood to mobilise it as a tool for navigating the Anthropocene. Certainly, transnational law is no panacea; but in light of the urgencies of planetary change, it is one avenue that legal scholarship can and should further explore. To this end, the paper argued that Jessup's conception of transnational law could function as a framework within which legal thinking can 'de-familiarise' itself from Holocene orthodoxies. A practical, progressive and pragmatic approach is needed to envision law for the new planetary epoch.

Disclosure statement

No potential conflict of interest was reported by the author(s).

ORCID

Laura Mai http://orcid.org/0000-0001-8975-1078

of the concept of transnational environmental law see Olaf Dilling and Till Markus, 'The Transnationalisation of Environmental Law' (2018) 30 *Journal of Environmental Law* 179; see also Heyvaert and Etty (n 19).

OPEN ACCESS

Urgent agenda: how climate litigation builds transnational narratives

Phillip Paiement

ABSTRACT
This article draws on the notion of co-production to assess the construction of transnational narratives in climate change litigation. Using the examples of recent cases from the Netherlands, Norway, and Ireland, the article identifies a common narrative regarding the temporal dimension of climate change and its governance. Litigants are shown to develop a notion of urgency for national climate policies with the help of symbols and discourses—including pathways, crossroads, milestones, thresholds and carbon budgets—in order to attribute meaning to complex models of the future climate, and the immediate responsibilities of states to limit future global warming. In response, states offer depictions of the future in which technological and economic evolutions render our current climate crisis less challenging and costly. This narrative approach helps make sense of the transnational legal strategies through which our understanding of responsibility and climate justice is unfolding.

1. Introduction

Since 2015, environmental lawyers have been emboldened by the affirmative judgments from the Dutch courts in the *Urgenda* case,[1] in which the State of the Netherlands has been ordered to pursue a more ambitious reduction of greenhouse gas emissions by 2020 than its climate policy had offered. The case provides a powerful example of how the courts could be used to demand adequate climate change mitigation policy. More importantly, it has been a rallying call for strategic climate litigation around the world. Tessa Khan, a co-director of the Climate Litigation Network, describes the importance of these litigation actions for the activists and attorneys involved:

---

[1] Rechtbank Den Haag, 24 juni 2015, ECLI:NL:RBDH:2015:7145. An unauthoritative English translation of the decision has also been provided by the court: The Hague District Court, 24 June 2015, ECLI:NL:RBDH:2015:7196. Hereinafter referred to as '*Urgenda* District Court decision'.

> Litigation that is driven by those most affected has personalized abstract injustices, put facts on the public record, and exposed misinformation and political spin ... For the global movement for climate justice, these cases also help to drive *a clear narrative of responsibility*: as much as we have been made to grapple with our individual guilt, the truth is that governments and the fossil fuel industry bear the real responsibility for this crisis.[2]

Climate litigation is thus a tool used by the global climate justice movement to gradually develop narratives of responsibility, science, right, and wrong. Above all else, it involves the building of narratives about time, the future, timelines for action and consequences, and the urgency with which societies should responsibly mitigate global warming, given the inevitable costs and difficult decisions that mitigation efforts will entail.

This article draws on the notion of co-production from science and technology studies, in order to demonstrate how climate litigation is involved in the creation of shared narratives about time and climate governance. Focusing on recent cases from the Netherlands, Norway and Ireland, the article explores how the litigants have developed a narrative of urgency which unfolds through a particular framing of both climate science and legal texts. At its core, the narrative demands that any State which has obliged itself to prevent more than 2°C warming in the long term also holds an obligation to substantially reduce emissions and the production of oil as soon as 2020 and 2030. The discussion below also illustrates how their narrative runs counter to depictions of the future, provided by the three States involved in the litigation, in which currently undiscovered technologies and strategies of mitigation and adaption will resolve our climate crisis. By approaching the current proliferation of climate litigation through the formation of narratives, the article offers a lens for making sense of such cases as elements of transnational legal strategy.

2. Methodological nationalism in climate change litigation research

In the past two decades both the amount of litigation concerning the causes and effects of climate change and the attention given by legal scholars to this litigation has quickly proliferated. Climate change litigation databases include records of more than 1100 cases from the United States (US),[3] and another 349 cases from other countries, figures which likely under-

---

2 Tessa Khan, 'Litigation is a Powerful Tool for Holding Those Responsible for the Climate Crisis to Account' *Time Magazine* (25 September 2019) <https://time.com/5686087/courtroom-climate-change-litigation/> accessed 13 October 2019 (emphasis added).

3 See the US Climate Change Litigation database maintained by the Sabin Center for Climate Change Law at Columbia Law School and Arnold & Porter Kaye Scholer LLP, online: <http://climatecasechart.com/> accessed 2 April 2020.

report the actual number of cases.[4] Likewise, Setzer and Vanhala's literature review on climate change litigation from 2019 found 130 scientific articles from the period 2000–2018.[5] Amid the growing field of climate change litigation, legal scholars have made exceptional progress in understanding the variety of types of cases which can be brought forward to contest, or push for, mitigation and adaptation policies, as well as to challenge measures that contribute indirectly to climate change. The impressive breadth of this scholarship extends well beyond the limits of this article. Despite the broad attention given to litigation of this complex global environmental challenge, the transnational character of climate change litigation has been largely overlooked. Instead, methodological nationalism permeates the literature, including comparative analyses and evaluations of litigation in supranational institutions.[6]

Early scholarship on climate change litigation featured in-depth analyses of case law from single jurisdictions or individual, high-profile, cases.[7] A 'second wave' of literature then focused more broadly on categorising climate change from a single jurisdiction, or comparatively across jurisdictions, and developing typologies about case properties, such as the nature of claims and whether they were focused on climate change mitigation or adaptation.[8] A 'third wave' has since shifted attention towards evaluating the regulatory impact of climate change litigation, both in single jurisdictions as well as comparatively.[9] At the same time, scholars have suggested that the current wave of litigation is best characterised by the increasing tendency to base claims on human or constitutional rights.[10] Notably, litigation from jurisdictions in the Global South may be leading this turn to rights-based claims.[11]

---

[4] See the Climate Change Laws of the World database maintained by the Grantham Research Institute on Climate Change and the Environment, online: <https://climate-laws.org/> accessed 2 April 2020.

[5] Joana Setzer and Lisa C Vanhala, 'Climate Change Litigation: A Review of Research on Courts and Litigants in Climate Governance' (2019) 10 *WIREs Climate Change* e580.

[6] On the shortfalls of methodological nationalism, see Eve Darian-Smith and Philip C McCarthy, *The Global Turn: Theories, Research Designs, and Methods for Global Studies* (University of California Press 2017) 154–8.

[7] This is sometimes referred to as the 'first wave' of literature on climate change litigation. Jacqueline Peel and Hari M Osofsky, *Climate Change Litigation: Regulatory Pathways to Cleaner Energy* (Cambridge University Press 2015) 14; Setzer and Vanhala (n 5) 5.

[8] Peel and Osofsky, *Climate Change Litigation: Regulatory Pathways to Cleaner Energy* (n 7) 14.

[9] For example, Lin identifies how it can be used for three purposes in broader climate governance: to press for regulation, to regulate existing regulatory responses, and to articulate marginalised concerns. Jolene Lin, 'Climate Change and the Courts' (2012) 32 *Legal Studies* 35; Peel and Osofsky, *Climate Change Litigation: Regulatory Pathways to Cleaner Energy* (n 7); Jacqueline Peel and Hari M Osofsky, 'Climate Change Litigation's Regulatory Pathways: A Comparative Analysis of the United States and Australia' (2013) 35 *Law & Policy* 150.

[10] Jacqueline Peel and Hari M Osofsky, 'A Rights Turn in Climate Change Litigation?' (2018) 7 *Transnational Environmental Law* 37; Setzer and Vanhala (n 5) 10–11.

[11] Jacqueline Peel and Jolene Lin, 'Transnational Climate Litigation: The Contribution of the Global South' (2019) 113 *The American Journal of International Law* 679, 711–14; Joana Setzer and Lisa Benjamin,

The three waves of climate change litigation scholarship have been largely defined by their methodological nationalism.[12] 'Big' cases that set influential precedents or extensively challenge existing regulatory frameworks have been the subject of overwhelming, some might say 'obsessive', attention.[13] Such isolated assessment of litigation tends to focus on problems of institutional failure that are particular to the jurisdiction in which it arises, as well as the doctrinal possibilities and constraints in the jurisdiction that gave rise to the case.[14] In addition, there has been a large bias in the literature towards litigation from the US, Australia, and the United Kingdom, as well as a small number of other jurisdictions in the Global North.[15] When studies have taken a comparative approach to analysis, they have often treated national jurisdictions as isolated spaces in which different models of litigation occur with varying degrees of success and regulatory consequences. Comparison allows for assessment of which 'models' of litigation succeed in which contexts, with an eye towards identifying opportunities for the transplantation or diffusion of strategies.[16] To use a scientific metaphor, such a comparative analysis treats each jurisdiction as an independent petri dish in which experimentation takes place, in order to then evaluate how litigation models interact with other independent variables found in the jurisdiction.[17] While these in-depth, single jurisdiction and comparative analyses have been undoubtedly helpful in developing our understanding of the potential, limitations, and

'Climate Litigation in the Global South: Constraints and Innovations' (2020) 9 *Transnational Environmental Law* 77.

12 Darian-Smith and McCarthy (n 6) 154–8.

13 See, for example, Fisher's review of the extensive attention given to the US Supreme Court's decision in *Massachusetts v. EPA*: Elizabeth Fisher, 'Climate Change Litigation, Obsession and Expertise: Reflecting on the Scholarly Response to Massachusetts v. EPA' (2013) 35 *Law & Policy* 236.

14 Fisher labels these the 'institutional failure' and 'legal reasoning' narratives of climate change litigation. ibid 240–2.

15 For example, Peel and Osofsky's comprehensive monograph is limited to a comparative analysis of Australian and US litigation. Peel and Osofsky, *Climate Change Litigation: Regulatory Pathways to Cleaner Energy* (n 7). Setzer and Vanhala note that the concentration of studies on a small number of jurisdictions in the Global North largely reflects the concentration and location of climate change lawsuits. Setzer and Vanhala (n 5) 5.

16 See, for example, the discussion of the '*Urgenda* model' of litigation in Peel and Osofsky, 'A Rights Turn in Climate Change Litigation?' (n 10) 61–4. See also the prescription of different litigation strategies for small and vulnerable countries in Setzer and Benjamin (n 11) 90–1. Although legal transplants are more often associated with the diffusion and transfer of positive law (eg model contracts or particular codes or statutes), or architectural features of a legal system (eg *ombudsman* or specialised courts), types of behaviour of both legal officers and laypersons have also been assessed within the conceptual terminology of a legal transplant. See, for example, the transplantation of public interest litigation strategies in Noga Morag-Levine, 'The Politics of Imported Rights: Transplantation and Transformation in an Israeli Environmental Cause-Lawyering Organization' in Austin Sarat and Stuart Scheingold (eds), *Cause Lawyering and the State in a Global Era* (Oxford University Press 2001) 334. For more on the use of transplants in the development of global environmental legal norms, see Jonathan B Wiener, 'Something Borrowed for Something Blue: Legal Transplants and the Evolution of Global Environmental Law' (2001) 2000–2001 *Ecology Law Quarterly* 1295; Natasha Affolder, 'Contagious Environmental Lawmaking' (2019) 31 *Journal of Environmental Law* 187.

17 Peel and Osofsky describe their comparative analysis as 'opening up opportunities for testing explanations of the broader regulatory impact of climate change case law'. Peel and Osofsky, *Climate Change Litigation: Regulatory Pathways to Cleaner Energy* (n 7) 24.

challenges of using litigation to effect change in climate governance, they have also largely overlooked the transnational character of climate change litigation.

While the predominant lines of inquiry in climate change litigation scholarship have focused on nation states as the principal units of analysis, there are exceptions which have begun to employ transnational approaches. First, a number of studies have concentrated on international climate change litigation, with particular focus towards complaints brought to international human rights bodies,[18] the coordination of requests submitted to the World Heritage Committee to list climate change-affected sites under an 'in danger' classification,[19] and the Court of Justice of the European Union.[20] While these efforts pursue regulatory change within supranational bodies, their innovative coordination of petitioners from multiple national jurisdictions makes them particularly relevant for transnational[21] accounts of climate change litigation.[22] Second, and related to the previous cases brought by plaintiffs spread across jurisdictions, various scholars have noted the role of transnational communities (sometimes referred to as transnational advocacy networks) in fostering and supporting climate change litigation, as well as developing political campaigns the mobilise alongside their litigation activities.[23] For example, Peel and Lin identified the role of transnational advocacy networks in driving litigation in the Global South, including South-South and South-North advocacy collaborations.[24] Third, Osofsky discussed the role that climate change litigation plays in fostering regulatory

[18] Consider, for example, the 2005 petition from Inuit communities from the US and Canada to the Inter-American Commission on Human Rights. Hari M Osofsky, 'The Inuit Petition as a Bridge? Beyond Dialectices of Climate Change and Indigenous Peoples' Rights' (2007) 31 *American Indian Law Review* 675; Lin (n 9) 53–4.

[19] In particular, a coordinated petition effort concerning glacial sites, coral reef, and coastal regions took place between 2007 and 2009. See, for example, 'Petition to the World Heritage Committee: The Role of Black Carbon in Endangering World Heritage Sites Threatened by Glacial Melt and Sea Level Rise', 29 January 2009. For scholarly commentary, see Erica J Thorson, 'On Thin Ice: The Failure of the United States and the World Heritage Committee to Take Climate Change Mitigation Pursuant to the World Heritage Convention Seriously' (2008) 38 *Environmental Law* 139; Lin (n 9) 54–6.

[20] The 'Peoples' Climate Case', currently under appeal to the Court of Justice of the European Union, includes petitioners from both EU Member States as well as non-member states who argue that the EU's current emissions reductions are insufficient in light of international and European environmental and human rights law. Case T-330/18, *Carvalho and Others* v *European Parliament and Council of the European Union*, ECLI:EU:T:2019:324. For commentary, see Gerd Winter, 'Armando Carvalho and Others v. EU: Invoking Human Rights and the Paris Agreement for Better Climate Protection Legislation' (2020) 9 *Transnational Environmental Law* 137.

[21] Note that the scholarly distinction between international public law and transnational law has been fluid over time. Philip Jessup's 1956 essay provides one of the broadest definitions of transnational law as 'all law which regulates actions or events that transcend national frontiers'. Philip Jessup, *Transnational Law* (Yale University Press 1956) 2.

[22] For an excellent overview of transnational cases involving parties or jurisdictions in the Global South, see Peel and Lin (n 11) 726.

[23] David Ciplet, 'Contesting Climate Injustice: Transnational Advocacy Network Struggles for Rights in UN Climate Politics' (2014) 14 *Global Environmental Politics* 75.

[24] Peel and Lin (n 11).

dialogues diagonally across multiple scales of governance—local, national and supranational—as well as across horizontal divisions of governance.[25] Likewise, Peel and Lin identified the growing body transjudicial dialogues in climate change jurisprudence, although it has yet to be the subject of comprehensive analysis.[26] These transnational dimensions of climate change litigation are unsurprising given its 'multiscalar' character, composed of actors, norms and procedures from subnational, national and supranational levels of governance.[27] Yet, these analyses are often limited to the transnational character of single, isolated cases, describing multiscalar interactions in the case, rather than the transnational character of litigation that permeates throughout a collection of cases.

The notion of 'co-production', as developed in science and technical studies, offers an analytic framework for describing the transnational character of climate change litigation writ large, including cases that are *prima facie* domestic cases in substance, parties, procedure and jurisdiction. Such a framework provides transnational and socio-legal scholars the vocabulary and concepts to identify how seemingly isolated litigation attempts in (sub-)national cases, as well as international and transnational cases, may be related and engaged in joint governance activities. It allows legal scholars to move beyond describing litigation 'models' for transplantation to other jurisdictions, and instead treats them as shared endeavours of combined legal, political and scientific strategy. If climate change is a localised globalism[28] *par excellence*, then the analysis of climate change litigation ought to aspire towards grasping the transnational character of its local manifestations, even if that requires legal scholars to break with the comfortable frames of the nation-state.[29]

3. Co-production as a transnational approach to litigation

In her 2013 article on the famous US climate case *Massachusetts v. EPA*, Fisher described a line of scholarship which analysed the case as 'a site for

[25] For a discussion of the transnational characteristics of such 'diagonal regulatory dialogue' see Hari M Osofsky, 'Is Climate Change "International"? Litigation's Diagonal Regulatory Role' (2009) 49 *Virginia Journal of International Law* 585, 634–7.

[26] Peel and Lin (n 11) 724. The concept of 'transjudicial dialogues' was first developed in Anne-Marie Slaughter, 'A Typology of Transjudicial Communication' (1994) 29 *University of Richmond Law Review* 99.

[27] Hari M Osofsky, 'The Geography of Climate Change Litigation: Implications for Transnational Regulatory Governance' (2005) 83 *Washington University Law Quarterly* 1789. The focus on this analytic triad corresponds with the transnational legal methodology developed in Peer Zumbansen, 'Where the Wild Things Are: Journeys to Transnational Legal Orders, and Back' (2016) 1 *UC Irvine Journal of International, Transnational, and Comparative Law* 161.

[28] Boaventura de Sousa Santos, *Toward a New Legal Common Sense: Law, Globalization, And Emancipation* (2nd edn, Butterworths LexisNexis 2002) 179–82.

[29] On breaking frames in transnational legal theory see Gunther Teubner, 'Breaking Frames: Economic Globalization and the Emergence of Lex Mercatoria' (2002) 5 *European Journal of Social Theory* 199.

co-production of understandings of the climate change problem and how it should be addressed by the socio-political order'.[30]

According to Fisher, the Supreme Court's decision presented simultaneously an authoritative account of the 'factual matrix' of climate change science, affirming the roles of different institutions and actors and their climate modelling, as well as 'an understanding of how regulatory responses are developed in response to specific factual situations'.[31] This notion of co-production provides an analytic framework for assessing 'how the social order and physical world are constructed in climate change cases'.[32] This section explores how the approach could be used not only within cases, but also across them as a method of transnational and socio-legal analysis. It focuses on the role of narratives (or 'frames') in co-production, and how they can be used to analyse the role that litigation plays in conceptualising the many transnational environmental problems related to climate change.[33]

The concept of 'co-production', developed by Jasanoff, embraces the mutually constructive relationship between descriptive science and the normative ordering of society:

> [C]o-production is shorthand for the proposition that the ways in which we know and represent the world (both in nature and society) are inseparable from the ways in which we choose to live in it. Knowledge and its material embodiments are at once products of social work and constitutive of forms of social life; society cannot function without knowledge any more than knowledge can exist without appropriate social supports.[34]

According to Jasanoff, co-production occurs in both constitutive and interactional forms, concerning, respectively, 'the emergence of new facts, things and systems of thought' and the 'knowledge conflicts within worlds that have already been demarcated, for practical purposes, into the natural and the social'.[35] By focusing on the instruments of identities, institutions, discourses and representations, the analysis of co-production processes 'sweeps back into the analyst's field of vision connections between natural and social orders that disciplinary conventions often seek to obliterate, thereby doing injustice to the complexity as well as strangeness of human experience'.[36] Narratives can play

[30] Fisher, 'Climate Change Litigation, Obsession and Expertise: Reflecting on the Scholarly Response to Massachusetts v. EPA' (n 13) 250. Her primary reference in this line of scholarship was Sheila Jasanoff, 'A World of Experts: Science and Global Environmental Constitutionalism' (2013) 40 *Boston College Environmental Affairs Law Review* 439.

[31] Fisher, 'Climate Change Litigation, Obsession and Expertise: Reflecting on the Scholarly Response to Massachusetts v. EPA' (n 13) 251.

[32] ibid 256.

[33] Elizabeth Fisher, 'The Rise of Transnational Environmental Law and the Expertise of Environmental Lawyers' (2012) 1 *Transnational Environmental Law* 43, 50–1.

[34] Sheila Jasanoff, 'The Idiom of Co-Production' in Sheila Jasanoff (ed), *States of Knowledge: The Co-Production of Science and the Social Order* (Routledge 2004) 2–3.

[35] Sheila Jasanoff, 'Ordering Knowledge, Ordering Society' in Sheila Jasanoff (ed), *States of Knowledge: The Co-Production of Science and the Social Order* (Routledge 2004) 18–19.

powerful roles in processes of co-production, as they seize upon existing instruments, adjust them for new purposes, and recognise new forms of scientific authority and social order that could lead to the emergence of new instruments of co-production.[37]

Climate change stands to dramatically reconfigure our world as we understand it today, both descriptively and normatively. Jasanoff has described how, through processes of abstraction, scientific representations of climate change have also been joined with new representations of communities, polities, spaces and time.[38] For example, scientific accounts of climate change inevitably engage in questions about the representation of how various places are linked to both the cause of climate change (through the emission of greenhouse gases) as well its consequences. Likewise, the science of climate change 'invites humanity to play god with time' by impressing new questions of: the past (when did humanity begin altering the course of global climatic systems and what does that tell us about historic responsibility for the current state of global warming?); the present (what is the significance of our current actions and decisions, and what evaluations of risk should we take into account?); and the future (whose future interests should be taken into consideration, and what future version of the world are we able to offer?).[39]

Climate change litigation is situated at the intersection of legal institutions and the 'disruptive'[40] character of climate change, where a focus on processes of co-production can help us make sense of what litigants and courts are doing:

> For legal scholarship … climate change offers a site not merely to consider how enforceable obligations may be constructed around trades in greenhouse gases, but also to reflect on deeper questions of rights and responsibilities, the criteria and correlates of citizenship, and the rebuilding of constitutional norms around a threat that cuts at the foundations of all civilized societies.[41]

This account of what is at stake in climate change litigation also extends beyond constitutional norms to include issues of tort law (eg public nuisance), administrative law (eg environmental impact assessments), and environmental law (eg public trust doctrine, precautionary principle),

---

[36] ibid 42.

[37] ibid 40–1. See also Sheila Jasanoff, 'Restoring Reason: Causal Narratives and Political Culture' in Bridget Hutter and Michael Power (eds), *Organizational Encounters with Risk* (Cambridge University Press 2005). The analysis of co-production shares characteristics of Boyd White's narrative analysis of law

> as a language and a community—a world, made partly by others and partly by ourselves, in which we and others shall live, and which will be tested less by its distributive effects than by the resources of meaning it creates and the community it constitutes.

James Boyd White, 'Law as Rhetoric, Rhetoric as Law' (1985) 52 *University of Chicago Law Review* 684, 699.

[38] Sheila Jasanoff, 'A New Climate for Society' (2010) 27 *Theory, Culture & Society* 233.

[39] ibid 241–2.

[40] Elizabeth Fisher, Eloise Scotford and Emily Barritt, 'The Legally Disruptive Nature of Climate Change' (2017) 80 *The Modern Law Review* 173.

[41] Jasanoff, 'A New Climate for Society' (n 38) 249.

among others. Climate litigation is stretched across these multiple fields because it is an area of 'hot' law, as Fisher describes, in which there are mutually incompatible understandings of the fundamental bases of both scientific knowledge and legal norms.[42] These areas of law each present possible frameworks—for creating agreements, establishing consequences of (in)action, and creating modes of responsibility—and 'no frame controls and contains everything'.[43] As a 'hot' situation, climate litigation offers a site where narratives can 'make climate change "real" within communities', through disputing both scientific descriptions of it and a society's normative responses to it, with judges providing closure to these disputes.[44]

The notion of co-production has been used already within the context of single climate change cases. As noted above, both Fisher and Jasanoff have used this framework in their analyses of the court's opinion in *Massachusetts v EPA*.[45] Likewise, Vanhala used co-production in her analysis of the Center for Biological Diversity's reframing of climate change as a biodiversity threat in their petitioning efforts in the US to protect the polar bear as an endangered species.[46] Her analysis illustrates the fruitfulness of applying co-production beyond single cases to examine the use of narrative and framing across a series of petitions. Notably, her combined approach of legal opportunity structures and co-production also shifts focus to include the strategies and actions of litigants, in addition to judges. This shift provokes us to consider how mutually incompatible narratives are presented at the site of litigation, narratives that offer different ways of 'organiz[ing] certain kinds of problems into a form that renders culturally meaningful both the problems and their possible resolutions'.[47] The proposal, therefore, is to extend the application of co-production transnationally onto groups of climate cases from different jurisdictions, in order to assess how common narratives about the science and governance of climate change are built by the litigants.[48] As a transnational method, co-production can aide in understanding how struggles

---

[42] Elizabeth Fisher, 'Environmental Law as "Hot" Law' (2013) 25 *Journal of Environmental Law* 347, 350–1. Fisher is borrowing the concept of 'hot situations' from Michel Callon, 'An Essay on Framing and Overflowing: Economic Externalities Revisited by Sociology' in Michel Callon (ed), *The Laws of the Markets* (Blackwell 1998).

[43] Fisher, 'Environmental Law as "Hot" Law' (n 42) 350.

[44] Fisher, Scotford and Barritt (n 40) 198.

[45] Jasanoff, 'A World of Experts: Science and Global Environmental Constitutionalism' (n 30); Fisher, 'Climate Change Litigation, Obsession and Expertise: Reflecting on the Scholarly Response to Massachusetts v. EPA' (n 13).

[46] Lisa Vanhala, 'Coproducing the Endangered Polar Bear: Science, Climate Change, and Legal Mobilization' *Law & Policy* forthcoming.

[47] Jane B Baron and Julia Epstein, 'Is Law Narrative?' (1997) 45 *Buffalo Law Review* 141, 147.

[48] For example, Hilson has traced political populist narratives in climate change litigation across numerous jurisdictions, albeit without the notion of co-production. Chris Hilson, 'Law, Courts and Populism: Climate Change Litigation and the Narrative Turn' in Susan M Sterett and Lee Demetrius Walker (eds), *Research handbook on law and courts* (Edward Elgar 2019).

over understanding and ruling the problems of climate change occur across jurisdictions, while keeping in account the diverse national cultures of risk, science and law.[49]

4. The 'urgent agenda' narrative in climate change litigation

In this section, we assess the narratives presented in three recent climate change cases from the Netherlands (*Urgenda Foundation v The State of the Netherlands*), Norway (*Greenpeace and Nature & Youth v The Government of Norway*) and Ireland (*Friends of the Irish Environment v The Government of Ireland*). The assessment focuses on co-production process in the litigants' arguments and the judicial decisions, through which scientific claims about climate change and connected with normative positions about the appropriate legal governance of climate change. In particular, the discourse and representation of time and timelines for mitigation are highlighted, to illustrate continuities across these three cases and jurisdictions and highlight how they serve as an example of a shared, transnational legal narrative that frames climate change and its corresponding legal framework. The cases were not selected to be representative of global climate change litigation writ large, an impossible goal for this short article. Instead, they were chosen to illustrate how continuities across jurisdictions can be identified despite considerable differences. The cases are based in tort, constitutional, and administrative law, and each challenge different actions taken by the corresponding national governments. There are notable similarities as well, including that they each come from the Global North and address climate change mitigation, rather than adaptation.[50]

4.1. Urgenda Foundation v State of the Netherlands (Ministry of Economic Affairs and Climate Policy

The *Urgenda* case in the Netherlands was one of the first successful climate change cases to gather worldwide attention. Following its initial success, it went on to spark a series of litigation attempts throughout a number of European countries (the '*Urgenda* effect').[51] Among the three cases reviewed here, it is received the most attention from legal scholars.

---

[49] For the importance of national legal and scientific culture when using co-production as a transnational legal methodology, see Fisher, 'The Rise of Transnational Environmental Law and the Expertise of Environmental Lawyers' (n 33) 49–50; Jasanoff, 'A World of Experts: Science and Global Environmental Constitutionalism' (n 30) 446–7.

[50] It is noteworthy that the literature on climate change litigation has been overwhelmingly focused on common law jurisdictions from the Global North, leaving both civil law jurisdictions and the jurisdictions from the Global South largely overlooked. The latter group has recently been the subject of growing attention. Setzer and Vanhala (n 5) 4; Setzer and Benjamin (n 11).

[51] Setzer and Vanhala (n 5) 3; Peel and Osofsky, 'A Rights Turn in Climate Change Litigation?' (n 10) 61. For coverage of a comparable case in Switzerland, see Cordelia Christiane Bähr and others,

In 2013, the Urgenda Foundation (its name derived from a portmanteau of 'urgent agenda') first filed a claim against the State of the Netherlands, in which they sought an order for the State to take necessary measures to reduce national emissions of greenhouse gases to 25–40 percent below the 1990 level by 2020.[52] The Foundation was created in 2008 with the purpose of 'accelerating the transition process to a more sustainable society, beginning in the Netherlands', and as a litigant it represents the shared interests of 886 Dutch citizens.[53] Their argument was premised on the stated importance of maintaining at least a 50 percent possibility of limiting global warming to 2°C, as agreed upon at the 2010 United Nations' (UN) Conference of Parties (COP) 16 under the Framework Convention on Climate Change (UNFCCC)[54] and later formalised in the 2015 Paris Agreement,[55] after the *Urgenda* case had been initiated.[56] Referring to UN's Intergovernmental Panel on Climate Change (IPCC) models, they claimed that a maximum threshold of 450 parts per million (ppm) CO_2-equivalent is essential for maintaining the 50 percent likelihood of preventing more than 2°C warming.[57] Urgenda referred to the IPCC's Fourth Assessment Report in its finding that, in order to remain under the 450 ppm threshold, Annex I countries (industrial economies and economies in transition, including all of the European Union (EU)) would need to reduce emissions in 2020 by 25–40 percent of the 1990 levels.[58] Notably, they also illustrated how these reductions had been endorsed by both the EU[59] and the Dutch government[60] in earlier years. Despite those earlier endorsements, by 2011 the Dutch State's policies

---

'KlimaSeniorinnen: Lessons from the Swiss Senior Women's Case for Future Climate Litigation' (2018) 9 *Journal of Human Rights and the Environment* 194.

52 Unofficial transnational of the Summons in the case of *Urgenda Foundation v The State of the Netherlands*, filed with the District Court of the Hague on 20 November 2013, §45.

53 *Urgenda* District Court decision (n 1). Note that the case has received much attention both in the Netherlands and abroad for its many controversies, including: its impact on the separation of power, the role of judicial law-making, the application of European human rights law for the consequences of climate change, questions of standing, and the European human rights law as indicative of duties of care under tort law. For more on these dimensions of the case, see: Floor Fleurke and Anne de Vries, 'Urgenda: Covergentie Tussen Klimaat En Mensenrechten?' [2016] Milieu & recht Article 42; Marc Loth and Rob van Gestel, 'Urgenda: Roekeloze Rechtspraak of Rechtsvinding 3.0?' [2015] Nederlands Juristenblad 2598; Laura Burgers and Tim Staal, 'Climate Action as Positive Human Rights Obligation: The Appeals Judgment in Urgenda v The Netherlands' in JE Nijdam and WG Werner (eds), *Netherlands Yearbook of International Law 2018: Populism and International Law* (Asser Press 2018); Suryapratim Roy and Edwin Woerdman, 'Situating Urgenda v the Netherlands within Comparative Climate Change Litigation' (2016) 34 *Journal of Energy & Natural Resources Law* 165; Roger Cox, 'A Climate Change Litigation Precedent: Urgenda Foundation v the State of the Netherlands' (2019) 34 *Journal of Energy & Natural Resources Law* 143.

54 (adopted 9 May 1992, entered into force 21 March 1994) (1993) UNTS vol 1771 p 107 <https://unfccc.int/resource/docs/convkp/conveng.pdf>.

55 (adopted 12 December 2015, entered into force 4 November 2016) (2015) FCCC/CP/2015/10/Add 1 <http://unfccc.int/paris_agreement/items/ 9485.php>.

56 *Urgenda* Summons (n 52) §358–63.

57 ibid.

58 ibid [363].

59 *Urgenda* District Court decision (n 1) [2.63]–[2.64].

60 ibid [2.72]–[2.74].

had been reduced to a target of 20 percent decrease in emissions compared to 1990 levels.[61] According to Urgenda, the Dutch State's failure to pursue a 25–40 percent reduction target by 2020 amounted to a tortious (or 'unlawful') act, and offered four grounds for its unlawfulness: the violation of the general 'no-harm' principle under international law; the violation of its obligations under the UNFCCC and COP agreements (and later, the 2015 Paris Agreement); the violation of its obligations under Articles 2 (right to life) and 8 (right to respect of private and family life) of the European Convention on Human Rights (ECHR);[62] and the torts of nuisance and endangerment in Dutch private law.[63] The Dutch State, however, argued in defence that its emissions reduction target was consistent with its obligations under EU law, that it opted to pursue a more ambitious reduction for 2030 and 2050 when mitigation measures would be least costly, and that the separation of powers prevents the Urgenda Foundation from ordering the Dutch State to take specific regulatory or legislative measures with respect to climate change policy.[64] The timing of reductions is the crux of the dispute, with the Dutch State positing ambitious 40 percent reductions by 2030 and 80–95 percent reductions by 2050 as 'milestones' that are 'sufficient for ensuring the 2°C target',[65] and Urgenda arguing that this delayed set of 'milestones' results in a greater amount of overall emissions and, therefore, an elevated risk of failing to remain under 450 ppm and 2°C warming in comparison to a pathway of 25–40 percent by 2020.[66]

The Hague District Court ruled in favour of the plaintiffs in 2015, ordering that the Dutch government must reduce the joint volume of Dutch annual greenhouse gas emissions by at least 25 percent by the end of 2020.[67] According to the Court, failing to meet this level of reduction, although nowhere explicitly prescribed by Dutch or EU legislation, amounted to a violation of the State's duty of care regarding mitigation measures. Notably, the court agreed that the 'postponement' of the reduction timeline was unacceptable in light of '*the scientifically proven and acknowledged* higher reduction path of 25–40% in 2020'.[68]

The Dutch government appealed the case to the Court of Appeal. In the interim period, the 2015 Paris Agreement came into effect, committing its signatories (including the Netherlands) to the goal of preventing global warming

---

61 Gerechtshof Den Haag, 9 oktober 2018, ECLI:NL:GHDHA:2018:2591, 30. An unauthoritative English translation of the decision has also been provided by the court: The Hague Court of Appeal, 9 October 2018, ECLI:NL:GHDHA:2018:2610, [47]. Hereafter referred to as '*Urgenda* Appellate decision'.

62 (adopted November 1950, entered into force 3 September 1953) (1950) ETS 5 https://www.echr.coe.int/Documents/Convention_ENG.pdf>

63 *Urgenda* Summons (n 52) [312].

64 *Urgenda* District Court decision (n 1) [3.3].

65 ibid [4.33].

66 ibid [4.32].

67 ibid [5.1].

68 ibid [4.85], emphasis added.

from eclipsing 2°C, with the stated ambition of a maximum of 1.5°C.[69] Furthermore, it requires each signatory to submit 'Nationally determined contributions' which lay out their intended path towards preventing the maximum global warming limit.[70] Within this framework, the European Union, on behalf of all of its Member States, committed to a 40 percent reduction of emissions by 2030 (compared to 1990).[71] For the Netherlands, this corresponds to a 36 percent decrease in emissions by 2030 (compared to 2005)[72] and a 16 percent decrease in emissions by 2020 (compared to 2005 levels).[73]

Before the Court of Appeal, the State argued that much of the emissions reductions should, and will, come in the 2020–2030 and 2030–2040 periods, with emphasis on the latter, when mitigation technologies are more advanced:

> There is no absolute need to reduce emissions by 25–40% by end-2020. The State's scope for policymaking includes, after considering all interests involved, such as those of the industry, finances, energy-provision, healthcare, education and defence, to choose the most appropriate reduction path.[74]

The state also suggested that the IPCC's 5th Assessment Report demonstrated that there were reduction pathways in which a 25–40 percent reduction by 2020 was not necessary. In its judgment, the Court of Appeal acknowledged the diversity of reduction pathways as projected by the IPCC, and noted that the linear reduction path used by the State to calculate its 2030 (49 percent) and 2050 (95 percent) reduction goals, 'would result in a 28% reduction by 2020', a far more serious reduction than the State's 2020 target.[75] It also noted that pathways which diverge from the 25–40 percent target for 2020 rely on the future use of CO_2 removal technologies that do not currently exist, and thus cannot be considered a realistic option. Furthermore, the Court acknowledged the IPCC's finding that the maximum 2°C warming equates to a maximum concentration of 450 ppm of CO_2 in the atmosphere in 2100, and that Annex I countries must reduce emissions by 25–40 percent by 2020 to realistically maintain a 'more likely than not' chance of remaining under the 450 ppm threshold.[76] In conclusion, the Court of Appeal found the State's current climate reduction policy amounted to a contravention of

69 Paris Agreement (n 55), Art 2(1)a.
70 Paris Agreement (n 55), Art 4(2).
71 'Submission by Latvia and the European Commission on behalf of the European Union and its Member States: Intended Nationally Determined Contribution of the EU and its Member States', 6 March 2015.
72 Regulation (EU) 2018/842 on binding annual greenhouse gas emission reductions by Member States from 2021 to 2030 contributing to climate action to meet commitments under the Paris Agreement and amending Regulation (EU) No 525/2013 [2018] L 156/26, Annex 1.
73 Decision (EU) 406/2009/EC on the effort of Member States to reduce their greenhouse gas emissions to meet the Community's greenhouse gas emission reduction commitments up to 2020 [2009] L 140/136, Annex II.
74 *Urgenda* Appellate decision (n 61) [30].
75 ibid [47].
76 ibid [48]–[50].

Articles 2 and 8 of the ECHR, that it was therefore deemed unlawful, and that the State must reduce emissions by at least 25 percent by 2020.[77]

The Supreme Court heard the case on appeal in cassation and issued its decision to uphold the appellate ruling in December 2019.[78] The Supreme Court's ruling clarified that, despite the lack of an explicit obligation under national or European Union climate law, the Dutch State was required to pursue a 25–40 percent reduction by 2020, and that failing to do so amount to a violation of Articles 2 and 8 of the ECHR. The Supreme Court decided the evolution of international climate change law and science was indicative of a 'common ground', shared by all societies, that the ECHR requires its signatories to limit climate change to a maximum 2°C warming in the long term.[79] This, in turn, requires at least a 25 percent reduction of emissions by 2020. Ultimately, the Urgenda Foundation successfully mobilised the IPCC's climate science, European human rights law, and Dutch tort law to compel the State to pursue a 25 percent reduction of emissions by the end of 2020, under the forecast that, 'otherwise it would be too late'.[80]

4.2. Greenpeace Nordic Association and Nature & Youth v Government of Norway (Ministry of Petroleum and Energy)

In 2016, the Norwegian branch of Greenpeace and Nature & Youth (*Natur og Ungdom*) challenged the constitutionality of a Royal Decree which awarded oil production licenses for forty new blocks in the Barents Sea.[81] The Decree offered Norway's first expansion of oil exploration and production into new territories since the turn of the twenty-first Century. The two environmental organisations sought to have the Decree invalidated, arguing that the expansion of oil exploration would amount to a violation of the

---

[77] ibid [76].

[78] Hoge Raad, 20 december 2019, ECLI:NL:HR:2019:2006. An unofficial English translation of the judgment has been provided by the Supreme Court: ECLI:NL:HR:2019:2007.

[79] ibid [5.4.1]–[5.4.3]. The Supreme Court stated:

> [I]t follows once again that there is a high degree of international consensus on the urgent need for the Annex I countries to reduce greenhouse emissions by at least 25–40% by 2020 compared to 1990 levels, in order to achieve at least the two-degree target, which is the maximum target to be deemed responsible. This high degree of consensus can be regarded as common ground … [which] must be taken into account when interpreting and applying the ECHR. [7.2.11]

[80] Considerable attention within Dutch legal scholarship has been spent on discussing whether these judgments violate traditional conceptions of the separation of powers. Loth & van Gestel convincingly suggest, however, that the more pressing question is whether the 'otherwise it will be too late' reasoning in the case is sufficient for judicial intervention. See Loth and van Gestel (n 53).

[81] Oslo District Court, Decision of 4 January 2018, *Föreningen Greenpeace Norden, Natur og Ungdom v Norges Rejgering, Olje- og energideapartementet*, 16-166674TVI-OTIR/06 (hereafter referred to as '*People v Arctic Oil* District Court decision', the moniker given to the case by the plaintiff organisations). The references in this text refer to an unofficial translation of the decision <https://www.greenpeace.org/norway/pressemelding/544/greenpeace-and-nature-and-youth-take-the-norwegian-government-to-the-supreme-court/> accessed 20 April 2020. For background on the case see Ivar Alvik, 'The First Norwegian Climate Litigation' (2018) 11 *Journal of World Energy Law and Business* 541.

new Article 112 'right to an environment' added to the Norwegian Constitution in 2014:

> Every person has the right to an environment that is conductive to health and to a natural environment whose productivity and diversity are maintained. Natural resources shall be managed on the basis of comprehensive long-term considerations which will safeguard this right for future generations.

Briefly summarised, the plaintiffs argued that the State's issuance of oil production licenses to previously unexploited zones amounted to a violation of their Article 112 rights, and posed a more 'traditional' climate litigation argument about procedural inadequacies in the impact assessment that preceded the Decree.[82]

Unlike the *Urgenda* case, this complaint targeted the role of the Norwegian State in the production, rather than consumption, of carbon-based energy. The plaintiffs' argument was premised on the notion of a global 'carbon budget', which corresponds to the amount of CO_2 emissions for which there is still 'room' in the atmosphere, before hitting the 450 ppm threshold to maintain a 50 percent likelihood of 2°C maximum warming.[83] Noting that, as of 2011, only 35 percent of a 2°C threshold carbon budget remained, the plaintiffs argued that the plans of long-term oil extraction associated with the exploration of new oil fields was inconsistent with Norway's Article 112 obligations, interpreted in light of the precautionary principle and Articles 2 and 8 of the ECHR.[84] They emphasised the confronting fact that 'there is not even room for emissions from discovered oil and gas reserves in the [global] carbon budget'.[85] As such, they demanded that a future with a limited or depleted carbon budget be given more weight in assessing the environmental impact of immediate decisions regarding oil exploration:

> The fact that the climate threat must be taken seriously, and that changes are urgently required to quickly reduce the climate threat can hardly be denied after the IPCC's report from 2014 … Calculations of the carbon budget show that there probably will not be 'space for' petroleum produced in the maritime areas in question.[86]

In effect, their strategy sought to include emissions caused abroad after export within the environmental assessment of Norwegian oil and gas exploration.

For its part, the Norwegian government, citing the framework for emissions reductions established under international climate change law, denies responsibility for emissions abroad that are associated with Norway's oil

82 *People v Arctic Oil* District Court decision (n 81) [6]–[9].
83 Greenpeace Nordic Association and Nature & Youth, 'Notice of Proceedings in Oslo District Court', 18 October 2016, [6.4.3].
84 ibid [9.2.2]–[9.2.5].
85 ibid [3.1].
86 ibid [9.2.6].

and gas exports.[87] Likewise, it opposed the use of the 'carbon budget' for understanding its constitutional obligations, noting the many uncertainties of the future which could affect such a budget calculation. These uncertainties included both the development of future technologies to remove and store emissions, as well as the volume and type of oil and gas that may be discovered through exploration of the new fields, and therefore how it would factor into a carbon budget.[88]

In its decision, the District Court appeared largely sympathetic with the plaintiffs' concerns, and acknowledged the 'crossroads' in climate governance where we currently stand:

> [The plaintiffs] have pointed out that these are the first licenses granted after there is reliable knowledge that the world's proven fossil fuel resources exceed what can be burned in order to reach the goals in the Paris Agreement. They have also emphasized that the Decision opens the way for petroleum activities further east and north than ever and have alleged that the purpose is to maintain petroleum production at the current level despite the fact that emissions must be reduced at a dramatic pace. They have also argued that the Decision [or "Decree"] contributes to extensive investments and technology development that contribute to increased fossil fuel production (the path argument) and that we are confronting a crossroads (the crossroads argument). They have pointed out that there is not even room for emissions from discovered oil and gas reserves in the carbon budget.[89]

Yet, the Court ultimately found that the State could not be held responsible for emissions resulting from oil and gas exports, and that the social and environmental consequences of Norway's domestic emissions, and the conservation risks associated with opening the new area for oil production, were too limited to constitute a violation of the plaintiffs' constitutional right.[90]

At the Court of Appeal, the plaintiffs were again unsuccessful.[91] Yet, the Court of Appeal engaged in a lengthy discussion about carbon budgets, acknowledging in more alarming terms how pressing the issue of emissions reductions has become:

---

87 The Government of Norway, 'Notice of Defence to Oslo District Court', 14 December 2016, [5.3].

88 ibid [1].

89 *People v Arctic Oil* District Court decision (n 81) [28]. The Court also critiqued these arguments in stating,

> none of these arguments are relevant in the assessment of whether the Decision [or 'Decree'] violated Article 112 of the Constitution. In part, it is talk of possible impacts from the Decision that are too remote in relation to the risk that is relevant to assess, and in part the issues involve overall assessments that are better assessed through political processes that the courts are not suited to reviewing.

90 ibid [18]–[25].

91 Borgarting Court of Appeal, Decision of 23 January 2020, *Föreningen Greenpeace Norden, Natur og Ungdom v Norges Rejgering, Olje- og energideapartemente*, 18-060499ASD-BORG/03 (hereafter refered to as '*People v Arctic Oil* Appellate decision'). An unofficial translation of the Court of Appeal's decision <http://www.xn--klimasksml-95a8t.no/en/2019/10/31/legal-documents-in-english/> accessed 15 April 2020.

> With annual emissions of approximately 42 GtCO2, this [carbon budget] means that there is only room for approximately 15 years of today's emissions before the world must switch to zero net emissions, ie not emitting more than the natural environment can absorb. With a gradual reduction, it will be approximately 30 years before the switch is required.[92]

While the Court of Appeal upheld the initial judgment, it also opened slightly towards to the plaintiffs' arguments, acknowledging that emissions associated with exported oil and gas should be included in the assessment of the Decree's conformity with Article 112 of the Constitution.[93] The appellate judgment, however, also downplayed the consequences of such calculations, in suggesting that, 'there is a greater likelihood that cuts in production will actually be significant the further into the future these arise, as it must be assumed that alternative energy sources will constitute a steadily larger competitor'.[94] Taking into account this future of uncertainty—about levels of emissions, rates of reduction, the size of oil reserves under exploration, technological mitigation possibilities, the competitiveness of alternative energy, and the impact of climate change for the Norwegian—the Court of Appeal found that there were not sufficient grounds to rule the Decree unconstitutional, in violation of the ECHR, or procedurally invalid.

4.3. Friends of the Irish Environment v the Government of Ireland and the Attorney General

In July 2017, the Friends of the Irish Environment challenged the constitutionality of the Irish Government's National Mitigation Plan ('the Plan'), which was created by the Government under its obligations from the Climate Action and Low Carbon Development Act 2015.[95] As a signatory to the Paris Agreement, Ireland committed itself to the maximum 2°C warming limit and the ambition to prevent greater than 1.5°C warming. It's commitments under EU law are a 20 percent reduction by 2020 (compared to 2005 levels),[96] and a 30 percent reduction by 2030 (compared to 2005 levels).[97] Friends of the Irish Environment argued, in echo of the *Urgenda* claims, that the State is obliged to meet interim reductions of 25–40 percent (compared to 1990 levels) by 2020, in accordance with the UNFCCC's reduction goals for Annex 1 countries necessary to maintain a 2°C maximum warming.[98] They argue that the failure of the Plan to meet Ireland's international obligations places it in breach of the corresponding Act,

---

[92] ibid [3.1].
[93] ibid [2.4].
[94] ibid [3.3].
[95] *Friends of the Irish Environment CLG v The Government of Ireland and the Attorney General* [2017 No. 793 JR] (Hereafter '*Friends of the Irish Environment*').
[96] Decision (EU) 406/2009/EC (n 73) Annex II.
[97] Regulation (EU) 2018/842 (n 72), Annex I.
[98] *Friends of the Irish Environment* (n 95), §23.

and that the Plan is both unconstitutional and a violation of Ireland's human rights obligations under the ECHR.[99] As such, the plaintiffs requested the Court to order the Plan to be quashed and remitted for redrafting. Similar to *Urgenda*, their claim includes an, 'emphasis on the path of reduction and the necessity to reach interim emission reduction targets', and the scientific position that, 'several reduction paths with the same starting point and the same end point can vary dramatically in the amount of cumulative or aggregate emissions'.[100]

The Irish Government admitted that it was unlikely to meet its 2020 targets, and that a considerable amount of the reduction in emissions in past years was (ironically) due to a milder climate rather than effective policy.[101] Focusing on near term goals for 2020 distracts attention from the key issue of climate policy, according to the State: 'The key national policy position on climate action and low carbon development was adopted by the government and published in 2014; the object being the transition to a competitive low carbon, climate resilient and environmentally sustainable economy by 2050'.[102] For the Irish Government, the primary goal lies in 2050, and the strategy is to choose the most cost effective pathway to arrive to that goal:

> [I]t is not feasible to prescribe precisely in 2017 which measures will be put in place by government to achieve the national transition objective for 2050 … The act provides for a formal update to the Plan at least once every five years and in this context, he [the Principal Officer in the Department of Communications, Climate Action and Energy] avers that the government has recognised the high likelihood that technology and innovation will continue to evolve over the coming decades. He also refers to the requirement to recognise the need to achieve the objectives of the Plan at the least cost to the national economy and to adopt measures that are cost effective which do not impose an unreasonable burden on the exchequer.[103]

The Irish State's defence suggests that the emissions reduction targets that really 'count' are those in 2050, not 2020.

---

99 ibid [12]. Notably, the plaintiff did not substantiate which convention rights were potentially violated by the Plan. They clarified that the allegedly violated constitutional rights included the rights to life, liberty, security, integrity of the person, property, children's rights, as well as an unenumerated constitutional right to a reasonable environment. ibid [24]. On the background of a right to an environment in Irish constitutional law, and its impact on climate change litigation see Eadbhard Pernot, 'The Right to an Environment and Its Effects for Climate Change Litigation in Ireland' (2019) 22 *Trinity College Law Review* 151.

100 *Friends of the Irish Environment* (n 95) [20].

101

> For 2017, the national greenhouse gas emissions are estimated to be 0.9 percent lower in 2017 than 2016, although he [the Principal Officer in the Department of Communications, Climate Action and Energy] does acknowledge that the decrease is mainly due to mild weather conditions. ibid [52]

102 ibid [45].

103 ibid [47].

The High Court acknowledged that this is a dispute about the urgency of climate action:

> [T]he essential difference of approach between the parties is one of immediacy —what measures are required to be taken immediately in order to maintain a trajectory which will result in the achievement of the objective of a low-carbon country by 2050.[104]

The Court found the Government to have considerable discretion in the formulation of the Plan, a policy document that is intended to be routinely updated, and noted that the legislative framework in which it develops the Plan does not impose a requirement to achieve intermediate targets (or 'milestones', to use the language in *Urgenda*).[105] The Court also offers a not so subtle suggestion that the plaintiffs might better contest the objectives and provisions in the overarching legislative Act, rather than the Plan, for their inadequacy to protect the fundamental rights of the organisation's members.[106] In February 2020, the Supreme Court agreed to hear the case on appeal directly from the High Court.

4.4. The transnational co-production of urgent climate action

These three cases illustrate a common strategy for the co-production of the time and governance of climate change. In his theory-building monograph on the role of time in environmental law, Richardson astutely observes that, 'time is not something that simply exerts an influence on law, but rather law itself also structures how we perceive of time, by disciplining and normalizing the experience of time'.[107] This observation resonates with the thesis of the co-production of natural and social order, and it draws attention to the interaction between representations of time (or timelines) and legal obligations in the above cases. Richardson notes that, among the many temporalities in environmental law, 'the pull of the future is a mirage … with the present exerting far greater rein over environmental decisions and habits'.[108] With respect to climate change, Richardson identifies the importance of a 'turning point' discourse for defining timelines of action and consequences, while also noting that climate change is exemplary of 'slow violence'—characterised by remote and uncertain relationships between causes and effects—which is fundamentally difficult to adjudicate.[109] Likewise, in a review of numerous climate change cases, Hilson identified

---

[104] ibid [107].
[105] ibid [111]–[116].
[106] ibid [140].
[107] Benjamin J Richardson, *Time and Environmental Law: Telling Nature's Time* (Cambridge University Press 2017) 80.
[108] ibid 123.
[109] ibid 115. The term 'slow violence' was first developed in Rob Nixon, *Slow Violence and the Environmentalism of the Poor* (Harvard University Press 2013).

representations of different types of time frames, including scientific, environmentalist policy, and generational time frames.[110] Notably, Hilson's analysis reveals tensions between time frames that emphasise immediate, or urgent, climate change consequences and policy action, in contrast to time frames that situate its impacts further off in the future.

While *Urgenda* remains the only of the three cases to succeed before the courts, each contribute to a growing narrative of urgent climate action. The plaintiffs in these cases share a common framing of how we understand the future climate, and thus also how constitutional and international norms—the Paris Agreement and the European Convention of Human Rights—need to be re-interpreted to govern our current actions with respect to that future climate. Notably, the interpretations used in the *Urgenda* decision were discussed at length in the judgments of the other two cases.[111] Each case builds on a common discourse about the vital importance of a maximum 2°C global warming, the 450 ppm threshold which corresponds with the likelihood of keeping under 2°C warming, and the Annex I countries' 25–40 percent reduction target for 2020 which is necessary to remain under the 450 ppm threshold throughout the coming eight decades. This discourse is built upon the importance of the IPCC as an institution of climate knowledge, with its Assessment Reports offering an authoritative account of the possible futures available to us, and the present actions required to attain them.

In addition, the arguments in the above cases use symbols and representations in order to reduce, simplify, and bring to life complex issues of climate policymaking. For example, they reduce the seemingly endless possible climate mitigation strategies into identifiable 'reduction pathways', and assert 'milestones' at key moments for evaluation. Indeed, the crux of the *Urgenda* and *Friends of the Irish Environment* cases lies in whether 2020 is such a key milestone, or whether 2050 ought to serve as the more definitive moment for evaluating success, and hence also our shared climatic destinies. While the differences between the various pathways appear fairly minimal for the time being—with arguments revolving around whether states must pursue 20 percent or 25 percent reductions by 2020—the narrative also positions us at a 'crossroads', from which the pathways will only continue to diverge. Regardless of which path we take, however, the metaphor of a 'carbon budget' reminds us that there is only so much carbon which the atmosphere can hold before the balance is in the red, and that each pathway is associated with different levels of risk of entering into debt. Through these representations, the narrative presented in these cases builds a case for taking urgent action to reduce both emissions and the production of oil and gas

---

[110] Chris Hilson, 'Framing Time in Climate Change Litigation' [2018] Oñati Socio-Legal Series 1.

[111] *People v Arctic Oil* Appellate decision (n 91) [3.2]; *Friends of the Irish Environment* (n 95) [76].

immediately, in order to reduce the likelihood of verging into a pathway with greater than 2°C.

In response, the three States in the above cases each posit their own narrative of the future. In the uncertainty of the future they see opportunity which coincidences with dramatic reductions in emissions before 2050, their prioritised milestone. These opportunities include the development of new technologies for removing emissions from the atmosphere, or geo-engineering technologies that can artificially keep warming under 2°C, despite emissions rising beyond the 450 ppm threshold, or future energy markets in which renewable sources are so competitive that they broadly outprice carbon-based sources and result in a rapid, market-driven energy transition.[112] With such an opportunistic future in mind, the corresponding States assert considerable discretion in choosing how much to sacrifice in the short term, when the costs of mitigation *might* be much less in the future.

Approaching litigation as a form of shared narrative building emphasises the underlying notion that such obligations flow not from idiosyncrasies in national or regional legislation, but from a transnational conception of (un)reasonableness with regards to the risks incurred by postponing emissions reductions. At the heart of the urgent agenda narrative is the claim that any political community which has obliged itself to prevent an excess of 2°C warming, through signing the Paris Agreement or via other instruments, has also created an obligation of urgent climate action with substantial reductions in 2020 and 2030. As seen throughout the cases above, this narrative is diffusible across jurisdictions insofar that it is a more general lens for interpreting obligations under EU climate law, international human rights law, and international environmental law.[113] For example, the Urgenda Foundation partner organisation, the Climate Litigation Network, is involved in providing legal assistance for climate change litigation throughout Europe, as well as corresponding grassroots political campaign support. One of the attorneys involved in the *Urgenda* case also provided assistance in the *Friends of the Irish Environment* case, and others spoke at events on climate litigation along with representatives from the *People v Arctic Oil* case. In pursuing these narratives through both legal and political strategies, these cases push for an evolution in the broader public understanding of the timeline of state responsibilities in addressing climate change that transcends jurisdictions.[114]

---

[112] See, for instance, the argument about the potential of future technological innovations which would make postponed mitigation measures far less disruptive than immediate measures; *Urgenda* District Court decision (n 1) [4.32].

[113] Roy and Woerdman highlight various 'diffusible' aspects of the *Urgenda* decision, particularly focusing on the court's interpretation of the precautionary principle in the decision. See Roy and Woerdman, 'Situating Urgenda v the Netherlands within Comparative Climate Change Litigation' (n 51).

[114] Roger Cox summarises this vision by comparing this field of litigation with the history of tobacco and asbestos litigation:

Yet, this analysis must also consider the contingency of any narrative and consider that alternative narratives in climate change governance could develop.[115] In the cases discussed above, we frequently see the urgency narrative confronted with narratives that emphasise the states' discretion in how and, more importantly, *when* to reduce emissions. Perhaps more critical, however, is the fissure within environmentalist organisations about the desirability of reifying the 2°C maximum warming threshold instead of the more stringent 1.5°C goal. For small island states, 2°C warming constitutes an existential threat to their continued existence with likely scenarios of ocean rising and severe weather patterns that would terminate the possibility of habitation on their sovereign territory.[116] If, as Cover postulates, 'legal interpretation takes place in a field of pain and death', then the interpretation of the Paris Agreement in the urgency narrative deals in the death of the small island states.[117] While environmentalists extol the success of the *Urgenda* case,[118] it also represents an uncomfortable compromise from the perspective of island states, who presumably would have argued for a far more radical 2020 reduction target and lower maximum warming threshold. It also perpetuates a (post-)colonial mentality whereby the sovereignty of small island states count for less than the national interests of European and North American states, among others. Along similar lines, the urgency narrative perpetuates a postcolonial mindset through which Global North states pass on the 'ecological debt' of their consumerism to the emissions accounts of Global South states where corresponding manufacturing occurs.[119] The failure of

---

> As we have seen in asbestos and tobacco lawsuits, momentum seems to be gained after an initial--and thus historic--ruling sets a precedent. It is almost a rule that more judgments will follow. Subsequent condemnatory rulings will then begin to change the public perception of the problem. Twenty years ago, the idea of a ban on smoking in cafés or public buildings would have been unimaginable. After various court rulings, however, it is now generally accepted that smokers should not be permitted to pose a risk to the health of others. It is to be hoped that cases dealing with the climate problem will follow the same course. That is why this ruling, the first of its kind in the world, is so important. It will hopefully help change the public perception of the problem and bring it in line with what climate scientists have been trying to make clear to us for so many years: climate change poses a major threat to society and states, and companies and citizens will have to do their share to stop it while the worst can still be avoided. States bear a special responsibility in this respect.

Roger Cox, 'A Climate Change Litigation Precedent: Urgenda Foundation v the State of the Netherlands' (n 53) 161–2.

115 Baron and Epstein (n 47) 177.

116 A spokesperson for small island states put it rather bluntly during the 2009 Copenhagen Summit: 'Some countries will flat-out disappear'. Bill McKibben, 'Global Warming's Terrifying New Math' [2012] *Rolling Stone*. For a broader discussion on the impacts of the Paris Agreement on small island states, see Ian Fry, 'The Paris Agreement: An Insider's Perspective - The Role of Small Island Developing States' (2016) 46 *Environmental Policy and Law* 105.

117 Robert Cover, 'Violence and the Word' in Martha Minow, Michael Ryan and Austin Sarat (eds), *Narrative, Violence, and the Law: The Essays of Robert Cover* (The University of Michigan Press 1993) 203.

118 See for instance, Cox (n 53); Burgers and Staal (n 53).

119 Anna Aseeva, 'Intergenerational Climate Justice' in Thomas Cottier, Shaheeza Lalani and Clarence Siziba (eds), *Intergenerational Equity: Environmental and Cultural Concerns* (Brill Nijhoff 2019) 135–6; J Timmons Roberts and Bradley C Parks, 'Ecologically Unequal Exchange, Ecological Debt, and

the above litigation to engage critically with the injustice of this attribution scheme places the narrative at odds with the lived realities of many communities in the Global South.

5. Conclusion

This article articulated a narrative of time and urgency that was developed across climate litigation in three countries. It employed the notion of co-production to assess litigation as sites for framing both our scientific understanding of climate change and how it is to be governed. In doing so, it has illustrated how seemingly isolated litigation from different jurisdictions can be approached transnationally, in order to assess how they contribute to common or competing narratives about our future climate. The mode of analysis offers legal scholars a tool for breaking out of our discipline's methodological nationalism in order to make sense of the transnational legal strategies through which our understanding of responsibility and climate justice is unfolding. While the article has grappled with the role of time and timelines in the three cases above, it has necessarily excluded another important dimension of time for climate governance: the rights and interests of future generations. It should be incumbent for any expansion of the analysis presented here to engage more comprehensibly with the dual temporal considerations of immediate urgency and long-term intergenerational justice that often structure climate litigation.

Disclosure statement

No potential conflict of interest was reported by the author(s).

Climate Justice: The History and Implications of Three Related Ideas for a New Social Movement' (2009) 50 *International Journal of Comparative Sociology* 385.

Litigation and regulatory governance in the age of the Anthropocene: the case of fracking in the Karoo

Melanie Murcott and Emily Webster

ABSTRACT

The demand for fossil fuels, and most recently natural gas, has resulted in large-scale intervention with the Earth both from its extraction and its overwhelming contribution to global greenhouse gas emissions, and so climate change. Adopting a transnational legal methodology, this article assesses the role of non-state actors in the regulation of fracking in the ecologically and socially sensitive area of the Karoo, South Africa. The litigation discussed reveals a constellation of actors including the government and transnational fossil fuels promoting fracking on the one hand, and various non-state actors, such as civil society, domestic business as well as the global anti-fracking movement, opposing fracking on the other. The role and power of the state to regulate fracking is significantly impacted by these actors, including by refocussing the minds of transnational corporations and the state on the centrality of public participation, by challenging regulations introduced to govern fracking, and through delaying the operationalisation of fracking in the Karoo.

1. Introduction

In the quest for energy security, humanity has spent centuries extracting fossil fuels from the Earth. Global energy demands continue to require cheap fuels, and natural gas has been touted as a fuel to 'bridge the gap' between coal and oil on the one hand, and clean energy on the other.[1] This has resulted in rapidly increasing consumption of this fuel; 'in 2018 gas accounted for almost half of the growth in total global energy demand' alone.[2] Hydraulic fracturing (fracking) is a process by which gas that is 'dispersed in the rock, rather than in a concentrated underground location' is extracted from shale

[1] see eg: IEA, 'The Role of Gas in Today's Energy Transitions' (2019) online: <https://webstore.iea.org/download/direct/2819?fileName=TheRoleofGas.pdf> accessed 11 March 2020; 'Majors Back Gas in Power Switch as a "Bridge Fuel" | Financial Times' <https://www.ft.com/content/811b38ae-c883-11e8-86e6-19f5b7134d1c> accessed 11 March 2020.

[2] IEA (n 1) 1–2.

rock through the injection of fluids that increase the pressure on the geological formations, fracturing them.[3] There are a multitude of environmental and social externalities associated with this activity, including localised geological tremors and pollution and contributions to global concentrations of methane and carbon dioxide from its extraction and use, thereby exacerbating the climate crisis.[4]

This article adopts a transnational legal methodology[5] to identify the actors, norms and processes involved in the response to fracking,[6] and the environmental and social harms posed by this activity in the Karoo, South Africa. We engage with the contestations and tensions amongst state and non-state actors that importantly, extend beyond the traditional territorial, jurisdictional, and regulatory boundaries of the state. By identifying who is involved in norm generation, how they are involved, and what the impact of their involvement is in practice, a new perspective on a legal development (in our case, the regulation of fracking in the Karoo) is revealed. This perspective allows us to acknowledge and engage with the crucial role that non-state actors can play in shaping legal and regulatory developments in response to the socio-ecological crisis of the Anthropocene.

We analyse litigation in South Africa related to fracking that has yielded, among others, the following judgments: *Normandien Farms (Pty) Limited v South African Agency for Promotion of Petroleum and Exploitation SOC Limited* (*Normandien Farms HC*) and *Minister of Mineral Resources v Stern* (*Stern SCA*).[7] Litigation pursued by private actors in response to the state's approach to the regulation of polluting operations is often resorted to as a

---

3 OA US EPA, 'The Process of Unconventional Natural Gas Production' (*US EPA*, 7 February 2013) online: <https://www.epa.gov/uog/process-unconventional-natural-gas-production> accessed 11 March 2020.

4 see eg: Robert W Howarth, 'Ideas and Perspectives: Is Shale Gas a Major Driver of Recent Increase in Global Atmospheric Methane?' (2019) 16 *Biogeosciences* 3033; M Saunois and others, 'The Growing Role of Methane in Anthropogenic Climate Change' (2016) 11 (120207) *Environmental Research Letters* 1; Pascal Peduzzi and Ruth Harding, 'Gas Fracking: Can We Safely Squeeze the Rocks?' (UNEP Global Environmental Alert Service 2012) online: <https://na.unep.net/geas/archive/pdfs/GEAS_Nov2012_Fracking.pdf> accessed 2 May 2020.

5 Peer Zumbansen, 'Defining the Space of Transnational Law: Legal Theory, Global Governance, and Legal Pluralism' (2012) 21 *Transnational Law & Contemporary Problems* 305; Peer Zumbansen, 'Transnational Law, Evolving' in Jan M Smits (ed), *Elgar Encyclopaedia of Comparative Law* (2nd edn, Elgar 2012).

6 We refer to fracking to include exploration (involving the identification of shale gas reservoirs and assessing the economic viability of extracting the gas), extraction (involving the production of gas), and post-extraction (involving the decommissioning of areas that are no longer productive), as discussed in Surina Esterhuyse and others, 'A Review of Biophysical and Socio-Economic Effects of Unconventional Oil and Gas Extraction – Implications for South Africa' (2016) 184 *Journal of Environmental Management* 419, 420.

7 *Normandien Farms HC* was taken on appeal, resulting in *Minister of Rural Development and Land Reform v Normandien Farms (Pty) Ltd* 2019 (1) SA 154 (SCA) (*Normandien Farms SCA*) and then *Normandien Farms (Pty) Ltd v South African Agency for Promotion of Petroleum Exportation and Exploitation (SOC) Ltd* (unreported, referred to as [2020] ZACC 5, 24 March 2020, online: <https://www.saflii.org/za/cases/ZACC/2020/5.html>) (*Normandien Farms CC*). *Stern SCA* is the result of the consolidated appeal against the judgments: *Stern NO and Others v Minister of Mineral Resources* (unreported, referred to as [2017] ZAECGHC 109, 17 October 2017; online: <https://www.saflii.org/za/cases/ZAECGHC/2017/109.html>) (*Stern HC*) and *Treasure Karoo Action Group v Department of Mineral Resources* [2018] 3 All SA 896 (GP) (*TKAG HC*).

way of limiting or preventing the negative environmental and social externalities associated with these activities.[8] Adopting a transnational legal methodology when analysing such litigation can reveal a complex, cross-border context in which non-state actors play a key role in confronting environmentally and socially harmful activity. Further, such litigation can influence the development of more appropriate regulatory responses to environmental problems.[9] Indeed, there has been a rise in the use of litigation specifically in the context of climate change,[10] pursuant to which lawyers and litigants are increasingly reaching beyond the boundaries of the state, linking with those who have preceded them, and sharing scientific research, legal arguments and expertise.[11]

The litigation discussed in this paper did not explicitly engage with the phenomenon of climate change, nor did it address arguments concerning climate change mitigation or adaptation. Accordingly, *Normandien HC* and *Stern SCA* would not, on narrow understandings, be viewed as 'climate change cases' or instances of 'climate litigation'.[12] Nonetheless, *Normandien HC* and *Stern SCA* are both concerned with better regulating fracking in the Karoo (an activity that will arguably exacerbate the global climate crisis), and in this sense, they impact upon the state's climate change mitigation efforts. *Normandien HC* and *Stern SCA* could therefore be construed as a sub-section of climate litigation.[13] Setzer and Vanhala, reviewing the mass of

[8] Eg see: Kim Bouwer, 'The Unsexy Future of Climate Litigation' (2018) 30(3) *Journal of Environmental Law* 483; see also Phillip Paiement, 'Urgent Agenda: How Climate Litigation Builds Transnational Narratives' (2020) 11(1–2) *Transnational Legal Theory* (this issue).

[9] Jacqueline Peel and Hari M Osofsky, *Climate Change Litigation : Regulatory Pathways to Cleaner Energy* (Cambridge University Press 2015); An example of tort law's regulatory potential see: Douglas A Kysar, 'The Public Life of Private Law: Tort Law as a Risk Regulation Mechanism' (2018) 9(1) *European Journal of Risk Regulation* 48.

[10] For example, in *Urgenda Foundation v The Netherlands* [2015] Rechtbank Den Haag, 24 juni 2015, ECLI: NL:RBDH:2015:7145 the NGO Urgenda brought successful climate litigation against the Netherlands for insufficient greenhouse gas reduction targets. The court ordered the Netherlands to pursue a 25% reduction in greenhouse gases by 2030, rather than the planned 17%. See also Peel and Osofsky (n 9); Bouwer, (n 8); Joyeeta Gupta, 'Legal Steps Outside the Climate Convention: Litigation as a Tool to Address Climate Change' (2007) 16(1) *Review of European Community & International Environmental Law* 76; LSE, 'Global Trends in Climate Change Legislation and Litigation: 2018 Snapshot' (*LSE*, 30 April 2018) online: <https://www.lse.ac.uk/GranthamInstitute/publication/global-trends-in-climate-change-legislation-and-litigation-2018-snapshot/> accessed 1 June 2020; Hari M Osofsky and Jacqueline Peel, 'The Role of Litigation in Multilevel Climate Change Governance: Possibilities for a Lower Carbon Future' (2013) 30 *Environmental and Planning Law Journal* 303; For litigation challenging shale gas see eg: Brian J Preston, 'Unconventional Natural Gas in the Courts: An Overview' (2014) 32 (4) *Journal of Energy & Natural Resource Law* 377.

[11] Keck and Sikkink describe this phenomenon in the context of civil society Margret E Keck and Kathryn Sikkink, 'Transnational Advocacy Networks in the Movement Society' in David S Meyer and Sidney Tarrow (eds), *The Social Movement Society: Contentious Politics for a New Century* (Rowman & Littlefield Publishers 1997); Margret E Keck and Kathryn Sikkink, *Activists beyond Borders* (Cornell University Press 2014); For an initiative in the context of climate litigation see: 'Global Climate Litigation' (*Urgenda*) online: <https://www.urgenda.nl/en/themas/climate-case/global-climate-litigation/> accessed 24 January 2020. See also: Paiement, (n 8).

[12] For a review of literature concerned with 'climate litigation' and what its focus is, see: Joana Setzer and Lisa C Vanhala, 'Climate Change Litigation: A Review of Research on Courts and Litigants in Climate Governance' (2019) 10(e580) *WIREs Climate Change* 1.

[13] Bouwer (n 8).

literature concerned with 'climate litigation', have noted the paucity of literature concerned with litigation in the global South.[14] A more inclusive understanding of 'climate change cases' serves to draw attention to efforts by litigants and the courts in the global South to respond to climate change, albeit not directly.

Before engaging with *Normandien HC* and *Stern SCA*, in part 2 of this article we discuss the relevance and value of the notion of the Anthropocene and we elaborate upon the transnational legal methodology that we adopt. In part 3 we discuss the Karoo as a site of contestation amongst state and non-state actors. Finally, in part 4, our analysis of *Normandien Farms HC* and *Stern SCA* invokes a transnational legal methodology and illustrates the role that non-state actors can play in responding to the conditions of the Anthropocene.

2. The Anthropocene, transnational law and litigation

The Anthropocene connotes a proposed geological epoch arising from 'the transformation of the Earth's surface environments by human activity'.[15] Climate change is one of the consequences of the Anthropocene and one of its distinct markers.[16] The imagery associated with this epoch is of 'planetary systems ... on the brink of human-induced ecological disaster that could change life on Earth as we know it'.[17] Although the effects of this disaster will be felt by all of humanity, impoverished people, principally in the global South, will be first and hardest hit.[18] At the same time, economic growth, benefitting (primarily) the global North, and driven, to a great extent, by transnational corporations, is largely responsible for the collapse of the planet's ecosystems.[19] The Anthropocene thus raises the spectre of a global socio-ecological crisis contributing towards grave injustices and profound patterns of differentially distributed vulnerability.[20] We adopt the perspective that regardless of whether or not the Earth is formally determined to

[14] Setzer and Vanhala (n 12) 4.

[15] Jan Zalasiewicz, Mark Williams and Alan Haywood, 'The Anthropocene: A New Epoch of Geological Time' (2011) *Philosophical Transactions of the Royal Society B* 369, 835, 838.

[16] Will Steffen and others, 'Planetary Boundaries: Guiding Human Development on a Changing Planet' (2015) 347(6223) *Science* 736; Anna Grear, 'Deconstructing *Anthropos*: A Critical Legal Reflection on "Anthropocentric" Law and the Anthropocene "Humanity"' (2015) 26 *Law Critique* 225.

[17] Louis J Kotzé, 'Preface: Discomforting Conversations in the Anthropocene' in Louis J Kotzé (ed), *Environmental Law and Governance for the Anthropocene* (Hart Publishing 2017) i, iv. On the concept of planetary boundaries see Steffen and others (n 16).

[18] Carmen Gonzalez, 'Global Justice in the Anthropocene', in Louis J Kotzé (ed) *Environmental Law and Governance for the Anthropocene* (Hart Publishing 2017) 219, 229–31; Rebecca Bratspies, 'Do We Need a Human Right to a Healthy Environment' (2015) 13(1) *Santa Clara Journal of International Law* 31, 34.

[19] Gonzalez (n 18) 227–9; Sally Wheeler, 'The Corporation and the Anthropocene' in Louis J Kotzé (ed), *Environmental Law and Governance for the Anthropocene* (Hart Publishing 2017) 289, 291–7.

[20] Grear (n 16) 227.

have entered into this epoch, the concept of the Anthropocene is of 'heuristic value' as humans endeavour to understand our impact on the Earth, and 'contemplate ways to confront Anthropocene exigencies, and our own destructive behavior'.[21]

As demonstrated by the companion articles in this special issue, scholars have increasingly engaged with the concept of the Anthropocene to reconfigure our understanding of the law in the face of the recognition of humanity's impact upon the Earth,[22] adopting, for instance, ecological law,[23] Earth system law,[24] Earth Trusteeship,[25] and socio-ecological justice,[26] as well as calls for the reconceptualisation of transnational law itself to account for the realities of the Anthropocene[27] in order to do so. We acknowledge the necessity of situating the law in the context of the Anthropocene. Indeed, as Viñualés argues in this issue, '[i]f we call 'law' the conscious or unconscious observance of certain prescriptions of conduct, then, law has never been as fundamental for the Earth system as it is today'.[28] He goes on to argue for the connection of narratives between the concepts of human self-regulation and biospheric self-regulation.[29] This perspective is apposite because how states utilise regulation to govern specific issues is grounded within the existing legal culture and traditions of the particular state, and environmental-economic paradigms expressed within contested concepts such as sustainable development.[30] The Anthropocene thus raises the spectre of a dichotomy between how law *should* be conceived, given the evidence of significant human impacts on the planet, and how it is currently deployed in practice within the existing legal order.[31] A transnational legal methodology, as

---

[21] Louis J Kotzé, 'Six Constitutional Elements for Implementing Environmental Constitutionalism in the Anthropocene' in Erin Daly and James R May (eds), *Implementing Environmental Constitutionalism: Current Global Challenge* (Cambridge University Press 2018) 13, 16.

[22] See eg: Afshin Akhtar-Khavari, 'Restoration and Cooperation for Flourishing Socio-ecological Landscapes' (2020) 11(1–2) *Transnational Legal Theory*, this issue.

[23] Peter Burdon, 'Ecolgocial Law in the Anthropocene' (2020) 11(1–2) *Transnational Legal Theory*, this issue.

[24] Louis J Kotzé, 'The Juridical Implications of the Anthropocene's Earth System Perspective: Towards Earth System Law?' (2020) 11(1–2) *Transnational Legal Theory*, this issue.

[25] Klaus Bosselmann, 'Earth Trusteeship and State Sovereignty: Can They be Reconciled?' (2020) 11(1–2) *Transnational Legal Theory*, this issue.

[26] Melanie Murcott, 'Towards a Social Justice-Oriented Environmental Law Jurisprudence in South Africa' (LLD thesis, North-West University).

[27] Laura Mai, 'Transnational Law for the Anthropocene: Revisiting Jessup's Move from "What?" to "How?"'(2020) 11(1–2) *Transnational Legal Theory*, this issue.

[28] Jorge Viñuales, 'Two Layers of Self-Regulation' (2020) 11(1–2) *Transnational Legal Theory*, this issue, 3.

[29] *Ibid.*

[30] see for example, United Nations, 'Transforming Our World: The 2030 Agenda for Sustainable Development' (2015) A/RES/70/1 online: <https://sustainabledevelopment.un.org/content/documents/21252030%20Agenda%20for%20Sustainable%20Development%20web.pdf>. On the contested nature of sustainable development, see Sam Adelman, 'The Sustainable Development Goals, Anthropocentrism and Neoliberalism' in Duncan French and Louis J Kotzé (eds), *Sustainable Development Goals: Law, Theory and Implementation* (Edward Elgar Publishing 2018) 15–40.

[31] For example of humanity's impact on the Earth in this issue: Pierre Cloutier de Repentigny, 'To the Anthropocene and Beyond: The Role of Law in Decimating and Protecting of Marine Life' (2020) 11

discussed next, takes into consideration the wider actors involved within the governance of particular issues, such as fracking, to understand what is happening in reality, while also providing the analytical space to view the socio-ecological problems posed by fracking and its regulation in the context of the Anthropocene.

Jessup, in his 1956 Storrs Lectures, adopted the concept of transnational law to account for developments in the global arena that were not sufficiently reflected in international law or the law of nations.[32] He proposed this approach as a means to also take into account 'other rules which do not wholly fit into [the] categories' of public and private international law.[33] This early reconceptualisation of what constitutes 'law', has seen a burgeoning of literature dedicated to diverging perspectives of what this theoretical account could entail[34] while also applying this lens to analyse different fields of law.[35] For instance, transnational environmental law scholarship has adopted an approach that takes into account the plurality of state and non-state actors involved in environmental regulation and decision-making.[36] According to Lin, shifting from 'international law to transnational environmental law ... may provide us with a more nuanced approach as we consider how we should deal with the effects of global human-induced

---

(1–2) *Transnational Legal Theory*, this issue; Michael Hennessy Picard and Tina Biegi, 'The (in)Visibility of Transnational Waste Law in the Anthropocene' (2020) 11(1–2) *Transnational Legal Theory*, this issue.

32 Phillip Jessup, *Transnational Law* (Yale University Press 1956, 2).

33 *Ibid*, 136.

34 eg see: Zumbansen, 'Transnational Law, Evolving' (n 5); Craig Scott, 'Transnational Law as a Proto-Concept: Three Conceptions' (2009) 10(6–7) *German Law Journal* 859; Harold Hongju Koh, 'Transnational Legal Process after September 11th' (2004) 22 *Berkeley Journal of International Law* 337; Terence C Halliday and Gregory Shaffer, 'Transnational Legal Orders', *Transnational Legal Orders* (Cambridge University Press 2015); Kenneth Abbott and Duncan Snidal, 'Strengthening International Regulation Through Transnational New Governance: Overcoming the Orchestration Deficit' (2009) 42(2) *Vanderbilt Journal of Transnational Law* 501; In the context of climate change see eg: Kenneth Abbott, 'Transnational Regime Complex for Climate Change' (2012) 30 *Environment and Planning C: Politics and Space* 571; Harriet Bulkeley and others, *Transnational Climate Change Governance* (Cambridge University Press 2014); Philipp Pattberg and Johannes Stripple, 'Beyond the Public and Private Divide: Remapping Transnational Climate Governance in the 21st Century' (2008) 8 *International Environmental Agreements* 367; Gregory Shaffer and Daniel Bodansky, 'Transnationalism, Unilateralism and International Law' (2012) 1(1) *Transnational Environmental Law* 31.

35 For example: investment law: Thomas Schultz, *Transnational Legality: Stateless Law and International Arbitration* (Oxford University Press 2014); International human rights law: Sigrun I Skogly and Mark Gibney, 'Transnational Human rights Obligations' (2002) 24(3) *Human Rights Quarterly* 781; Corporate governance: Peer Zumbansen, 'Neither "Public" Nor "Private", "National" Nor "International": Transnational Corporate Governance from a Legal Pluralist Perspective' (2011) 38(1) *Journal of Law and Society* 50.

36 Eg see: Thijs Etty and others, '[T]he Maturing of Transnational Environmental Law' (2017) 6 *Transnational Environmental Law* 193; Thijs Etty and others, 'Expanding the Scope of Transnational Environmental Law' (2017) 6 *Transnational Environmental Law* 391; Veerle Heyvaert and Thijs Etty, 'Introducing Transnational Environmental Law' (2012) 1 *Transnational Environmental Law* 1; Jolene Lin, 'The Emergence of Transnational Environmental Law' in Louis Kotze (ed), *Environmental Law and Governance for the Anthropocene* (Hart 2017); Kenneth Abbott, 'Strengthening the Transnational Regime Complex for Climate Change' (2013) 3(1) *Transnational Environmental law* 57; Emily Webster, 'Transnational Legal Processes, the EU and RED II: Strengthening the Global Governance of Bioenergy' (2020) 29(1) *Review of European Community & International Environmental Law* 86.

climate change, including how we promote sustainable energy use'.[37] She goes on to argue that transnational law offers a normative framework that moves beyond the state, and embraces the possibility of multi-level and multi-actor governance.[38] This transnational approach to environmental law is consonant with the Anthropocene imagery, and an appreciation that environmental problems and their solutions are increasingly complex, requiring multifaceted responses.[39]

Precisely because of the diverging perspectives that have emerged regarding transnational law, the development and use of this conception of law is fraught with contestation.[40] This complexity invites us to clearly identify exactly how we are using it. Rather than viewing transnational law as an emerging field, Zumbansen has urged its use as a methodological lens that identifies the actors involved in norm generation—be they state or non-state—the processes by which they are generated, and the nature of the legal norms themselves.[41] By doing so, he asserts, we shift perspective away from a state-centric view of the law to take account of the influence wielded by non-state actors.[42] We adopt Zumbansen's approach to transnational law for purposes of our analysis of *Normandien Farms HC* and *Stern SCA* to consider the actors, norms and processes involved in response to the socio-ecological risks of fracking in the Karoo. This approach allows us to trace the variety of actors involved either directly or indirectly in the regulation of fracking in South Africa. The analysis unveils the effect of non-state actors on the regulation of fracking within South Africa, the implications of the turn to litigation in South Africa for other jurisdictions, and contribution to the development of global climate governance. Furthermore, the analysis exposes the ways in which non-state actors can organise themselves in learning networks in order to reach common goals.

3. The Karoo, an ecologically significant site of contestation amongst state and non-state actors

There are believed to be vast shale gas reserves in the Karoo, a region that covers much of South Africa's land area.[43] As 'the only place in the world

---

[37] Lin (n 34) 330.
[38] *Ibid*, 331.
[39] *Ibid*.
[40] Peer Zumbansen, 'Can Transnational Law Be Critical? Reflections on a Contested Idea, Field and Method' in Emilios Christodoulidis, Ruth Dukes and Marco Goldoni (eds), *Research Handbook on Critical Legal Theory* (Edward Elgar 2019).
[41] Zumbansen, 'Defining the Space of Transnational Law: Legal Theory, Global Governance, and Legal Pluralism' (n 5); Zumbansen, 'Transnational Law, Evolving' (n 5).
[42] Zumbansen, 'Transnational Law, Evolving' (n 5) 899.
[43] David Morris, Bruce Rubidge and Jan Glazewski, 'The Internationally Significant Karoo Archaeology and Palaeontology Record: Short-Term Threats and Long-Term Responsibilities' in Jan Glazewski and Surina Esterhuyse (eds), *Hydraulic Fracturing in the Karoo* (Juta and Company 2016) 302.

with an extended fossil record from 300 to 180 million years ago of the early evolution of tortoises, dinosaurs and mammals',[44] the geology of the Karoo is internationally significant and unique.[45] Biogeographically, the Karoo comprises two biomes, the Succulent Karoo, which experiences winter-rainfall, and the Nama-Karoo, which experiences summer-rainfall.[46] The Succulent Karoo has 'unparalleled' plant biodiversity, and is an internationally recognised biodiversity hotspot.[47]

The prospect of fracking in the Karoo is evocative of the Anthropocene imagery, not least because by increasing seismicity levels, fracking will disturb the geology of the Karoo, and leave behind a lasting human-induced geological imprint.[48] For instance:

> The rocks of the Karoo Basin preserve one of the most remarkable and extended sequences of terrestrial tetrapod development from the Permian to the Jurassic and provide the most complete documentation of the evolutionary development of early mammals in the world. In addition they provide a record of the evolving palaeoenvironments in which these changes in biodiversity occurred, and record the devastating effects of the "mother of all mass extinctions" ... and the subsequent biotic recovery.[49]

Seismic activity which might result from fracking could thus damage important fossil records.

Moreover, fracking is predicted to cause immense socio-ecological harm, and to intensify climate change, including by causing air and water pollution and destroying biodiversity.[50] In the Succulent Karoo, for example, succulent plants can withstand only a limited range of environmental conditions and are therefore limited to those particular conditions. Any environmental changes could therefore be severely detrimental to these plant species.[51] Bird, mammal and reptile diversity is also high, with critically endangered, De

---

44 Morris (n 43) 303.

45 See for example, Bruce S Rubidge, 'Re-Uniting Lost Continents – Fossil Reptiles from ancient Karoo and Their Wanderlust' (2005) *South African Journal of Geology* 108, 135; and Morris (n 43).

46 Joh R Henschel, M Timm Hoffman and Cherryl Walker, 'Introduction to the Karoo Special Issue: Trajectories of Change in the Anthropocene' (2018) 35(3–4) *African Journal of Range & Forage Science* 151, 151–52.

47 United Nations Educational, Scientific and Cultural Organisation, 'Succulent Karoo Protected Areas' online: <https://whc.unesco.org/en/tentativelists/5458/>.

48 Morris (n 43) 315, Esterhuyse (n 6) 421–22 and 424.

49 Bruce Rubridge, 'The Karoo, A Geological and Palaeontological Superlative: Economic Potential of Deep History' (2009) online: <https://www.researchgate.net/publication/242120361_THE_KAROO_A_GEOLOGICAL_AND_PALAEONTOLOGICAL_SUPERLATIVE_ECONOMIC_POTENTIAL_OF_DEEP_HISTORY> accessed 2 May 2020.

50 Surina Esterhuyse, Fanie de Lange and Jan Glazewski, 'Potential Impact of Unconventional Oil and Gas Extraction on Karoo Aquifers' in Jan Glazewski and Surina Esterhuyse (eds), *Hydraulic Fracturing in the Karoo* (Juta and Company 2016) 206; Marinda Avenant and others 'Potential Impact of Unconventional Gas Mining on Surface Water Systems of the Karoo' in Jan Glazewski and Surina Esterhuyse (eds), *Hydraulic Fracturing in the Karoo* (Juta and Company 2016) 222; Simon W Todd and others 'The Potential Impacts of Fracking on Biodiversity of the Karoo Basin, South Africa' in Jan Glazewski and Surina Esterhuyse (eds), *Hydraulic Fracturing in the Karoo* (Juta and Company 2016) 278.

51 'Succulent Karoo – Species | CEPF' (*CEPF*) online: <https://www.cepf.net/our-work/biodiversity-hotspots/succulent-karoo/species> accessed 2 May 2020.

Winton's golden mole and riverine rabbit particularly vulnerable to environmental changes such as those caused by fracking.[52]

The Karoo is sparsely populated with around one million people living in the whole region. In the Succulent Karoo 90% of the land is used for sheep grazing,[53] while around 100,000 people work in agriculture across the whole of the Karoo.[54] Poverty is widespread in the Karoo. For instance, in 2011 Statistics South Africa reported that in the Prince Albert Local Municipality, an area located in the western part of the Karoo with a population of around 130,000 people, more than 19% were unemployed, only around 63% of households had a flush toilet connected to sewerage, and approximately 30% of the population did not have access to piped water inside their dwelling.[55] These figures are not likely to have improved in the last 10 years. A Statistics South Africa study on poverty trends in South Africa between 2006 and 2015 reveals that poverty was on the rise, with over 30.4 million South Africans (more than half of the population) living in poverty, mainly black Africans, women and people from rural areas.[56] Many of South Africa's poor are 'water poor', in that they 'regularly experience insufficient access to water [and] inevitably also suffer from myriad associated consequences, including problems relating to health, as well as pressures on finance and time'.[57] As Cooper pointed out in 2017, 'a significant proportion of South Africans still do not have access to sufficient water, 24 years after the formal end of apartheid'.[58] The nature and extent of poverty in South Africa is further inextricably linked to historical land alienation arising from conquest and past and current racial oppression, as Mkhize illustrates in the context of the town of Cradock in the Karoo and the tenure insecurity experienced by farm workers and farm dwellers.[59] As a result of South Africa's problematic history, around 71% of privately-owned farmland (roughly 26 million hectares) is still owned by white people, who make up less than 10% of the country's population.[60]

---

[52] *Ibid.*

[53] 'Succulent Karoo – Threats | CEPF' (*CEPF*) online: <https://www.cepf.net/our-work/biodiversity-hotspots/succulent-karoo/threats> accessed 2 May 2020.

[54] Julienne du Toit, 'Karoo by Numbers' (*Karoo Space*, 7 October 2014) online: <https://karoospace.co.za/karoo-numbers/> accessed 2 May 2020.

[55] Statistics South Africa, 'Prince Albert' online: <https://www.statssa.gov.za/?page_id=993&id=prince-albert-municipality> accessed 26 May 2020.

[56] Statistics South Africa, 'Poverty Trends in South Africa: An Examination of Absolute Poverty Between 2006 and 2015' online: <https://www.statssa.gov.za/publications/Report-03-10-06/Report-03-10-062015.pdf> 2017, accessed 26 May 2020.

[57] Nathan J Cooper, 'Grassroots Responses to Poverty, and the Limitations of a Right to Water in South Africa and Malawi' (2017) 23 *South African Journal of Environmental Law and Policy* 31, 34, 67–68.

[58] *Ibid*, 34, 36–38.

[59] Nomalanga Mkhize, 'Game Farm Conversions and the Land Question: Unpacking Present Contradictions and Historical Continuities in Farm Dwellers' Tenure Insecurity in Cradock' (2014) 32(2) *Journal of Contemporary African Studies* 207–19.

[60] South African Institute of Race Relations, 'Who Owns the Land? A Critique of the State of Land Audit' (March 2018) online: <https://irr.org.za/reports/occasional-reports/files/who-owns-the-land-26-03-

Land ownership and security of tenure generally translates into wealth and better living conditions for white farmers.[61]

One of the biggest threats of fracking in the Karoo is to the extensive agricultural production, given that it is a water stressed area[62] in which:

> the dryer central and western parts of the [Karoo] farming communities rely exclusively on boreholes for the provisioning of water for humans and livestock consumption, elsewhere both surface and groundwater are used for livestock and irrigation purposes. [Fracking] poses potential risks to both the quantity and agricultural usability of surface and groundwater resources.[63]

Fracking is an extremely water-intensive activity that can result in competition for access to water.[64] In addition, fracking can result in contamination of water resources.[65] The potential impacts of fracking on the already scarce water resources in the Karoo are of concern for wealthy farm-owners, whose operations could be threatened, but more particularly for 'water poor' communities, who fear that fracking could jeopardise their already limited access to water and their subsistence farming activities, and thus their water and food security.[66]

Fracking as a means to generate energy from shale gas, a fossil fuel, is reported to result in high greenhouse gas (GHG) emissions, especially relative to the generation of solar and wind energy, and thus represents a climate change mitigation challenge with which the South African government ought to grapple, as discussed in more detail below.[67] According to the Report of the UN Special Rapporteur on Extreme Poverty and Human Rights, addressing climate change requires 'decoupling improvements in

---

2018.pdf> accessed 24 May 2020. As the study points out, the farmland owned by whites makes up approximately 21.9% of the total extent of South Africa.

61 Kalie Pauw and others, 'A Profile of the Northern Cape Province: Demographics, Poverty, Inequality and Unemployment' (Background Paper Series – Provide Project 2005: 1(3)). The 2005 study found that in the Northern Cape Province, which to a considerable extent forms part of the Karoo, there is 'virtually no poverty among White and Asian people', but '53.3% of Coloured and 58.7% of African people are classified as poor'.

62 Esterhuyse (n 6) 421; Nola Redelinghuys, 'Effects on Communities: The Social Fabric, Local Livelihoods and the Social Psyche' in Jan Glazewski and Surina Esterhuyse (eds), *Hydraulic Fracturing in the Karoo* (Juta and Company 2016) 345.

63 Selwyn Adam and others 'Summary for Policy-Makers' in Bob Scholes and others (eds) *Shale Gas Development in the Central Karoo: A Scientific Assessment of the Opportunities and Risks* (CSIR 2016) 40.

64 Hennie Coetzee and Louis J Kotzé, 'Shale Gas Development and Water in South Africa: Regulatory Aspects' in Erkki J Hollo (ed) *Water Resource Management and the Law* (Edward Elgar Publishing 2017) 369, 377–9.

65 *Ibid*, 369, 379–86.

66 See for example: Saliem Fakir, 'Groups Opposed to Fracking in the Karoo Must Forge Stronger Links' *SACSIS* (12 March 2015) online: <https://sacsis.org.za/site/article/2308>; 'Karoo Communities Fear Long-Term Effects of Fracking' *Legalbrief Environmental* (2019) online: <https://legalbrief.co.za/diary/legalbrief-environmental/story/karoo-communities-fear-long-term-effects-of-fracking/print/>.

67 Jeremy Wakeford, 'The South African Energy Context' in Jan Glazewski and Suria Esterhuyse (eds) *Hydraulic Fracturing in the Karoo: Critical Legal and Environmental Perspectives* (Juta and Company 2019) 157–63.

economic well-being from fossil fuel emissions'.[68] The Report indicates that failing to adopt appropriate mitigation measures will not only have 'devastating consequences for people in poverty', but will also 'pull vast numbers into poverty'.[69] This observation is apt in the context of fracking in the Karoo, since it is predicted that jobs created by fracking will likely be offset by job losses in other sectors such as agriculture and tourism.[70] Job losses and changes to the environment are also predicted to result in disruption of social cohesion as well as a loss of a sense of place, which are likely to intensify conditions of poverty for poor and vulnerable people in the Karoo.[71] The impacts of climate change on the Karoo, including higher temperatures, longer and more frequent droughts, and general desertification,[72] will also impact upon the poor first and hardest.

In spite of the socio-ecological risks associated with fracking in the Karoo, the South African government, acting through the Minister of Mineral Resources and the authority designated to perform various functions on his behalf, the South African Agency for Promotion of Petroleum and Exploitation SOC Ltd (also known as the Petroleum Agency of South Africa or PASA), is in favour of exploiting the shale gas reserves.[73] The government, while responsible for authorising and regulating fracking in the Karoo, must grapple with competing priorities. South Africa is a party to the Paris Agreement and its first National Determined Contribution (NDC) under that instrument sets out that it is trying to balance climate change mitigation with developmental needs 'with overriding priorities to eliminate poverty and eradicate inequality'.[74] The NDC highlights that currently South Africa is dependent on coal, such that transitioning to natural gas may be consistent with its commitments.[75] South Africa as a 'Developing State' is yet to reach its peak GHG emissions, which it estimates will occur between 2020 and 2025.[76] However, the development of fracking does not seem consistent with this goal

[68] 'UN Expert Condemns Failure to Address Impact of Climate Change on Poverty' (*United Nations Human Rights Office of the High Commissioner*, 25 June 2019) online: <https://www.ohchr.org/EN/NewsEvents/Pages/DisplayNews.aspx?NewsID=24735&LangID=E>.

[69] *Ibid.*

[70] Esterhuyse (n 6) 421; Nola Redelinghuys, 'Effects on Communities: The Social Fabric, Local Livelihoods and the Social Psyche' in Jan Glazewski and Surina Esterhuyse (eds), *Hydraulic Fracturing in the Karoo* (Juta and Company 2016) 345.

[71] Esterhuyse (n 6) 421; Loretta Feris, 'Making Legal Sense of a "Sense of Place" in the Karoo' in Jan Glazewski and Surina Esterhuyse (eds), *Hydraulic Fracturing in the Karoo* (Juta and Company 2016) 395. Surina Esterhuyse and others (n 50); Marinda Avenant and others (n 50).

[72] M Timm Hoffman and others, 'Drought, Climate Change and Vegetation Response in the Succulent Karoo, South Africa' (2009) 105(1–2) *South African Journal of Science* 54–60.

[73] Wakeford (n 67) 142, 153–54.

[74] 'South Africa's Intended Nationally Determined Contribution (INDC)' 2, online: <https://www4.unfccc.int/sites/ndcstaging/PublishedDocuments/South%20Africa%20First/South%20Africa.pdf> accessed 6 November 2019; Paris Agreement (adopted 12 December 2015, entered into force 4 November 2016) FCCC/CP/2015/10/Add.

[75] *Ibid.*

[76] *Ibid*, 7.

due to the release of methane from its extraction, and the carbon dioxide emissions associated with the extraction infrastructure and its combustion for energy.[77] This is especially so given the renewable energy resources—sunlight and wind in particular—that are at the disposal of the State.[78] Although the development of solar and wind farms would also require vast infrastructure development to transmit and store the energy produced, by developing the fracking industry in the Karoo, emissions associated with fracking may be 'locked in' for much longer than the NDC provides for emissions growth. Furthermore, the gas would need to replace coal domestically rather than be exported out of the South Africa. Balancing these competing priorities and controlling the actions of private companies once they have extracted the shale gas, therefore presents a highly complex and uncertain picture that may be inconsistent with international climate commitments.

Notwithstanding its international climate commitments, the state has regulated the extractive industry through the Minerals and Petroleum Resources Development Act 28 of 2000 (MPRDA), and granted exploration permits to various transnational corporations, thus allowing them to assess the viability of extracting shale gas. The corporations include Shell South Africa Upstream BV, a subsidiary of Royal Dutch Shell PLC (Shell), Bundu Gas and Oil Exploration (Pty) Ltd (Bundu), Falcon Oil and Gas Ltd (Falcon), Rhino Oil and Gas Exploration South Africa (Pty) Ltd (Rhino Oil and Gas), a subsidiary of Rhino Resources Ltd (Rhino Resources). The state and these transnational corporations are in favour of fracking on the grounds that it will facilitate economic development and energy security, including for the benefit of the poor.[79] Shell, for instance, has stated that the extraction of shale gas represents 'a public good in the form of abundant supplies of clean energy and potential significant local job opportunities'.[80]

Collectively, these transnational corporations hold a great deal of political and economic capital in South Africa. They offer significant development opportunities for the state, including by investing in South Africa and thereby providing jobs and other economic benefits to the country, among other things through income generated from the production of natural gas.[81] They are in powerful positions to influence the state's energy policies by 'locking in' fossil fuels for decades to come. The energy security and the

---

77 Howarth (n 4).

78 Anna Pegels, 'Renewable Energy in South Africa: Potentials, Barriers and Options for Support' (2010) 38 (9) *Energy Policy* 4945.

79 Esterhuyse, (n 6) 420–21.

80 Willem EgginkDeur Jan, 'Shale Gas – Myths and Facts' (South Africa, November 2011) online: <https://www.shell.co.za/about-us/projects-and-sites/the-karoo/Karoo-communications/_jcr_content/par/textimage.stream/1464105376598/9ad866e2a52520b122a46b699a8b1f719527a00a/karroo-comms-shalegas.pdf>.

81 'Econometrix Karoo Shale Gas Report' online: <https://www.shell.co.za/about-us/projects-and-sites/the-karoo/econometrix-karoo-shale-gas-report.html> accessed 24 January 2020.

alleviation of poverty that these companies promise is often perceived to outweigh GHG reductions through the development of clean energy, especially given the costs involved with scaling up their use. Non-state actors are therefore potentially the 'David' to the transnational fossil fuel companies and South African government's 'Goliath', as we will illustrate with reference to *Normandien Farms HC* and *Stern SCA*. In this role, non-state actors can play a pivotal role in restraining environmentally and socially damaging activities in an area of particular vulnerability.

Local communities in the Karoo have expressed concerns that short-term economic benefits could be far outweighed by negative long-term socio-ecological impacts.[82] Some community members have joined forces with international non-governmental organisations (NGOs), scientists and lawyers in an attempt to prevent, or at least improve the regulation of fracking, including, with some success, through the courts.[83] Alongside the activism of local communities, NGOs and lawyers, price decreases in the international market for gas have also played a part in slowing down transnational corporations, including Shell's, campaign to begin fracking in the Karoo.[84] As discussed above, the local communities opposing fracking represent a diverse range of interests and are by no means homogenous, as '[d]ivisions along the fault-lines of class, race and ethnicity are strongly evident, as are severe social challenges to human well-being'.[85] Further, the ability of some community members to participate in efforts to oppose fracking is no doubt hampered by, among other things, the area's 'aridity and sparse population' (of fewer than a million people), which 'have rendered it a politically and economically marginal region of South Africa, despite its spatial extent'.[86] For instance, although poor communities oppose fracking on the basis that it could jeopardise their already limited access to water and their subsistence farming activities, and thus their water and food security,[87] their interests and concerns do not emerge from the litigation we discuss. As we discuss below, instead the interests of wealthy white farmers who are land owners in the Karoo are represented, and seem to have driven the litigation that resulted in *Normandien Farms HC* and *Stern SCA*, largely to the exclusion of those of poor communities.

---

82 Legalbrief Environmental 2019 (n 66).

83 As we discuss with reference to *Normandien Farms HC* and *Stern SCA* below. 'Treasure Karoo Action Group – Home' online: <https://www.treasurethekaroo.co.za/> accessed 23 January 2020; 'AgriSA – Home' <https://www.agrisa.co.za/> accessed 23 January 2020. 'SAFCEI – About us' <https://safcei.org/about-us/> accessed 3 March 2020.

84 Joe Brock, 'Shell Pulls Back from Shale in South Africa' *Reuters* (16 March 2015) online: <https://uk.reuters.com/article/uk-shell-shale-idUKKBN0MC0G920150316> accessed 23 January 2020.

85 Henschel, Hoffman and Walker (n 46) 152.

86 *Ibid.*

87 See for example: Fakir (n 66).

4. Climate litigation and the Karoo

In *Normandien Farms HC*, the owner of various farms in the Karoo instigated judicial review proceedings on administrative law grounds to challenge the acceptance of a permit to explore for shale gas by PASA. The exploration permit application was submitted by and for the benefit of Rhino Oil and Gas in terms of section 79 of the MPRDA, but without having given Normandien prior notice as required by the Act. On 3 May 2017, the High Court found that the failure by Rhino Oil and Gas to comply with the notice requirements of the MPRDA in the decision-making process rendered PASA's acceptance of the permit application invalid, and the court thus set the acceptance aside.[88]

Rhino Oil and Gas is a subsidiary of Rhino Resources, a transnational corporation based in the British Virgin Islands, that claims to be 'one of the largest holders of both onshore and offshore oil and gas rights in South Africa with over twenty five million acres granted by [PASA]'.[89] In terms of the Corporate Social Responsibility Policy of Rhino Resources, it is required to 'strive to promote environmental stewardship' in areas that they work, to 'minimize environmental impacts', and to 'comply with all relevant local, national and international laws and regulations in countries where [they] operate'.

Normandien conducts timber farming on several of its properties, and had recently established a water bottling plant on another property, representing a R40 million capital investment.[90] Its litigation was thus motivated primarily by economic concerns, and the desire to protect its land ownership rights.[91] The court was sympathetic to Normandien's rights as land owner, and recognised that the MPRDA had 'corroded the right of ownership of land'.[92] For the court, these ownership rights rendered compliance with the MPRDA's consultation process essential in the context of the application by Rhino Oil and Gas for an exploration permit.[93] The court noted that these procedures require 'communities being informed and consulted on any mining activities applied for by mining companies (such as [Rhino Oil and Gas]) in their area'.[94] Consultation would enable good faith attempts to accommodate affected parties whose rights would be interfered with by mining activities.[95]

88 *Normandien Farms HC* [29].
89 'Rhino Resources Ltd' online: <https://www.rhinoresourcesltd.com> accessed 2 February 2020.
90 *Normandien Farms HC* [2] and [26].
91 *Normandien Farms HC* [2], [25]–[26] and [30].
92 *Normandien Farms HC* [30].
93 *Ibid.*
94 *Ibid.*
95 *Ibid.*

Interestingly, the court and Normandien framed *Normandien Farms HC* as an administrative law case in which a procedural error committed by PASA had hampered public participation. There is no indication in the judgment that the court was scrutinising the validity of conduct that could ultimately lead to fracking, and there are no direct or indirect references to climate change. News coverage of the judgment revealed its broader environmental significance in the context of fracking in the Karoo.[96] The court made no more than a passing comment that obliquely links the granting of an exploration permit and harm to the environment by acknowledging Normandien's fear that if the exploration right were to be granted, it could impact upon Normandien's planned water bottling operation and 'the water extracted from the earth'.[97] For these reasons, *Normandien Farms HC* would not fall within narrow understandings of climate litigation. Nonetheless, by setting aside the acceptance of the permit application of Rhino Oil and Gas, the court's order in *Normandien Farms HC* had the effect of requiring the company to start the application process from scratch, and delayed the possibility of exploring for, and ultimately exploiting shale gas in the Karoo. Two years later, on 31 May 2019, the Supreme Court of Appeal upheld an appeal by Rhino Oil and Gas against the judgment and order of the High Court on the basis that Normandien could not review the mere acceptance by PASA of the application for an exploration right.[98] According to the Supreme Court of Appeal:

> As a general rule, a challenge to the validity of an exercise of public power that is not final in effect is premature. An application to review the action will not be ripe, and cannot succeed on that account.[99]

Subsequently, the Constitutional Court found that the litigation had become moot, as Rhino Oil and Gas withdrew its exploration right application on 24 July 2019, and no longer intends to pursue fracking in the Karoo.[100] Even though it dismissed Normandien's appeal against the Supreme Court of Appeal's judgment on the basis of mootness, the Constitutional Court emphasised that should Rhino Oil and Gas wish to apply for an exploration right in the future it would have to comply with the MPRDA's procedural requirements.[101] The Constitutional Court also found that the Supreme Court of Appeal's reasoning should not be viewed as undermining 'the fundamental importance of public participation in the process for an exploration right

[96] See for example, Sipho Kings, 'Court Throws Out Fracking Application for KZN' *Mail & Guardian* (8 May 2017) online: <https://mg.co.za/article/2017-05-08-00-court-throws-out-fracking-application/> accessed 2 March 2020.
[97] *Normandien Farms HC* [26].
[98] *Normandien Farms SCA* [32]–[35].
[99] *Normandien Farms SCA* [33].
[100] *Normandien Farms CC* [27], [30], [46]–[58].
[101] *Normandien Farms CC* [54]–[55].

application'.[102] The value of *Normandien Farms HC* is that it demonstrated to Rhino Oil and Gas and Rhino Resources (and by extension other fossil fuel companies) the importance of compliance with national laws regulating the approval process for fracking and in particular, public participation. By emphasising the value of public participation, the court arguably protected the interests not only of Normandien as a land owner who wished to be given proper notice before PASA accepted the application of Rhino Oil and Gas to explore for shale gas, but also, in a theoretical or abstract sense, the interests of the broader community, including poor and vulnerable people who might wish to participate in the decision-making process from the outset. Rhino Resources was further arguably held to the standards of corporate social responsibility that it set for itself in its own policy. Should Rhino Resources wish to pursue fracking in the Karoo in the future, the court's approach in *Normandien* makes it plain that comprehensive public participation will be required, which could in turn ensure that the interests of all members of the community, including poor and vulnerable people, are heard and addressed.

Stern SCA involved a challenge by civil society actors against the promulgation of Regulations for Petroleum Exploration and Production, 2015 (the Petroleum Regulations). The Petroleum Regulations were promulgated by the Minister of Mineral Resources, who purported to exercise regulation-making powers conferred by section 107 of the MPRDA. The purpose of the Petroleum Regulations was to augment the regulatory regime governing fracking in South Africa. Extensive governmental studies had revealed significant gaps in the regulatory regime.[103] John Douglas Stern (on behalf of the Stern Family Trust), together with several other farm owners in the Karoo, instituted a review application to challenge the promulgation of the Petroleum Regulations in the High Court, Grahamstown.[104] Meanwhile, two civil society actors, Treasure the Karoo Action Group (TKAG) and Afriforum, instituted a similar application in the High Court, Pretoria.[105] Whilst the application launched by Stern and others was successful, the application launched by TKAG and Afriforum was unsuccessful. *Stern SCA* was a consolidated appeal to the Supreme Court of Appeal in respect of both matters.

At issue in *Stern SCA* was not whether fracking ought to proceed in South Africa, but the narrow question of whether the correct authority had promulgated the Petroleum Regulations. Therefore *Stern SCA* was, like *Normandien Farms HC*, framed as an administrative law case. However, in *Stern SCA* the environmental context of the litigation was far more apparent. For instance, the court noted that:

---

102 *Normandien Farms CC* [54].
103 *Stern SCA* [12]–[15].
104 *Stern HC.*
105 *TKAG HC.*

> Hydraulic fracturing may have a variety of adverse effects on the environment ... Access roads and manoeuvring space for trucks would be required. This would generate dust and noise. Hydraulic fracturing may also have seismic effects. Large quantities of water would be used. Waste water containing chemicals or heavy or radioactive metals would have to be disposed of.
>
> It is common cause, however, that the major potentially adverse impacts of hydraulic fracturing on the environment are the emission of pollutants and the contamination of surface water and groundwater. This may be caused by uncontrolled gas or fluid flows arising from blowouts or spills, linking of hydrogeological systems, well failures (corrosion of the casing or cementing failure), leaking of fracturing fluids and uncontrolled waste water discharge. The contamination of groundwater in a water-scarce area may, in particular, be disastrous.[106]

Further, *Stern SCA* was aimed at improving the regulation of the impacts of fracking, including GHG emissions, so as to give effect to South Africa's constitutional right to an environment not harmful to health or well-being.[107] *Stern SCA* therefore potentially falls within at least some (broader) understandings of climate litigation. The Supreme Court of Appeal reasoned that the Minister of Mineral Resources was not authorised by the MPRDA to promulgate the Petroleum Regulations, and that the Minister of Environmental Affairs was the proper authority to do so, acting in terms of powers conferred upon her by the National Environmental Management Act 107 of 1998.[108] Accordingly, the Supreme Court of Appeal found that the Minister of Mineral Resources had acted unlawfully, and set aside the Petroleum Regulations. Although not forming part of its order, the court remarked in conclusion that 'the ... argument that exploration for petroleum by hydraulic fracturing should not take place at all before it is lawfully regulated, is compelling'.[109]

Although *Stern SCA* was resolved with reference to a narrow administrative law issue, it has had significant implications for the development of fracking in South Africa. The proposed fracking activities of Shell, Bundu and Falcon were brought to a halt as a result of the uncertainty created by the litigation,[110] and no fracking has taken place following the setting aside of the Petroleum Regulations.[111] Shell's involvement is particularly intriguing, given its status as a one of a very small number of transnational fossil fuel companies that has (through investor action) made certain commitments to

106 *Stern SCA* [7]–[8].
107 *Stern SCA* [42]–[43].
108 *Stern SCA* [48].
109 *Stern SCA* [52].
110 *Stern SCA* [16].
111 Tshegofatso Mathe, 'Gwede Keeps Options Open Despite Anti-Fracking Ruling' *Mail & Guardian* (12 July 2019) online: <https://mg.co.za/article/2019-07-12-00-gwede-keeps-options-open-despite-anti-fracking-ruling/> accessed 10 March 2020.

climate mitigation, which seem at first glance to be inconsistent with its efforts to frack in the Karoo.[112] Shell had lobbied for fracking in the Karoo for over a decade, and despite scaling down (in reaction to the fluctuating global gas market), the team dedicated to this mission is still active. However, Shell also committed to climate action as part of the Climate 100+,[113] introduced climate risk disclosure, energy transition reports,[114] and has expressed an ambition to reduce its net carbon emissions by 50% by 2050 with 'executive pay linked, in part, to this target'[115] and has publicised its ambition to reach net zero GHG emissions by 2050.[116] While it is making these commitments on the one hand, on the other the company 'believes' that GHG emissions will not need to be eliminated until 2070, despite scientific consensus that this should be 2050 at the latest,[117] is promoting natural gas as a 'low carbon alternative' to oil and coal, and has several shale gas assets around the world.[118] Indeed, more recently, concerns have been raised regarding Shell's climate ambition with asset manager Sarasin & Partners divesting around 20% of its shares in protest of a failure to meet the 2°C global temperature target of the Paris Agreement.[119] Establishing new fracking sites, rather than only operating existing ones, seems inconsistent with both Shell's (albeit rather weak) commitment to the Paris Agreement collective targets, and the position of several of its large investors who are concerned

---

[112] Andrew Ward, 'Shell Faces Shareholder Push on Climate Change Goals' *Financial Times* (25 March 2018) online: <https://www.ft.com/content/fae8e478-2eba-11e8-9b4b-bc4b9f08f381>; Shell, 'Shell Energy Transition Report' online: <https://www.shell.com/energy-and-innovation/the-energy-future/shell-energy-transition-report/_jcr_content/par/toptasks.stream/1524757699226/3f2ad7f01e2181c302cdc453c5642c77acb48ca3/web-shell-energy-transition-report.pdf> accessed 24 January 2020; Damian Carrington, 'Shell Urges Shareholders to Accept Climate Resolution' *The Guardian* (29 January 2015) online: <https://www.theguardian.com/environment/2015/jan/29/shell-urges-shareholders-to-accept-climate-change-resolution> accessed 17 August 2019.

[113] 'About Us' (*Climate Action 100+*, 2 July 2018) online: <https://climateaction100.wordpress.com/about-us/> accessed 24 January 2020.

[114] Shell (n 111).

[115] 'Shell's Net Carbon Footprint Ambition: Frequently Asked Questions' online: <https://www.shell.com/energy-and-innovation/the-energy-future/what-is-shells-net-carbon-footprint-ambition/faq.html> accessed 24 January 2020.

[116] 'Shell's Ambition to Be a Net-Zero Emissions Energy Business' online: <https://www.shell.com/energy-and-innovation/the-energy-future/shells-ambition-to-be-a-net-zero-emissions-energy-business.html> accessed 17 April 2020.

[117] Valérie Masson-Delmotte and others (eds), 'IPCC, 2018: Summary for Policymakers', *Global Warming of 1.5°C. An IPCC Special Report on the Impacts of Global Warming of 1.5°C Above Pre-Industrial Levels and Related Global Greenhouse Gas Emission Pathways, in the Context of Strengthening the Global Response to the Threat of Climate Change, Sustainable Development, and Efforts to Eradicate Poverty* (World Meteorological Organization 2018); IPCC, 'Climate Change 2014: Synthesis Report Summary for Policymakers' (World Meteorological Organization 2015) online: <https://www.ipcc.ch/site/assets/uploads/2018/02/AR5_SYR_FINAL_SPM.pdf>.

[118] 'Shell's Net Carbon Footprint Ambition: Frequently Asked Questions' (n 114); 'Tight and Shale Gas' online: <https://www.shell.com/energy-and-innovation/natural-gas/tight-and-shale-gas.html> accessed 24 January 2020.

[119] Anjli Raval, 'Asset Manager Sarasin Cuts Shell Stake Over Climate Worries' *Financial Times* (9 July 2019) online: <https://www.ft.com/content/446ba6ca-a189-11e9-a282-2df48f366f7d> accessed 24 January 2020; Paris Agreement (n 73) Article 2.

with both climate change and, more broadly, ethical investing including limiting the environmental impact of their investments.[120]

By preventing Shell and others from fracking in South Africa, even if only temporarily, *Stern SCA* represents a significant victory on the part of civil society actors seeking to ensure improved environmental protection and governance in an era of climate change. Amongst the relevant actors, TKAG is an example of the way in which civil society has connected with the global anti-fracking movement.[121] After forming TKAG, which consists of a partnership of scientists, lawyers and other actors, its founder, Jonathan Deal, reached out to American's Against Fracking, a coalition of NGOs—including Greenpeace —business and other actors addressing fracking in the USA, thereby entering a global coalition of anti-fracking campaigners.[122] In this way Deal was arguably able to establish a network of expertise to strengthen the approach taken in *Stern SCA* through sharing experiences. This approach could be especially valuable in climate litigation to draw on scientific evidence compiled elsewhere, the observable impacts of fracking in jurisdictions where it is already occurring, and legal expertise in those jurisdictions. However, the experiences of the different actors within such networks will invariably not be homogenous; locality, context and legal culture can materially influence success in litigation and, thus, must be taken into account.

Despite the victory, it is important to acknowledge that the perspectives and concerns of poor and vulnerable local communities were noticeably absent in *Stern SCA*. Apart from TKAG, the litigation was driven by Afriforum, 'a civil rights organisation that mobilises Afrikaners, Afrikaans-speaking people and other minority groups in South Africa and protects their rights'.[123] Afriforum, controversially, thus primarily represents the interests of South Africa's white Afrikaans minority, who were hugely privileged during apartheid. In addition, Stern and other farmers acted from the privileged position of landowners, rather than in the interests of poor and vulnerable communities in the Karoo, whose livelihoods and sense of place are likely to be most affected by fracking. Although litigation potentially offers affected people, environmental and human rights NGOs and other interested parties a

---

120 eg see: 'Our Story | Follow This' (*Follow This*) Online: <https://follow-this.org/our-story/> accessed 11 March 2020; 'How We Invest' (*The Church of England*) online: <https://www.churchofengland.org/about/leadership-and-governance/church-commissioners-england/how-we-invest> accessed 11 March 2020; 'Responsible Investment' (*The Church of England*) online: <https://www.churchofengland.org/about/leadership-and-governance/church-commissioners-england/how-we-invest/responsible-investment-1> accessed 11 March 2020.

121 'South African Anti-Fracking Activist Calls for Global Alliance' *National Geographic Society Newsroom* (13 May 2013) online: <https://blog.nationalgeographic.org/2013/05/13/south-african-anti-fracking-activist-calls-for-global-alliance/> accessed 23 January 2020.

122 *Ibid*; 'Americans Against Fracking' online: <https://www.americansagainstfracking.org/> accessed 24 January 2020; 'About the Coalition | Americans Against Fracking' online: <https://www.americansagainstfracking.org/about-the-coalition/> accessed 24 January 2020; 'Treasure Karoo Action Group – Home' (n 82).

123 'Who is Afriforum' online: <https://www.afriforum.co.za/en/> accessed 10 March 2020.

significantly stronger voice—and as a result influence—on the state's regulation of fracking in the Karoo, it is important that interests of marginalised communities be brought to the fore. Those interests could include justice-related concerns about water and food security, job losses in agriculture and tourism, and a loss of social cohesion. They could also include concerns about the impacts of fracking on climate change and the impacts of climate change, in turn, on livelihoods. While transnational (or global) litigation or advocacy networks represent a significant and recognisable phenomenon that may in turn impact upon transnational regulation concerned with the energy transition,[124] it remains important to question the extent to which their litigation strategies recognise and address the concerns of poor and marginalised people who stand to be directly, and most immediately impacted by the development of fracking in the Karoo.

5. Conclusion

Fracking represents a significant threat to the Karoo's socio-ecological systems, among other things, due to its negative impact on biodiversity and resulting habitat loss and fragmentation, contamination of surface water and aquifers and air pollution.[125] The economic benefits and contribution towards energy security and South Africa's energy transition proposed by transnational fossil fuel companies hoping to exploit the vast gas reserves of the Karoo, and the government, must therefore be balanced with the environmental and social costs of its extraction. Given the number of corporations that have either expressed interest in operating well sites in the Karoo and those who have already applied for permits, the damage could be significant. Furthermore, while it could be argued that this issue is a domestic one, both the contribution of methane emissions from fracking to global concentrations, the contribution of carbon dioxide from its extraction, transport and combustion as well as its likely export out of the country, makes this issue one of a global nature. The wide variety of actors involved—state, civil society and NGOs, transnational fossil fuel companies, domestic companies and the involvement of the global anti-fracking movement—truly reveals the transnational dimensions of what appears to be a purely domestic issue, as well as the impact that litigation has on the regulatory capacity of the state itself.

In this article we have illustrated, adopting a transnational legal methodology, that the power of the state to authorise fracking through domestic

[124] Hari M Osofsky, 'The Geography of Climate Change Litigation: Implications for Transnational Regulatory Governance' (2005) 83 *Washington University Law Quarterly* 1789; Osofsky and Peel (n 9); Hannah L Buxbaum, 'Transnational Regulatory Litigation' (2006) 46(2) *Virginia Journal of International Law* 251.

[125] Esterhuyse (n 6); Esterhuyse, de Lange and Glazewski (n 50) 206; Avenant and others (n 50) 222;

regulation may be weakened by non-state actors who engage in litigation in order to prioritise the protection of this area. By so doing, these non-state actors also act as a counterbalance to the powerful transnational corporations who have immense economic power and incentives to exploit untapped shale gas. While the Department of Mineral Resources had expected to issue the first permits to extract shale gas in the Karoo during 2019, this did not happen, and it remains unclear whether and when permits will be issued.[126] This is in large part due to the role of non-state actors, including civil society, who mobilised to influence the manner in which fracking is regulated and the Karoo is developed. The turn to litigation, as illustrated by *Normandien HC* and more particularly *Stern SCA*, has resulted in much greater scrutiny and evaluation of the impacts of fracking in the area, and highlighted the need for proper public participation, which represent important and necessary regulatory shifts in the context of the Anthropocene's imagery of planetary destruction.

Environmental litigation—encompassing as it does the use of the court to pursue either directly or indirectly environmentally beneficial outcomes—has the capacity as a form of regulatory governance to address and attempt to limit humanity's impact upon the Earth. The turn to litigation both strategically and in pursuit of specific goals has burgeoned over the last decade and, especially with regard to climate change, plays a role in the governance of this problem.[127] Ultimately, the cases discussed in this article may serve to include more voices in this type of environmental decision-making on the local level as well as form the basis of stronger resistance to fracking in the Karoo and beyond. Indeed, the power of litigation to delay may become its best form of attack; as the global gas market fluctuates and the energy transition moves beyond the use of this fuel, the economic incentive for its exploitation may wane thereby preserving the Karoo and its people.

ORCID

Melanie Murcott http://orcid.org/0000-0001-8311-2195
Emily Webster http://orcid.org/0000-0003-1360-6071

Disclosure statement

No potential conflict of interest was reported by the author(s).

---

126 'South Africa Commits to Shale Gas despite Adverse Court Ruling' *Reuters* (19 October 2017) online: <https://www.reuters.com/article/us-safrica-shale-idUSKBN1CO0XV> accessed 23 January 2020.

127 eg see: Osofsky and Peel (n 10); Setzer and Vanhala (n 11); LSE (n 10); Bouwer (n 8); *Urgenda* (n 10).

The myth of mermaids and stewardship of the seas

Emily Barritt

ABSTRACT
Mermaids have become increasingly present in popular culture. At the same time as this mermaid renaissance, states have been negotiating a new international legally binding instrument on the sustainable use and conservation of marine biodiversity in areas beyond national jurisdiction. Faced with increased pressures on ocean ecosystems—fisheries depletion, ocean acidification and plastics pollution—urgent action is required to remedy gaps in the current regime. However, although the problems with this regime are well rehearsed—it is fragmented and based a fictionalised account of ocean space that does not accurately reflect the ecological complexities of the seas and there appears to be little appetite for the root and branch changes necessary to remedy these problems. In appealing to the transnational mythology of mermaids, I seek to reinvigorate calls for a more ecologically sensitive narrative of the seas that will better protect marine biodiversity both within and beyond areas of national jurisdiction.

> Far, far out in the sea the water is as blue as the petals of the most beautiful cornflower, and as clear as the purest glass. But it is very deep, deeper than any cable will sound; many steeples must be placed one above the other to reach from the ground to the surface of the water. And down there live the sea people.[1]
>
> We are in a certain sense amphibious, not exclusively connected with the land, but with the sea as well.[2]

I. Introduction

Mermaids have experienced something of a renaissance in recent years. With films like *The Shape of Water*, books such as *The Mermaid and Mrs Hancock* and a growing job market for professional mermaids, merfolk are in vogue. At

---

[1] *The Complete Illustrated Stories of Hans Christian Andersen* (Henry W Dulcken tr, Chancellor Press 1984) 32.

[2] Ellen C Semple, *The Geography of the Mediterranean Region: Its Relation to Ancient History* (Henry Holt 1931) 59

the same time as the growth of this 'mermaid economy',[3] states have been engrossed in negotiations for the text of a new treaty on the conservation and sustainable use of marine biodiversity in areas beyond national jurisdiction (BBNJ).[4] Proposals for this new agreement recognise that the current stewardship paradigm for the oceans does not adequately safeguard ecological integrity in areas beyond national jurisdiction (ABNJ).[5] Amongst other things, the existing legal framework provides an unsatisfactory patchwork of sectoral provisions, creates damaging divisions of ocean space and fails to appreciate the intricacies of marine ecosystems, all of which contributes to diminishing biological diversity and ecological integrity.[6] What is more, the very notion that ocean space can be divided into areas within and beyond national jurisdiction exacerbates this fragmentation.

Ocean governance is of course a profoundly challenging enterprise. The oceans are vast and infinitely complex, they traverse national jurisdictions and their inhabitants occupy ocean space with no concern for human borders. And for many of us the oceans are a remote, unknowable expanse that bears little connection to our day to day lives. The task of addressing marine biodiversity depletion is therefore an enormous one. In this contribution to the special 'Anthropocene' issue of Transnational Legal Theory, I want to enter the realms of fantasy and fable, deep into the world of mermaids, to see what lessons we might learn from the tales of merfolk for our relationship with the oceans. In so doing, I hope to understand how we can become better stewards of marine biodiversity, both within the context of the formal negotiations of the new international legally binding instrument (ILBI) and in terms of ocean governance more generally. Although for reasons of space, I focus on ABNJ in this contribution, the challenges I identify extend to the entire enterprise of dividing up the oceans.

The imaginative exercise that I undertake in this contribution is not to entertain the further fiction that mermaids would be perfect oceans stewards. No doubt, mythical sea creatures like land dwellers have the capacity to exploit, degrade and destroy their aquatic environment. Indeed, in the

---

[3] Elizabeth Sergan, 'Inside the Mermaid Economy' (*Fast Company*, 9 Septemebr 2015) <www.fastcompany.com/3050847/inside-the-mermaid-economy-2> (accessed 7 May 2020).

[4] United Nations General Assembly, (2015) Resolution 69/292—Development of an International Legally Binding Instrument under the United Nations Convention on the Law of the Sea on the conservation and sustainable use of marine biological diversity of areas beyond national jurisdiction UN Doc A/RES/69/292, 19 June 2015; United Nations General Assembly, (2017), Resolution 72/2490 International Legally Binding Instrument under the United Nations Convention on the Law of the Sea on the conservation and sustainable use of marine biological diversity of areas beyond national jurisdiction A/Res/72/249, 24 December 2017.

[5] For example, UNGA Resolution 69/292 stresses 'the need for the comprehensive global regime to *better address* the conservation and sustainable use of marine biological diversity of areas beyond national jurisdiction … ' (emphasis added).

[6] Dire Tladi, 'Ocean Governance: A Fragmented Regulatory Framework' in Pierre Jacquet, Rajendra Pachauri and Laurence Tubiana (eds), *Oceans: The New Frontier – A Planet for Life* (Teri Press 2011) 99–111.

Bhagavata Purana, Krishna banishes the sea creature Naga from the river Yamuna because his venom pollutes the water, singeing birds and scorching trees.[7] And in European accounts of merfolk, they are often so greedy for precious resources that their worlds can come crumbling down in pursuit of a shiny trinket.[8] Nevertheless, tales of water peoples do help us to think about our complicated relationship with the oceans. Instead of lauding mermaids as the exemplar ocean steward, I appeal to the renewed 'fascination with mermaids' in order to 'breathe new life and possibilities' into how human beings understand their relationship with the seas.[9]

I do this for two reasons. First, mermaids help expand our imaginative capacities, a capacity that can be tested by the vast, unknowable expanse of the oceans. As Rachel Carson remarked, 'the sea has always challenged the minds and the imagination' of human beings.[10] Our perception of the 'otherness' of the oceans, as a 'void between societies' allows us to separate ourselves from the oceanic consequences of our actions.[11] Following the hunch of Jane Bennett, I suggest that it is this dislocation from the oceans that 'feeds human hubris ... [and] our [ocean]-destroying fantasies of conquest and consumption' that have so scarred our relationship with the seas.[12] Second, by exploring the watery realms of merfolk I am appealing to the explanatory power of myths. As Cristina Bacchilega and Marie Alohalani Brown claim, stories of mermaids are not mere fairy tales, fictions developed to entertain and enthral, rather these stories represent a powerful, transnational mythology that helps 'to explain how and why things are the way they are and who is accountable for what'.[13] Thus mermaids provide 'mythological resources' for re-examining our relationship with the oceans.[14]

Neither of these tasks is typically one we envisage for lawyers. Lawyers are generally relegated to the mundane, to the practical, to the law and its defined black letters. Yet, if we are to address the existential challenges we face as inhabitants of this planet, even lawyers need to enter the realms of fantasy and fable.[15] In developing his ideas about the legal rights of trees, Christopher Stone calls for the law to coalesce into a 'radical new theory or myth' in order to revaluate humanities relationship to the rest of nature.[16] It would be a

---

[7] 'Kāliya, the Snake' in Cristina Bacchilega and Marie Alohalani Brown (eds), *The Penguin Book of Mermaids* (Penguin Books 2019) 5–8.

[8] 'Storia d'una Sirena', *ibid*, 75–79

[9] *Ibid*, xxii

[10] Rachel Carson, *The Sea Around Us* (Introduction by Sylvia Earle, Oxford University Press 2018) x

[11] Phillip E Steinberg, *The Social Construction of the Ocean* (Cambridge University Press 2001) 14

[12] Jane Bennett, *Vibrant Matter: A Political Ecology of Things* (Duke University Press 2010) ix.

[13] *Ibid*, xvi–xvii.

[14] Michel Foucault, 'Of Other Spaces: Utopias and Heterotopias' (1986) 16 *Diacritics* 22 (Kay Miskowiec (tr)) 22.

[15] A cynic might argue that we never leave those realms.

[16] Christopher D Stone, *Should Trees Have Standing? Law, Morality and the Environment* (Oxford University Press, 3rd edn 2010) 29.

vanity attributable to the sirens themselves for me to assume that I could develop this new mythology in a single article, or indeed in a lifetime of scholarship. Instead, I will do as all good story tellers tend to and build on the storytelling capacities of those before me to unpick how we might reimagine our stewardship of the seas.

To begin, I examine the way that human beings, through the medium of international law in particular, have constructed the oceans. In so doing, I show that ocean space has been fictionalised such that it may run counter to the professed ecological aims of the new internationally legally binding instrument. Second, I turn to the transnational mythology of mermaids to identify the key themes that might illuminate a more ecologically nuanced understanding of humanities relationship with ocean space. Principally, I suggest that mermaids help to populate the characterless narrative of the law of sea, a narrative which contributes to fragmentation and dislocation. Finally, I consider three practical ways in which we might shape a story of ocean governance to produce a human-ocean relationship that is less fractured and less remote through the appointment of an ocean guardian; a more serious commitment to public participation in ocean spaces; and by paying more attention to the possibilities of marine rights. The question at the heart of these cumulative enquiries is thus, can the mythology of mermaids help us to reimagine the existing stewardship paradigm of ocean governance?

This contribution is necessarily light on concrete legal ideas, dwelling as it does in the watery worlds of mythical sea creatures. My hope, therefore, is to provoke further thinking on how a mythology of the oceans that is more sensitive to their ecologically complexity might shape ocean governance. I point to a few places where I think this mythology can play a role, for example, by reemphasising the role of the public in marine spatial planning, but these examples are illustrative rather than comprehensive. There is therefore much more that can be said, and indeed more that I would have liked to say.

II. Ocean space and legal fiction

Throughout history, humans have constructed the oceans in a way that reflect culturally embedded ideas about how we relate to the vast expanse of the seas.[17] Such ideas are often represented in mermaid mythology.[18] Early Micronesians, for example, saw the seas as an extension of the land and operated with a very fluid sense of territory, crossing the seas like many of us would cross the road.[19] By contrast, peoples surrounding the Indian Ocean

[17] Steinberg (n 11) 40.
[18] Bacchilega and Alohalani Brown (n 7) x
[19] Steinberg (n 11) 53–60.

had a more remote appreciation of the seas, as a void to be traversed for the purposes of trade.[20] During the period when the Ancient Greeks and Romans sailed the Mediterranean Seas, the oceans were viewed as a space over which to gain power and control (*imperium*), whilst remaining immune from claims of ownership (*dominium*).[21] In modern times, the most persistent paradigm has been of stewardship,[22] originating in this Greco-Roman era and shaped by the Grotian crafting of control over ocean space.[23] It is this paradigm that established the foundations for our legal framework of marine governance in international law and which set the course for our current conservation challenges.[24] However, it is a paradigm that is very far removed from the realities of ocean space, focused as it has been on navigating the line between freedom and control. The very separation of areas of the ocean to within and beyond national jurisdiction, for example, developed as a matter of diplomatic necessity, creates harsh and unsensitive dividing lines that ignore ecological reality.[25] Therefore, rather than allowing law to be informed by observations and understandings about marine space, the pursuit of power and resources has wrought how the oceans are constructed and governed.[26]

In many ways, ocean space has been treated like a Heterotopia,[27] a space 'of alternate ordering ... that ... marks [it] out as Other and allows [it] to be seen as an example of an alternate way of doing things', a playground free from the limits of the land.[28] This is understandable: the physical distance that most of us experience with the oceans allows us to view them as spaces immune from our terrestrial lives and therefore a space where we can experiment with 'alternate ordering' without consequence.[29] Carson wrote in 1950, despite the discouraging history of human stewardship of the land 'there has long been a certain comfort in the belief that the sea, at least, was inviolate, beyond man's ability to change and to despoil'.[30] As Carson knew then, and we certainly know now, our record in the sea is just as dismal as on land. With rising sea levels, ocean acidification, microplastics, trash islands and species

[20] *Ibid*, 41–52.
[21] *Ibid*, 60–67.
[22] I would argue that this stewardship paradigm represents an impoverished picture of stewardship, for a more nuanced understanding of stewardship see Emily Barritt, 'Conceptualising Stewardship in Environmental Law' (2014) 26 *Journal of Environmental Law* 1.
[23] Steinberg (n 10) 90–5.
[24] Robert Jay Wilder, *Listening to the Seas: The Politics of Improving Environmental Protection* (University of Pittsburgh Press 1998) 28.
[25] *Ibid*, 3–28.
[26] See for example the jurisdictional struggle over the seas following World War II: Elizabeth Mendenhall, 'The Ocean Governance Regime: International Conventions and Institutions' in Paul G Harris (ed), *Climate Change and Ocean Governance* (Cambridge University Press 2019) 33.
[27] As Phillip Steinberg describes '[a]s a heterotopia, the ocean is a space of ordering and limits, but, as those orders and limits themselves stretch the bounds of social norms and systems, it is also a space for imagining the actualizing social change'. Steinberg (n 11) 205.
[28] Kevin Hetherington, *The Badlands of Modernity: Heterotopia and Social Ordering* (Routledge 1997) viii.
[29] *Ibid*, viii.
[30] Carson (n 10) xxiii.

depletion, humanities' mark on the oceans has been as devastating as many mermaid myths foretold. However, the belief that the oceans are somehow impervious to what human beings could throw at (and in) them has been a persistent one.[31] Buttressed by idea that the seas are 'merely a void between societies',[32] the great immutable 'otherness' of the oceans has contributed to a social construction and legal architecture driven more by the whims of statecraft than by the complex realities of the marine environment.[33]

Through law we have fictionalised an account of the seas that has entrenched ideas of remoteness, divisibility and impermeability. For example, as Surabhi Ranganathan explains, the legal limits created for the continental shelf do not reflect the geological truths of these underwater masses.[34] Other fictions include, separating the sea floor from its waters (and as a result the species that occupy those spaces),[35] treating fish separately as commodities and as desirable genetic resources,[36] persisting in the use of fishing subsidies whilst fish stocks are dangerously depleted[37] and the pursuit of fantastical floating communities that can operate without limits or regulation.[38] All of these artifices contribute to a picture of ocean space that is far removed from the realities of ocean ecosystems and biodiversity. International law has thus perpetuated a colonisation ideology about how we can divide up the oceans[39] and has exacerbated the physical remoteness of the oceans through legal complexity.[40]

It is against this background that states are attempting to establish a new framework for the conservation and sustainable use of marine biodiversity, the ILBI. Despite the wish to safeguard the health of the oceans however,[41] states do not seem to have acknowledged that the problem is not just a

---

31 Glen Wright and others, *The Long And Winding Road: Negotiating a Treaty for the Conservation and Sustainable Use of Marine Biodiversity in Areas Beyond National Jurisdiction* (IDDRI, Studies No 08/18, 82 p 2018) 9

32 Steinberg (n 11) 14

33 For example, the consequences of United States President Harry Truman's two proclamations expanding the authority of the beyond its territorial waters: *ibid*, 139–43.

34 Surabhi Ranganathan, 'Ocean Floor Grab: International Law and the Making of an Extractive Imaginary' (2019) 30 *The European Journal of International Law* 573, 577 and 586.

35 In UNCLOS the High Seas are governed by the principle of 'freedom' and the seabed the idea that it is the 'common heritage of mankind' see *ibid*, 596.

36 David Leary, 'Agreeing to Disagree on What We Have or Have Not Agreed On: The Current State of Play of the BBNJ Negotiations on the Status of Marine Genetic Resources in Areas Beyond National Jurisdiction' (2019) 99 *Marine Policy* 21, 26.

37 Stone (n 16) 91.

38 Kent M Keith, 'Floating Cities: A New Challenge for Transnational Law' (1977) 1 *Marine Policy* 190; Surabhi Ranganathan, 'Seasteads, Land-grabs and International Law' 32 *Liden Journal of International Law* 205.

39 Ranganathan, 'Ocean Floor Grab: International Law and the Making of an Extractive Imaginary' (n 34) 582.

40 Richard Barnes, 'Environmental Rights in Marine Spaces' in Sanja Bogojević and Rosemary Rayfuse (eds), *Environmental Rights in Europe and Beyond* (Hart Publishing 2018) 70–3.

41 The Future We Want (2012) UNGA Resolution A/66/288, section 158; see also: CBD Cop 10, Decision X/2 Strategic Plan for Biodiversity 2011/2020 (Aichi Targets), Targets 3, 6 and 11; United Nations Sustainable Development Goals, Goal 14.

matter of gaps in the exiting framework, but that the framework itself may be contributing to biodiversity loss.[42] Critically, negotiations for the new agreement are bound by the principle that it 'should not undermine' existing legal regimes.[43] It is therefore difficult to fathom how marine biodiversity can genuinely be protected if the damaging fictions of the current regime are not addressed. As Ranganathan warns, the new initiative, committed as it is to not undermine exiting regimes, will continue to privilege extraction and thus perpetuates the problems it is attempting to solve.[44] Whilst it is entirely possible that this principle could be treated lightly and interpreted flexibly,[45] the novelty of the terminology, and therefore the lack of explanatory material to aide its interpretation, has allowed some states to use it to block progress particularly in relation to the architecture of the agreement.[46] Indeed, in an ongoing assessment of the current negotiating process, researchers have identified the dictum as noticeably 'inhibit[ing] movement towards a consensual and effective agreement'.[47] The uncertainty that surrounds the appropriate meaning that should be given to the commitment to not undermining, and its restrictive interpretation, therefore appears to be limiting the scope of the final agreement, opening up the possibility that the ILBI will not adequately addressed issues of marine biodiversity protection.[48]

Another challenge posed by the framing of the negotiations is the emphasis that is placed on 'sustainable use'. Whilst this is understandable—fish are the main source of protein for a significant portion of the world's population—there is something jarring about this being a focus of a treaty intended to remedy diminishing biodiversity.[49] This is especially evident in the

---

42 Mendenhall (n 26) 39–40; Deqiang Ma, Qinhua Fang and Song Guan, 'Current Legal Regime for Environmental Impact Assessment in Areas Beyond National Jurisdiction and its Future Approaches' (2016) 56 *Environmental Impact Assessment Review* 23, 24–5.

43 UNGA Resolution 69/292 (n 4) para 3; UNGA Resolution 72/249 (n 4) para 7.

44 Ranganathan, 'Ocean Floor Grab: International Law and the Making of an Extractive Imaginary' (n 34) 576.

45 As was the case in relation to negotiations surrounding the 1995 Fish Stocks Agreement, which despite being bound by a similar principle—'that the work and results of the conferenced should be fully consistent' with UNCLOS—were able to introduce stronger environmental principles and to limit fishing rights through mandatory membership of the Regional Fishing Management Organisations. United Nations General Assembly, (1993) Resolution 47/192 United Nations conference on straddling fish stocks and highly migratory fish stocks, UN Doc A/RES/47/192, 29 January 1993, 2.

46 Elizabeth Mendenehall and others, 'A Soft Treaty, Hard to Reach: The Second Inter-Governmental Conference for Biodiversity Beyond National Jurisdictions' (2019) 108 *Marine Policy* 1, 1.

47 *Ibid*, 2.

48 *Ibid*, 7.

49 The Convention of Biological Diversity, Article 10 similarly promotes sustainable use alongside conservation and protection of biodiversity. However, this is not a central theme of the Convention, whereas 'sustainable use of marine biological diversity' is one set alongside conservation as one of the two focuses of the IBLI, UNGA Resolution 69/292 (n 4). Further, the notion of sustainability in the boarder context of environmental governance is embedded with tension, whether it be sustainable use or sustainable development, it is a term that must contain and balance competing objectives and that balance is not always obvious: John Dryzek, *The Politics of the Earth: Environmental Discourses* (Oxford University Press 2005) 145–61; see also Erika J Techera, *Marine Environmental Governance: From International Law to Local Practice* (Routledge 2012) 29–30.

intransigence over the limited role a new regime might play in relation to fishing, a significant contributor to BBNJ depletion.[50] Further, the profound challenges presented by Marine Genetic Resources, and the need to ensure equity in the global division of benefits, means that marine biodiversity is frequently spoken about using the language of commodities, rather than of biodiversity. All of this contributes to a narrative that portrays the seas simply as a provider of resources and not as an ecosystem requiring protection.

Apart from the challenges related to the use of marine resources, other entrenched aspects of the existing regime are likely to limit the ecological potential of the ILBI. Speaking specifically about treatment of the seabed, for example, Ranganathan is sceptical that the law 'as the medium that facilitated the grab of the ocean floor' can be used to 'serve as the medium [to] return it to the common benefit'.[51] There is also significant unwillingness on the part of many states to establish a new overarching governance body, for fear it will undermine existing bodies such as the International Seabed Authority or Regional Fisheries Management Organisations.[52] Therefore, fragmentation caused by a dependence on the existing regional and sectoral framework will likely persist. It is difficult to see, for example, how an holistic, ecosystems-based approach might be channelled without an overarching body to coordinate such an approach.[53] Finally, as Mendlenhall and others, reflecting on their observations of the negotiations, conclude, the commitment to not undermining is likely to produce a soft legal instrument that will be light on substantive obligations thus limiting the potency of the IBLI.[54] Therefore, 'by preventing the emerging agreement from contributing to the evolution of the ocean governance regime, and minimizing the compliance and implementation functions that a BBNJ instrument could feasibly adopt' the ILBI may have limited meaningful consequences for the conservation of BBNJ.[55]

As with very many stories of sea creatures, the narrative of ocean governance is dominated by exploitation, extraction[56] and accumulation.[57] Unless and until this narrative is altered, and the neutered conception of stewardship that permeates our historical construction of the oceans is addressed, it seems

[50] Alex G Oude Ekferink, 'Exploring the Future of the Institutional Landscape of the Oceans Beyond National Jurisdiction' (2019) 28 *Review of European, Comparative & International Environmental Law* 236, 238.

[51] Ranganathan, 'Ocean Floor Grab: International Law and the Making of an Extractive Imaginary' (n 34) 600.

[52] Mendenhall and others (n 46) 6; Oude Ekferink (n 50) 241.

[53] Mendenehall and others (n 46) 6.

[54] *Ibid*, 7.

[55] *Ibid*, 3

[56] Ranganathan, 'Ocean Floor Grab: International Law and the Making of an Extractive Imaginary' (n 34) 580.

[57] Wesley Flannery, Jane Clarek and Benedic McAteer, 'Politics and Power in Marine Spatial Planning' in Jacekt Zaucha and Kira Gee (eds), *Maritime Spatial Planning: Past, Present, Future* (Palgrave Macmillan 2019) 207.

unlikely that the new ILBI will result in meaningful protection for marine biodiversity. This is of course a profoundly pessimistic portrait of what is an ongoing process, and it may be that the final draft seriously commits to the protection of marine biodiversity. Given reports of the current process however, it is difficult to see how the persistent idea that the ocean is simply 'a socially significant space providing crucial resources' will meaningfully shift to an idea that the ocean is an ecologically significant space, vulnerable to human exploitation and therefore in need of considerable protection.[58]

III. The mythology of mermaids

At this point in my contribution, you might understandably ask yourself, if the problem identified is the fictionalisation of ocean space, why turn to mythology as a possible solution, surely fiction should be countered with fact. This is easier said than done. The realities of ocean space are infinitely complex, and even unknowable, developing a legal regime in tandem with that will necessarily require some degree of imagination. Therefore, the goal should not be meticulous (and ultimately unattainable) scientific perfection. Rather, it should be a fuller story that recognises the connections and nuances of ocean space. Indeed, the problem with the heterotopic approach to oceans is that they are treated merely as inert spaces, without adequately considering the creatures and characters that occupy them. The mythology of mermaids and other water spirits allows us to populate ocean heterotopias in a way that reminds us of the consequences of our legal choices. The solution, to the poor fiction of ocean governance, therefore, is to create a better story. What lessons then can we draw from the rich, transnational mythology of mermaid that can help to create such a story?

The first, is that in the end human attempts at domination rarely work out well for any of those involved; either the marine creature is destroyed (sometimes eliciting remorse from her human captor), or the mermaid takes its bitter and exacting revenge.[59] In the Japanese legend Yao Nikuni, for example, in the ultimate act of domination a father serves the flesh of a mermaid to his young daughter in order that she might have a long life.[60] She does, but after living no less than eight hundred years, the daughter is left lonely and weary, preferring to be buried alive than to continue living her mermaid prolonged existence. This riff of failed dominion over mercreatures has its counterparts in European and Australian mythology, often involving forced marriages that end in unhappiness. Each myth tells that

[58] Steinberg (n 11) 176
[59] Bacchilega and Alohalani Brown (n 7) xix.
[60] 'Yao Bikuni', *ibid*, 210–11

attempting to dominate, rather than coexist with mermaids is rarely a wise choice.[61]

Second, many mermaid myths explore the problems of uneven power dynamics. In the stories about the selkies of Scotland and seal women of Ireland, men, wanting merwives, take the marine essence of a selkie (their seal skin or their scales) and hide it so that the selkie is forced to live with them on land.[62] Each tale illustrates that when one party holds all the power it is difficult for the other to make meaningful choices, the selkies may well operate as dutiful wives and mothers while on land, but the minute they have their skin or scales back they return forever to the sea.

Finally, the human-merfolk relationships which dominate mermaid mythology allows us to think beyond the binary of anthropocentrism and eco-centrism. As Bacchilega and Alogalani Brown explain of the non-European mermaid mythology in particular, these stories show that 'our place as humans in the world is negotiated with a set of social relations that … encourage reciprocity and humility when interacting with other species and nature'.[63] Indeed the consequences of failing to respect the boundaries of mer-creatures can be significant. In the Persian story of a sea fairy, fishermen are blessed with bountiful supplies of fish, so long as they keep the secret of the sea fairy but are left hungry when they do not.[64] Similarly, the Pincoya, a water spirit from the Chiloé Archipelago, will summon abundant fish to help fisherman, but will quickly cause waters to become barren if the fishers are greedy and overfish.[65]

These are not the only themes represented in mermaid mythology. For example, the gendered dimensions of many mermaid myths speak of the work of ecofeminists, and the long-life spans of mermaids remind of us our intergenerational responsibilities. Further, the duality of many mermaids, able to exist both on land and at sea, reminds us of our own human incapacities, both in terms of physical abilities but also in terms of how we can conceive of ocean space:

> we humans do not deal well with betwixt and between—liminality makes us anxious. We prefer our world organized into well-ordered and sharply defined categories, and we prefer to be in charge of it.[66]

Indeed, it is human anxiety about the fluidity of ocean spaces that has led us to develop a highly fragmented and intractable legal regime. Each of these themes helps to illuminate a new perspective of ocean governance and would therefore be interesting to explore. For now, however, I focus on the

---

[61] Contrast these stories with that of the 'Hairy Chinese Mermaid or hai nü', *ibid*, 201–3.
[62] *Ibid*, 27–39.
[63] *Ibid*, xx.
[64] 'The Sea Fairy' *ibid*, 187–6.
[65] 'The Pincoya' *ibid*, 269–70.
[66] *Ibid*, xi.

three key themes identified as a starting point for examining how the mythology of mermaids might remedy the fictions of ocean governance.

IV. Stewardship, participation and the rights of mermaids

The first lesson identified from the global review of mermaid mythology, is that where humans treat merfolk as a thing to possess or control, the relationship always ends in tragedy. The dominant stewardship paradigm of the oceans is characterised by a perception of human control over ocean space.[67] In the children's story, *The Fate of Fausto*, Fausto believes that he can own and control all things in his sight, one day he announces to the sea that it is his and to prove it steps out of his boat to stomp on the sea, only to plunge into its depths and disappear forever.[68] Whilst the story highlights human hubris in relation to natural resources, it masks the reality that in exercising this hubris, humans are still able to exact significant harm. It is necessary therefore to develop a stewardship paradigm for the oceans that moves away from ideas of control and resource extraction, to those of care and guardianship.

Writing about the guardianship of the Whanganui River, Randal Abate attributes significance to the shift from rights to responsibility in ensuring adequate protection for the river as a natural being.[69] Indeed, if such a shift were to happen in relation to ocean governance, it is likely to produce a far more ecologically balanced approach to marine biodiversity. One way to achieve this shift, is to appoint a guardian for the ocean as has been done in relation to the guardianship of other natural entities. Such a guardian, proposes Stone, would be endowed in international treaties with 'standing to initiate legal and diplomatic action on the ocean ecosystem's behalf'.[70] Achieving this is of course no easy task, and the creation of an Ocean Guardian is an ambitious proposal. However, high ambition is needed 'to offer the world of statecraft a sounder vision' of how we interact with the natural world.[71]

The second lesson teaches about the damaging consequences of uneven power dynamics. When it comes to ocean space, states and powerful private actors, such as the fishing industry and extractive enterprises, are able to dominate the narrative and chose how the oceans are treated and controlled, individuals have very little say.[72] Yet, one of the fundamental ideas of international environmental law is that 'environmental decisions are best

[67] Steinberg (n 11) 172.
[68] Oliver Jeffers, *The Fate of Fausto: A Painted Fable* (Philomel Books 2019).
[69] Randall S Abate, *Climate Change and the Voiceless* (Cambridge University Press 2020) 220.
[70] Stone (n 16) 101.
[71] *Ibid*, 102.
[72] Although environmental non-governmental organisations do play an important role in monitoring and decision-making. See for example Solène Guggisber, 'The Role of Nongovernmental Actors in Improving Compliance with Fisheries Regulation' (2018) 28 *Review of European, Comparative and International Environmental Law* 314.

handled with the participation of all concerned citizens'.[73] Crucially, participation is not envisaged as a territorially bounded idea. Participation is instead premised on an interest in environmental values and their protection. For example, the participatory rights enshrined in the Aarhus Convention are available regardless of citizenship, nationality or domicile.[74] The profound inclusivity of participation should also extend therefore to oceanic regions because public participation is a powerful tool to reorder power dynamics, by empowering those otherwise excluded from decision-making.

There are of course difficulties in facilitating public participation in relation to ocean spaces, for many individuals there is often a 'degree of cultural, epistemic and legal disconnect with the material nature of the marine environment'.[75] Without an identifiable class of concerned citizens, it is difficult to facilitate participation in ocean governance. Even where it is possible to identify those with an interest in participating in marine governance decisions, there are additional complexities. Critical to participation is information, for example, and the scientific complexities of the oceans can mean that there is either a paucity of information or the information is impenetrable to a non-expert, thus hindering authentic participation. And even when public participation is made possible 'it may simply repackage power dynamics in the rhetoric of participation to legitimise the agendas of dominate actors'.[76] Facilitating public participation in marine spaces, particular in relation ABNJ, therefore requires careful thinking about how to translate participatory processes developed for land based decisions.

There are number of ways in which the power shifting possibilities of participation can be incorporated into ocean governance, for now I highlight just one technique: Marine Spatial Planning (MSP)—a collaborative process that brings together various actors, including in theory the public, to make decisions about how marine space is used.[77] For example, MSP might be used to decide the path of a new shipping route or whether to open a new fishery. Whilst MSP is common within waters governed by national jurisdiction, it does have transnational application and there are increasing calls for it to be used in ABNJ.[78]

---

[73] United Nations Rio Declaration on Environment and Development (13 June 1992) 31 ILM 874 (1992), Principle 10.

[74] Convention on Access to Information, Public Participation in Decision-Making and Access to Justice in Environmental Matters, Aarhus, (adopted 25 June 1998, entered into force 30 October 2001) (1998) 38 ILM 517, Article 3(9).

[75] Barnes (n 37) 52.

[76] Flannery, Clarek and McAteer (n 57) 32.

[77] UNESCO classified MSP as a public process: Vasco Becker-Weinberg, 'Preliminary Thoughts on Marine Spatial Planning in Arras Beyond National Jurisdiction' (2017) 32 *The International Journal of Marine and Costal Law* 570, 579.

[78] Susanne Alvater, Ruth Fletcher and Cristian Passarello, 'The Need for Marine Spatial Planning in Areas Beyond National Jurisdiction' in Jacekt Zaucha and Kira Gee (eds), *Maritime Spatial Planning: Past, Present, Future* (Palgrave Macmillan 2019).

As presently conceived however (although practises do vary across jurisdictions) there are aspects of MSP that limit its capacity for serious power redistribution from powerful actors to citizens and NGOs.[79] For example, the economic aspects of MSP are often privileged over other aspects of the process, limiting space for the consideration of ecological and social sustainability issues.[80] And, as Wesley Flannery and others have identified, the process is frequently depoliticised thus nullifying the 'radical potential' of MSP.[81] Therefore, considerable work is needed in order to ensure that public participation in relation to ocean space is satisfactorily achieved.

The final lesson learned from merfolk tales relates to another major preoccupation of modern environmental law, that is the development of a jurisprudence of substantive environmental rights. However, as Richard Barnes explains, marine environmental rights have tended to drift towards the 'margins of environmental rights discourse'.[82] Indeed the narrative of *freedom* of the High Seas seems to denote a space free from the normal rules and strictures of the land.[83] A place free from rights. Further, as I acknowledged earlier, the focus on rights, particularly those of states and powerful industry actors, can exacerbate biodiversity challenges of the oceans, by displacing considerations about responsibility.

Nevertheless, carefully articulated, rights can contribute to shifting the focus away from narrow anthropocentric considerations, to a more ecologically conscientious approach. Environmental rights can take many different forms, they can be procedural or substantive, positive or negative and they can extend to individuals, communities, future generations, of natural beings.[84] For now I want to highlight the burgeoning movement of the rights of nature and to point to the possibility of establishing ocean rights as a tool to protect marine biodiversity. Like Stone's proposal for a Guardian of the Oceans, the movement towards the rights of oceans dilutes the anthropocentric narrative of the present ocean governance regime, recognising the intrinsic value of the oceans.[85]

I recognise that in highlighting these lessons, I have not dealt in detail about how they might apply to the different parts of the oceans nor how

---

[79] For a comparative analysis of different approaches see Sarah Twomey and Cathal Mahony, 'Stakeholder Process in Marine Spatial Planning: Ambitions and Realities from the European Atlantic Experience' in Jacekt Zaucha and Kira Gee (eds), *Maritime Spatial Planning: Past, Present, Future* (Palgrave Macmillan 2019).

[80] Fred P Saunders, Michael Gilek and Ralph Tafon, 'Adding People to the Sea: Conceptualizing Social Sustainability in Marine Spatial Planning' in Jacekt Zaucha and Kira Gee (eds), *Maritime Spatial Planning: Past, Present, Future* (Palgrave Macmillan 2019); Flannery, Clarek and McAteer (n 57) 207.

[81] Mendenehall and others (n 57) 202.

[82] Barnes (n 40) 50.

[83] *Ibid*, 67.

[84] For a more detailed discussion of environmental rights see Emily Barritt, *The Foundations of the Aarhus Convention: Environmental Democracy, Rights and Stewardship* (Hart Publishing 2020) ch 4.

[85] Michelle Bender, *The Earth Law Framework for Protected Areas: Adopting a Holistic, Systems, and Rights-based Approach to Ocean Governance* (Earth Law Centre 2018).

they relate to the different elements of the package deal of the IBLI, partly this is a product of limited space, but it also stems from a conviction that thinking about ocean space in compartmentalised ways contributes to many of the significant problems that the oceans are enduring. Indeed, a regime for the protection of BBNJ will only truly be effective if it can have spill over effects for the protection of marine biodiversity across all ocean spaces. These three lessons are therefore not limited to how we think about ABNJ, but about how we construct and govern ocean space more generally.

V. Conclusion

In response to the mounting ecological problems that face us in this Anthropocene era, Anna Grear warns that nothing could be more urgent than the quest of 'worlds other' than the unsustainable status quo.[86] The worlds other that are occupied by mermaids, are often marred by human activity but by turning to these stories, I hope to retune and embellish the narrative of ocean space that is told by international law. The BBNJ negotiation process is an opportunity to seek out these worlds other in relation to the oceans, to embrace a new mythology of ocean space that better reflects the ecological and cultural realities of the seas, and in so doing, to achieve meaningful protection of marine biodiversity.

Sadly, little of what I have said in this contribution is new. The warning calls of those who fear the negative consequences of our fragmented ocean governance regime for conservation have gone unheeded for several decades.[87] Even with the promise of the ILBI as being designed to address marine biodiversity challenges, the commitment to not undermining the existing regime, dampens the promise of a genuine commitment to protecting ocean ecosystems. By appealing to the seductive powers of the mermaids, I hope that some of these warnings might be heard. That, unlike Odysseus' crew, those with the power to effect these changes will not stuff their ears with wax but will pay attention and respond to the song of the sirens.

Acknowledgements

I am grateful to Jorge Viñuales for helping to set me on the path of marine biodiversity protection, although he could not have realised it would have led me to mermaids, to Benjamin Richardson for his encouragement during IUCN-AEL 2017 to respond to the mermaid's lure and to Randal Abate for his invaluable thoughts and guidance on an early iteration of this piece. Thanks must also go to Megan Bowman and Leslie-Anne Duvic-Paoli for nurturing my fascination with mermaids. Finally, I am

[86] 'Anna Grear, 'Should Trees Have Standing: 40 Years On?' (2012) 3 *Journal of Human Rights and the Environment* 1, 1.

[87] See for example the work of Robert Jay Wilder written in 1998: Wilder (n 24).

very grateful to the anonymous reviewer for engaging seriously and thoughtfully with the paper, their comments were invaluable in helping me to refine my ideas.

Disclosure statement

No potential conflict of interest was reported by the author.

Funding

The genesis of this paper was prompted by research into legal options for a new international agreement on biodiversity in areas beyond national jurisdictions funded by the Cambridge Conservation Initiative.

To the Anthropocene and beyond: the responsibility of law in decimating and protecting marine life

Pierre Cloutier de Repentigny

ABSTRACT
As marine life spirals towards mass extinction in this age of the Anthropocene, law seems incapable of preventing negative human impacts on marine biodiversity. As humanity realises its geological agency, what is the responsibility of law for marine life within the Anthropocene? This article explores this question by first theorising the concept of the Anthropocene within law, focussing on the concept of responsibility. It then analyses, based on critical environmental law theory, the core marine biodiversity norms from a historical and structural perspective. The article finds that the law of the sea is moulded by liberal constitutive processes, namely economic growth. Law is not passive in the Anthropocene; it is one of the institutions that brought the era forth. The article concludes that to ensure responsible human geological agency, law must be used strategically to destabilise the dominant paradigm and reform it in something that recognises our responsibility towards the oceans and the biosphere.

I. Introduction

Over approximately 3.7 billion years ago, the first lifeform of our planet began to appear in the oceans.[1] Around 400 million years ago, early marine lifeforms began to spread on land and eventually, what we now call biodiversity (humans included), covered the entirety of planet Earth.[2] Despite the spread of biodiversity and the focus of human attention on terrestrial species (specifically, a minority subset of it), the oceans continue to be home to the majority of lifeforms; covering 70 percent of the Earth's

---

[1] Ben KD Pearce et al, 'Constraining the Time Interval for the Origin of Life on Earth' (2018) 18(3) *Astrobiology* 343.
[2] William A Shear, 'The Early Development of Terrestrial Ecosystems' in Henry Gee (ed), *Shaking the Tree: Readings from Nature in the History of Life* (UCP, 2000) 169–84.

surface and containing an even greater percentage of its biodiversity.[3] Indeed, the abundance of life in the oceans was once thought to be inexhaustible[4]; this belief even formed the part of Grotius's argument for free seas in his seminal work *Mare Liberum*.[5] It is now trite to state that this is not the case; marine life is in fact exhaustible and fragile. As we enter a period of mass extinction of marine life,[6] one of our own doing,[7] and search for solutions, it is important to question the role of law in the preservation and destruction of marine life.

Despite the proliferation of norms to conserve marine life, law, specifically the law of the sea, has proven ineffective in stopping or even slowing marine biodiversity decline.[8] Given this ineffectiveness, this article interrogates the role of law in the Anthropocene, focusing on the case of marine life. To answer this question, I first theorise the concept of the Anthropocene within the legal context. Specifically, I look at what this new epoch means in terms of law's responsibility towards the oceans and its inhabitants. Second, drawing from critical environment law, I offer a brief overview of the historical and structural failures of the core marine biodiversity protection regime. I analyse the constitutive impact of economic profit and territoriality on the law of the sea. The article ends by highlighting the responsibility of the marine biodiversity protection regime in creating the Anthropocene, hinting at the possible role law could play in transforming humanity into a responsible geological agent.

II. Theorising the Anthropocene: of geological agents and anthropocenic responsibility

The Anthropocene denotes 'the present geological time interval, in which many conditions and processes on Earth are profoundly altered by human impact'.[9] If the International Commission on Stratigraphy (ICS) adopts it as an official geological era, it will follow the Holocene, an era known for its stability and for having fostered human life. The starting point of the Anthropocene, as recently agreed by the ICS's Anthropocene Working

[3] Census of Marine Life International Secretariat, *Scientific Results to Support the Sustainable Use and Conservation of Marine Life: A Summary of the Census of Marine Life for Decision Makers* (Consortium for Ocean Leadership, 2011) 2.

[4] Lawrence Juda, *International Law and Ocean Use Management: The Evolution of Ocean Governance* (Routledge, 1996) 20.

[5] Hugo Grotius, *Mare Liberum*, in Robert Feenstra (ed), *Hugo Grotius Mare Liberum 1609–2009* (Brill, 2009) 60–63.

[6] UNEP Regional Seas Programme, *Global Synthesis—A report from the Regional Seas Conventions and Action Plans for the Marine Biodiversity Assessment and Outlook Series* (UNEP, 2010) 7.

[7] *Ibid*, 5.

[8] Rebecca M Bratspies and Anastasia Telesetsky, 'Marine Environmental Law: UNCLOS and Fisheries' in Shawkat Alam et al (eds), *Routledge Handbook of International Environmental Law* (Routledge, 2013) 260.

[9] Subcommission on Quaternary Stratigraphy, *Working Group on the 'Anthropocene' (International Commission on Stratigraphy)*, online: <http://quaternary.stratigraphy.org/working-groups/anthropocene/> (accessed 25 November 2019).

Group, is the mid-twentieth Century, in other words, the Great-Acceleration.[10] The intensification of human activities that characterises the Great-Acceleration period has resulted in the modification, at unprecedented rate, of the biosphere's components, and of its water, energy and biological cycles.[11] The impacts resulting from this era are multiple; climate change and mass extinction being two of them. Marine biodiversity has been hit particularly hard. The main culprits for the decline of marine life are overfishing, habitat destructions, pollution and climate change.[12] Ocean acidification (caused by the absorption of carbon dioxide by oceans) and increase in water temperature threaten the stability of marine ecosystems.[13] On average, based on historic levels, the decline of large marine animals reached 90 percent, while 65 percent of wetland and seagrass habitats, 85 percent of oyster reefs and 20 percent of mangrove forests have disappeared.[14] The majority of fisheries are either overfished or depleted (31.4 percent), or fully fished to their alleged maximum sustainable yield (MSY) (58.1 percent).[15] The situation is so dire that some studies have predicted that marine harvested fish could disappear by 2048.[16] Thus, regardless of whether the Anthropocene becomes an official era or not, our impact on the Earth system makes one thing clear: humanity has achieved the status of geological agent.[17]

But what does it mean to be a geological agent? It means that humanity possesses the capacity to change the Earth system on a geological level through our collective agency. That is, our collective intentional actions can alter basic geological processes previously thought unchangeable by human hands.[18] Conceptualising humanity as a geological agent means putting humanity as the central actor in the 'story of "the Anthropos" that has conquered the planet and now is humanizing the natural environment in

---

[10] *Ibid*; Will Steffen et al, 'The Trajectory of the Anthropocene: The Great Acceleration' (2015) 2(1) *The Anthropocene Review* 81.

[11] Will Steffen et al, 'The Anthropocene: Conceptual and Historical Perspectives' (2011) 369 *Philosophical Transactions of the Royal Society A* 842, 843.

[12] UNEP (n 6) 5.

[13] Sebastian Hennige, J Murray Roberts and Phillip Williamson (eds), *An Updated Synthesis of the Impacts of Ocean Acidification on Marine Biodiversity*, CBD Technical Series No 75 (CBD Secretariat 2014) 11; Census of Marine Life International Secretariat (n 3) 5; Food and Agriculture Organization, *State of the World Fisheries and Aquaculture 2010* (FAO 2010) 115.

[14] Census of Marine Life International Secretariat (n 3) 4; Secretariat of the Convention on Biological Diversity, *Global Biodiversity Outlook 3* (CBD Secretariat 2010) 46–48.

[15] Food and Agriculture Organization, *State of the World Fisheries and Aquaculture 2016* (FAO 2016) 38.

[16] Boris Worm et al, 'Impacts of Biodiversity Loss on Ocean Ecosystem Services' (2006) 314(5800) *Science* 787.

[17] Colin N Waters et al, 'The Anthropocene is Functionally and Stratigraphically Distinct from the Holocene' (2016) 351(6269) *Science* 137; Dipesh Chakrabarty, 'The Climate of History: Four Theses' (2009) 35(2) *Critical Inquiry* 197, 206–07.

[18] Naomi Oreskes, 'The Scientific Consensus on Climate Change: How Do We Know We're Not Wrong?' in Joseph FC Dimento and Pamela Doughman (eds), *Climate Change: What It Means for Us, Our Children, and Our Grandchildren* (MIT Press, 2007) 93.

dangerous and unforeseeable ways'.[19] This is in line with the goal of Crutzen and Stoermer, who coined the term Anthropocene, to 'emphasize the central role of mankind in geology and ecology'.[20] Nonetheless, geological agency means more than simply recognising our role as a geological force. The concept of human agency links our ability to make conscious actions to the sense of responsibility associated with these actions.[21] Geological agency thus brings forth a 'human species-responsibility' towards the current socio-ecological state of the world.[22] Pottage puts it in clear legal terminology: anthropocenic responsibility is akin to determining the liability of a tortfeasor at a geological level.[23] Just as tort law entails considering past actions, attributing responsibility in the present and anticipating social behaviour in the future in response to liability, so does anthropocenic responsibility. This entails a retrospective component (who and what caused the ecological crisis) and a prospective one (how to ensure actions that ensure the maintenance of the biosphere). In terms of legal thinking, anthropocenic responsibility creates 'a powerful framework that allows us to re-interrogate our regulatory institutions, including juridical institutions, with a view to devising a different approach to mediating the human-environment interface'.[24] In other words, what is the responsibility of law regarding the actions that lead to the Anthropocene and, learning from the past, how can law be changed in order to better take into account humanity's geological agency?

Looking at these questions of anthropocenic responsibility is not a neutral endeavour however; it is a deeply political.[25] This is made evident by the proposition of some scholars that 'Capitalocene' is a more appropriate name for the new geological epoch because capitalism—and those who control it (white, wealthy, heterosexual, abled cis-males)—is the institution responsible for endangering the Earth system.[26] The Capitalocene evokes ideology; it points its fingers at something larger and more 'constitutive' than a subset of humans. This underlines the socio-political and subjective context of anthropocenic responsibility. In terms of legal theory, this context is what

---

[19] Eva Lövbrand et al, 'Who Speaks for the Future of Earth? How Critical Social Science Can Extend the Conversation on the Anthropocene' (2015) 32 *Global Environmental Change* 211, 213.

[20] Paul Crutzen and Eugene Stoermer, 'The Anthropocene' (2000) 41 *IGBP Newsletter* 17.

[21] Chris D Frith, 'Action, Agency and Responsibility' (2014) 55 *Neuropsychologia* 137; David P Schweikard and Hans Bernhard Schmid, 'Collective Intentionality' in Edward N Zalta (ed), *The Stanford Encyclopedia of Philosophy* (Summer 2013 Edition), online: <https://plato.stanford.edu/archives/sum2013/entries/collective-intentionality/>.

[22] Anna Grear, 'Deconstructing Anthropos: A Critical Reflection on "Anthropocentric" Law and Anthropocene "Humanity"' (2015) 26 *Law & Critique* 225, 227.

[23] Alain Pottage, 'Holocene Jurisprudence' (2019) 10(2) *Journal of Human Rights and the Environment* 153, 158–59.

[24] Louis J Kotzé, *Global Environmental Constitutionalism in the Anthropocene* (Hart Publishing, 2016) 23.

[25] Cameron Harrington, 'The Ends of the World: International Relations and the Anthropocene' (2016) 44 (3) *Millennium* 478, 483.

[26] Jason W Moore, 'Introduction: Anthropocene or Capitalocene? Nature, History, and the Crisis of Capitalism' in Jason W Moore (ed), *Anthropocene or Capitalocene? Nature, History, and the Crisis of Capitalism* (PM Press, 2016); Harrington (n 25) 482–83.

M'Gonigle and Takeda calls the constitutive processes of the law,[27] or what Pottage refers to as super-jurisprudence.[28] Constitutive processes refer to the upstream dynamics of material and cultural production of law.[29] They act as a constraining framework, one that shapes law and prevents it from steering away from the aims of the relevant processes.[30] Given that law's dominant paradigm is liberalism, M'Gonigle and Takeda identifies economic growth as one of the primary constitutive processes of law, particularly environmental law.[31] Economic growth gives law a larger (political) purpose, which it contributes to by offering legitimacy (eg outlining and protecting institutions that are central to economic growth such as private property).[32] This is in line with Pottage's suggestion that the Capitalocene acts as super-jurisprudence.[33] Legal anthropocenic responsibility thus lies squarely within the ambit of critical legal theory.

In terms of the retrospective anthropocenic responsibility of the law, we are thus looking at the how the constitutive process of economic growth influences the development of the law, and how law has solidified this process. For law's prospective responsibility, we are concerned with law's ability to participate in the creation of a new paradigm and associated constitutive processes to ensure the *responsabilisation* (French for making someone aware of their responsibility) of humanity through law. In other words, anthropocenic responsibility can help deconstruct the role of law within humanity's geological agency and can assist us in reflecting on law's potential role in reconstituting itself as a tool for responsible collective geological agency. The next two sections explore this theoretical framework further through the example of marine biodiversity law.

III. The original sins: liberalism and territoriality in the law of the sea

The first step in applying the concept of anthropocenic responsibility to the law of the sea and the decline of marine biodiversity is retrospective. Reflecting upon the history of law is a common tool of critical legal theory; one that is central for understanding the impact of constitutive processes on the law of the sea.[34] The law of the sea is a fertile ground for this exploration given that its evolution has been driven by two intertwined aspects associated

[27] Michael M'Gonigle and Louise Takeda, 'The Liberal Limits of Environmental Law: A Green Legal Critique' (2013) 30 *Pace Environmental Law Review* 1005, 1020.
[28] Pottage (n 23) 164.
[29] M'Gonigle and Takeda (n 27) 1059.
[30] *Ibid*, 1060.
[31] *Ibid*, 1054–68.
[32] *Ibid*, 1019–20, 1059–65, 1109–10.
[33] Pottage (n 23) 164.
[34] Michael M'Gonigle and Paula Ramsay, 'Greening Environmental Law: From Sectoral Reform to Systemic Re-Formation' (2004) 14 *Journal of Environmental Law and Practice* 333, 345; Markus D Dubber, 'Legal

with liberalism and economic growth: territoriality and economic profit.[35] This section explores each aspect and highlights the impact of economic growth as a constitutive process on the development of the law of the sea as it relates to marine life. It focusses primarily on fisheries as an example given its predominant place within the law of the sea and given that over-exploitation remains the primary cause of marine biodiversity decline.

A. Economic profit and the law of the sea: the case of marine life

The development of the modern law of the sea technically began right before the emergence of liberalism. Nonetheless, the early authors of international law (in the sixteenth and seventeenth centuries), Grotius being a prominent one, participated in the creation of a world-view that would lead to the Industrial Revolution and subsequently to the Great-Acceleration.[36] Commerce and thus economic profit were the main motivators for these authors. Of great importance to commerce is a core principle of the law of the sea: the freedom of the sea. Grotius makes the argument for a free sea in his famous tract *Mare Liberum*. The idea of the free sea predated Grotius' tract,[37] but it is that text which provoked the discussion among jurists of different nations—ie the battle of the books—that crystallised the concepts of the freedoms of the sea and established the foundation of the modern law of the sea.[38] The aim of Grotius was not the free sea *per se*, but securing the rights for free trade and unhindered economic use of the oceans.[39] In other words, the aim was to ensure economic growth through a free market approach, what would become a central tenet of liberalism. The two freedoms discussed by Grotius were the freedom of navigation and the freedom of fishing. The first ensures the exchange of goods. The second allowed for the free economic exploitation of a resource hypothesised to be limitless (a hypothesis Grotius himself admitted could be wrong).[40]

The freedom of fishing went on to be integrated in the corpus of customary international law and was relatively undisturbed until the creation of the Exclusive Economic Zone (EEZ) and the expansion of conservation

History as Legal Scholarship: Doctrinalism, Interdisciplinarity, and Critical Analysis of Law' in Markus D Dubber and Christopher Tomlins (eds), *The Oxford Handbook of Legal History* (OUP, 2018) 114–15.

35 Davor Vidas, 'The Anthropocene and the International Law of the Sea' (2011) 369(1938) *Philosophical Transactions of the Royal Society A* 909, 912–13.

36 *Ibid*, 913–14; Ileana Porras, 'Appropriating Nature: Commerce, Property, and the Commodification of Nature in the Law of Nations' (2014) 27 *Leiden Journal of International Law* 641; Will Steffen, Paul J Crutzen and John R McNeill, 'The Anthropocene: Are Humans Now Overwhelming the Great Forces of Nature?' (2007) 36(8) *Ambio* 614, 617.

37 Vidas (n 35) 912.

38 Tullio Treves, 'Historical Development of the Law of the Sea' in Donald Rothwell et al, (eds), *The Oxford Handbook of the Law of the Sea* (OUP, 2012) 3–6.

39 Vidas (n 35) 920.

40 Grotius (n 5) 92–93.

obligations.[41] This stability is due in part to the fact that the freedoms of the sea corresponded to the commercial interest of the great maritime powers of the eighteenth and nineteenth centuries.[42] It is not surprising that the unqualified freedom to fish eventually ended up in the depletion of certain species. By the end of the nineteenth century, depletion led to a dispute between the United States and the United Kingdom over the exploitation of fur seals in the Bering Sea. The resulting arbitration award—the 1893 *Bering Fur Seal* Arbitration award[43]—was the first reference in international law to the conservation of 'marine living resources'. The tribunal reaffirmed the freedom of fishing, but 'recognized the need for restraint and called upon both states to co-operate in regulating the seals' over-exploitation on the high seas'.[44] This decision can be seen as the emergence of what would eventually become the customary conservation duty.[45] It is also around this time that the first treaty dealing with conservation emerged: the 1882 North Seas Overfishing Convention.[46]

With the rapid decline of whales due to commercial whaling, the early twentieth century saw the first global scale marine biodiversity issue. This led to the adoption of a succession of treaties regulating whaling, culminating with the still in force 1946 International Convention for the Regulation of Whaling[47] (ICRW).[48] The preamble of the convention clearly indicates that whales are viewed as a natural resource and that the aim of conservation was to sustain continued exploitation. The failure to halt the decline through conservation measures and the perception change of whales as highly intelligent beings in many states led to the adoption of a moratorium on commercial whaling in 1982.[49] The moratorium led to the death of the whaling industry in most of the world and to a slow recovery of many whale species (although many remain endangered).[50] Nonetheless,

---

[41] Michaela Young, 'Then and Now: Reappraising Freedom of the Seas in Modern Law of the Sea' (2016) 47 (2) *Ocean Development & International Law* 165.

[42] Treves (n 38) 5–6.

[43] Award between the United States and the United Kingdom relating to the rights of jurisdiction of United States in the Bering's sea and the preservation of fur seals (1893) 28 RIAA 263.

[44] Simone Borg, 'The Influence of International Case Law on Aspects of International Law Relating to the Conservation of Living Marine Resources beyond National Jurisdiction' (2012) 23(1) *Yearbook of International Environmental Law* 44, 46.

[45] *Ibid*, 47.

[46] Simone Borg, *Conservation on the High Seas – Harmonizing International Regimes for the Sustainable Use of Living Resources* (Edward Elgar, 2012) 96.

[47] (adopted 2 December 1946, entered into force 10 November 1948) 161 UNTS 72 (ICRW).

[48] Patricia W Birnie, 'Marine Mammals: Exploiting the Ambiguities of Article 65 of the Convention on the Law of the Sea and Related Provisions: Practice under the International Convention for the Regulation of Whaling' in Richard Barnes, David Freestone and David M Ong (eds), *The Law of the Sea, Progress and Prospects* (OUP, 2006) 268–70.

[49] *Ibid*, 267.

[50] See Phillip J Clapham and C Scott Baker, 'Whaling, Modern' in Bernd Würsig, JGM Thewissen and Kit M Kovacs (eds), *Encyclopedia of Marine Mammals* (Academic Press, 3rd edn 2018).

commercial whaling continues in three states with socio-economic ties to the industry, namely Norway, Iceland and Japan.

The continuation of overfishing and developments in technology after World War II—around the time of the Great-Acceleration—induced two major developments in the law of the sea. One was the codification of the law of the sea in 1958 through a series of treaties, including the Convention on Fishing and Conservation of the Living Resources of the High Seas,[51] the first treaty creating global but weak conservation obligations. The aim of the convention was to ensure the maximum supply of marine products through optimum sustainable yield of marine living resources.[52] The other development was the increase in unilateral actions to take control over coastal resources, including fisheries.[53] This practice—started by the United States though President Truman's Proclamation in 1945—eventually evolved into customary law and was widely adopted by states.[54] This vast development of customs coupled with the inefficiency of the 1958 Convention quickly led to the negotiation for a new agreement on the law of the sea in 1960 and in 1973–1982.[55]

The last prolonged round of negotiation resulted in the adoption of the 1982 United Nations Convention on the Law of the Sea (UNCLOS).[56] One of the goal of the negotiation and adoption of UNCLOS was to insure better conservation of 'marine living resources'.[57] Conservation duties are split between two regimes: the EEZ and the high seas. The growing jurisdiction of states over their coastal water was codified and expended to form the EEZ. States control over the marine living resources in this zone was balanced by the imposition of several conservation measures.[58] The main duty is the setting of total allowable catches based on MSY taking into account stocks interdependence and the impact on associated species, with the objective of attaining optimum utilisation of the resource.[59] UNCLOS maintained the freedom to fish in the high seas while codifying the duty of conservation.[60] These obligations are similar to the EEZ, that is achieving MSY, and include a duty to cooperate in the conservation of marine living resources.[61]

[51] (adopted 29 April 1958, entered into force 20 March 1966) 559 UNTS 285.
[52] Borg (n 46) 98–99.
[53] Treves (n 38) 10–12.
[54] Fisheries Jurisdiction Case (Federal Republic of Germany v Iceland) (Merits) [1974] ICJ Rep 175; Borg (n 46) 99–100.
[55] Treves (n 38) 17–21; Francisco O Vicuña, *The Changing International Law of High Seas Fisheries* (CUP, 1999) 19–23.
[56] (adopted 10 December 1982, entered into force 16 November 1994) 1833 UNTS 3 (UNCLOS).
[57] Borg (n 46) 27–28.
[58] Vicuña (n 55) 30.
[59] UNCLOS (n 56) art 61, 62.
[60] *Ibid*, art 87(1)(e), 116–20.
[61] *Ibid*, art 118, 119.

More stringent conservation measures can be adopted for marine mammals in both zones (eg the moratorium on commercial whaling).[62]

UNCLOS was inconclusive in terms of the conservation of highly migratory species and straddling stocks, imposing vague obligations of cooperation to set conservation measures.[63] As stocks continue their decline, an implementing agreement was negotiated for these species.[64] The result, the United Nations Agreement Relating to the Conservation and Management of Straddling Fish Stocks and Migratory Fish Stocks[65] (UNFSA), pushed fisheries conservation in line with modern developments in international environmental law.[66] The agreement's goal is the long term conservation and sustainable use of the covered species.[67] It is aimed at ensuring participation in Regional Management Fisheries Organisations (RMFOs), and establishes conservation obligations based on, *inter alia*, the precautionary principle, minimising pollution, data collection, enforcement measures, the compatibility of conservation measures between the EEZ and high seas, and optimum utilisation of the resource.[68] One of its main features is the introduction of the ecosystem approach to fisheries management.[69] Another implementing agreement is currently in negotiation to palliate for UNCLOS' weak protection of marine biodiversity beyond national jurisdiction (BBNJ). As it currently stands, this agreement will have three components: (1) area-based protection and management measures (ABPMM); (2) environmental impact assessments; and (3) sustainable use of genetic resources.[70]

Despite the *prima facie* progress in terms of conservation obligations brought by UNCLOS and UNFSA, the decline of marine biodiversity in both zones continues to worsen.[71] There is thus a disjunction between the increase in conservation obligations and the critical state of marine biodiversity. This is due to what M'Gonigle and Takeda term the law of mitigated production.[72] This concept relates to the inability of the law to truly address the cause of environmental degradation (eg marine biodiversity exploitation) and instead concentrating on the symptoms (eg bycatches). The law, under the constitutive process of economic growth, facilitates exploitation, including

---

[62] *Ibid*, art 65, 120.
[63] *Ibid*, art 63, 64.
[64] Borg (n 46) 51.
[65] (adopted 4 August 1995, entered into force 11 November 2001) 2167 UNTS 3 (UNFSA).
[66] Borg (n 46) 13.
[67] UNFSA (n 65) Art. 2.
[68] *Ibid*, art 5–23.
[69] *Ibid*, art 5(d),(e),(g).
[70] Intergovernmental Conference on Marine Biodiversity of Areas Beyond National Jurisdiction, 'Fourth substantive session' (*United Nations*) <www.un.org/bbnj/content/fourth-substantive-session> (accessed 2 April 2020).
[71] Borg (n 46) 50; Bratspies and Telesetsky (n 8) 265–66.
[72] M'Gonigle and Takeda (n 27) 1054–59, 1067–71, 1081–86.

the adoption of measures that soften the harshest edges of exploitation (eg measures based on *sustainable* use) to increase legitimacy. While we are far from the days of absolute freedom of fishing based on evidently commercial interests, the evolution of the law of the sea has been concerned with maintaining 'marine living resources' at an exploitable level. The 'wicked' problem here is that reduction and possibly elimination of commercial exploitation of marine biodiversity seem to be sorely needed, but such solutions are inconsistent with economic growth and its manifestation through law.

UNCLOS' economic paradigm is evident in its division of the sea between different regimes to exploit, *inter alia*, marine biodiversity. Exploitation is then mitigated through conservation measures, mainly MSY and sustainable use. These measures do not exist for the benefit of marine life, but for the 'optimum utilisation of the resource'.[73] In fact, economic factors are explicitly integrated in MSY and have led states to prioritise economic considerations to the detriment of marine biodiversity.[74] RFMOs have to resort to economic incentives, such as the higher market value of fish caught within their regime, to ensure participation by fishing states.[75] Current measures do not limit fisheries to what is necessary considering the overall ecosystem and what we need in terms of survival, and does not truly consider the needs or perspective of marine life.[76] Furthermore, the characteristic of the freedom of fishing as a fundamental principle of the law of the sea, even qualified, and the economic growth paradigm has led states who resists even mitigated conservation to rely on this freedom as a justification to continue their relatively unhindered exploitation of marine biodiversity.[77] One of the rare economically disruptive measures adopted—the whaling moratorium—has been thwarted by states hosting what is left of the whaling industry by simply refusing to participate in the regime or by having initially opted out of the moratorium as allowed by the ICRW.[78]

Concepts like the ecosystem approach—'a strategy for the integrated management of land, water and living resources that promotes conservation and sustainable use'[79]—may hold some promise to initiate a paradigm shift since they can potentially put ecosystems as the central focus of environmental

[73] UNCLOS (n 56) art 62; UNFSA (n 65) art 5(a); Usha Natarajan and Kishan Khoday, 'Locating Nature: Making and Unmaking International Law' (2014) 27 *Leiden Journal of International Law* 573, 588.
[74] UNCLOS (n 56) art 61(3); Bratspies and Telesetsky (n 8) 263.
[75] See Jaye Ellis, 'Fisheries Conservation in an Anarchical System: A Comparison of Rational Choice and Constructivist Perspectives' (2007) 3 *Journal of International Law & International Relations* 1.
[76] Patricia Birnie, Alan Boyle and Catherine Redgwell, *International Law and the Environment*, (OUP, 3rd edn 2009) 589; Bratspies and Telesetsky (n 8) 262–63.
[77] Young (n 41) 166.
[78] ICRW (n 47) art V(3).
[79] Secretariat of the Convention on Biological Diversity, 'Ecosystem Approach' (*Convention on Biological Diversity*, 8 August 2019) <www.cbd.int/ecosystem/> (accessed 29 May 2020).

decision-making rather than purely anthropocentric concerns.[80] Nevertheless, even a concept like the ecosystem approach is currently engulfed by the constitutive processes of liberalism by focussing on the primacy of human interests, especially economic considerations.[81] This anthropocentric interpretation relegates it to a management tool, one that is deemed consistent with the traditional fisheries management approach entrenched in the liberal paradigm. The BBNJ negotiation could improve the situation, but one of its core principle, the ecosystem approach, is currently undefined and thus subject to existing anthropocentrism. There is a high risk that the eventual BBNJ agreement will be constrained by the same economic growth paradigm as its predecessors. Nonetheless, in-depth analysis will have to wait for a final version of the agreement's text and its eventual implementation. Overall, economic growth has overtly and covertly influenced the development and application of the law of the sea regarding marine biodiversity, rendering this body of law partly responsible in bringing forth the Anthropocene.

B. Drawing lines in the oceans: appropriating the sea

Territorialisation has played an important role in the shaping of international law and in creating barriers to effective regulation of environmental issues, such as marine biodiversity, that do not respect juridico-political boundaries.[82] As the short history of the law of sea above demonstrates, territorialisation was avoided for a long time until the expansion of the territorial sea[83] and the creation of the EEZ. Territory is demarcated and exploited through the process of appropriation. This appropriation grounds the legal order, conditioning its operation within it.[84] Sovereignty, the core concept of international law, is premised on appropriation of territory, on exploitation of the 'land'.[85] This process emerged and evolved through colonisation, as apparent by the concept of *terra nullius*.[86] Land was 'free' and 'up for grabs'. The law entered after the event, justifying and ordering actions. The ordering is threefold: appropriation (through demarcation and exploitation), distribution (of the appropriated land) and production (from the fruit of the land). Overall, this ordering process creates fertile conditions for economic growth.

Appropriation of the sea is not as straight forward as that of land; the sea cannot be occupied in the same manner. In terms of marine life, exploitation

---

80 Vito De Lucia, 'Competing Narratives and Complex Genealogies: The Ecosystem Approach in International Environmental Law' (2015) 27 *Journal of Environmental Law* 91, 104–06.
81 *Ibid*, 104–16; Convention on Biological Diversity, COP 5 Decision V/6 (May 2000).
82 M'Gonigle and Ramsay (n 34) 349.
83 Treves (n 38) 7–14.
84 Pottage (n 23) 165.
85 Natarajan and Khoday (n 73) 586–87.
86 Pottage (n 23) 166.

takes the familiar form of fisheries, but also increasingly the form of marine genetic resources extraction. Grotius did envisage that fishing could be subject to appropriation if a person/state was able to 'enclose' a small area of the sea.[87] As technology progressed, geographically exclusive fishing rights became possible (eg through the ability to identify and track vessels). Technology now also allows for the demarcation of boundaries at sea (eg through GPS). Thus, the appropriation of the sea, as it is done today, was a near impossibility at the time of Grotius. Interestingly, claims over extended areas of the oceans began around the start of the Great-Acceleration.[88] Thus, once that technology allowed for appropriation, combined with the proper economic motivation of states, the law emerged to legitimise it and establish order. Now there are lines drawn in the sea, calculated from the coast (baseline), to demarcate what is the 'sovereign right' of the coastal state (ie the EEZ) and what is still 'free' (ie the high seas); all neatly codified in UNCLOS. The sea could, even more than land, be seen as empty and subject to appropriation —a *terra nullius* or *mare nullius*—as until a certain point in time, the freedoms of the sea had insured that the oceans could not belong to any particular state.

As with land, once the sea has been 'appropriated', fishing rights are 'distributed' and fishers can 'produce' from the sea.[89] Following the logic of economic growth, fishing rights are concentrated in industrial capitalist hands and thus mainly benefits them (distributive violence),[90] while the socio-ecological impacts—marine biodiversity decline—are felt by non-human marine life and coastal communities who rely on fishing for their survival (productive violence).[91] Therefore, the EEZ regime leads to 'asymmetries that are manifested in the distribution of "environmental goods and environmental bads" … produced by processes of appropriation'.[92] This trifecta—appropriation, distribution and production—shapes the socio-legal order of coastal waters. They are part of the economic growth constitutive process and its liberal paradigm.[93] The territorialisation of the sea has thus strengthened the economic exploitation of marine life rather than heightened the level of protection of marine life that was initially associated with the EEZ.[94]

---

[87] Grotius (n 5) 68–73.
[88] Treves (n 38) 10–11.
[89] Pottage (n 23) 171.
[90] FAO, State of the World Fisheries and Aquaculture 2016 (n 15) v, 32 & 52; Paul Hallwood, *Economics of the Oceans – Rights, rents and resources* (Routledge, 2014) 92–95.
[91] FAO, *State of the World Fisheries and Aquaculture 2010* (n 13) 10–11; Richard Barnes, 'Fisheries and marine biodiversity' in Malgosia Fitzmaurice, David M Ong and Panos Merkouris (eds), *Research Handbook on International Environmental Law* (Edward Elgar, 2010) 549.
[92] Pottage (n 23) 167.
[93] M'Gonigle and Ramsay (n 34) 344.
[94] Bratspies and Telesetsky (n 8) 262–65.

IV. Marine life in the Anthropocene: the responsibility of law

Looking at the formation and evolution of the law of the sea through processes of economic profit and territoriality paints a different picture than the usual doctrinal critique of ocean governance. This picture reveals that the anthropocenic responsibility of the law of the sea is not just for failing to prevent marine life decline; it is also for facilitating the decline. Law is not a powerless bystander; rather, it forms part of humanity's geological agency. Law is partly responsible for this agency through the creation of the framework for marine biodiversity exploitation, complete with a system of conservation measures participating in the law of mitigated production. Understanding the retrospective aspect of law's anthropocenic responsibility is crucial for imagining its prospective aspect. If law is to become an instrument of anthropocenic *responsabilisation*, it must use the lessons learned from its retrospective responsibility to imagine a new constitutive paradigm and new boundaries to our geological agency.[95] As the current state of marine life demonstrates, the status quo cannot persist. Concretely, what this means is that changes in positive laws (reform) must be accompanied and even preceded to some extent by a change of paradigm, what green legal theory calls legal re-formation.[96] This rethinking of the law and of its constitutive processes will require a great deal of imagination, particularly because none of the main traditions of political philosophy would accept limits to economic growth or degrowth as a core tenet.[97] While radical change would ensure the most thorough re-formation of constitutive processes, 'the structural transformation of the capitalist growth economy and the consumer culture … regard[ed] as indispensable if large-scale catastrophe and social collapse are to be averted, is nowhere in sight'.[98] If not revolution or reform, then what?

There is a potential middle way, one based on concrete actions aimed at shifting the paradigm we are in. This approach could be called 'strategic revolution'. This approach is based on actions, which individually might not institute radical change, but that aim at destabilising the system and promote a new way of thinking about society and law. De Lucia stated that such an approach

> should perhaps be conceptualized as a form of internal resistance and as a strategy, one that may need to be discarded as soon as it becomes a hindrance. Such an understanding arguably keeps alive the important tension between practical

95 Luc Semal, 'Anthropocene, Catastrophism and Green Political Theory' in Clive Hamilton, Christophe Bonneuil and François Gemenne (eds), *The Anthropocene and the Global Environmental Crisis: Rethinking modernity in a new epoch* (Routledge, 2015) 88.

96 M'Gonigle and Ramsay (n 34) 344.

97 Andrew Dobson et al, 'Andrew Dobson: Trajectories of Green Political Theory' (2014) 22(2) *Natures Sciences Sociétés* 132, 134.

98 Ingolfur Blühdorn, 'A Much-needed Renewal of Environmentalism? Eco-politics in the Anthropocene' in Hamilton, Bonneuil and Gemenne (n 95) 156.

> action and radical cultural change – which is the level and kind of change essential for a deep, long-term shift of our cultural vision and of our juridical forms.[99]

This strategy does not abandon environmental law. Rather it contextualises it, provides it with a better understanding of the hegemonic structures in which it operates, and thus allows the strategic use of the law to instigate deeper changes.[100] Examples of existing strategic actions for the law of the sea include legitimising and revitalising Indigenous legal orders, instituting the public trust doctrine, and Earth Jurisprudence approaches.

Indigenous legal orders have the benefit of being based on a worldview exogenous of liberalism and thus of offering an alternative—one that is currently practised and not simply theoretical—to the dominant liberal legal order.[101] Having maintained close relationships with the environment, Indigenous worldviews conceptualise nature very differently; for coastal peoples, these relationships relate to the seas.[102] For examples, Hawaiians view the ocean as kin (*'ohana*) and as the source of life (*ke kumu*).[103] The ocean is considered alive and interconnected with other lifeforms. These relationships translate into an obligation to care for the land (inclusive of the ocean) named *mālama 'aina*. The concept of *mālama 'aina* may appear vague and difficult to apply, but so do many western legal concepts such as 'natural justice'. It is through its application in various contexts (praxis) via customary governance processes that the contour of the concept becomes clearer.[104] This praxis and deep knowledge of the marine environment resulted in detailed and strictly enforced laws (*kānāwai*) and codes of behaviour (*kapu*) for fishing.[105] Given colonisation and the imposition of American law on Hawaiians, there is currently little space for Hawaiians to practice their laws.[106] Nonetheless, Techera offers many contemporary examples of Pacific Island states that have recognised, to varying degrees, Indigenous law to great effect in terms of marine biodiversity protection and socio-economic outcomes.[107] Given that the constitutive processes that resulted in the degradation of the oceans also caused the deterioration of Indigenous cultures,[108]

99 Vito De Lucia, 'Towards an Ecological Philosophy of Law: A Comparative Discussion' (2013) 4(2) *Journal of Human Rights and the Environment* 167, 190.
100 M'Gonigle and Ramsay (n 34) 356.
101 Williamson B C Chang, 'Indigenous Values and the Law of the Sea' in Jon M Van Dyke et al (eds), *Governing Ocean Resources: New Challenges and Emerging Regimes* (Martinus Nijhoff, 2013) 427–28; Erika J Techera, *Marine Environmental Governance: From International Law to Local Practice* (Routledge, 2012) 165; M'Gonigle and Ramsay (n 34) 352.
102 See Chang (n 101) 432–36; Techera (n 101) 165–67.
103 Chang (n 101) 429–34.
104 Chang (n 101) 436–39; see also Techera (n 101) 247.
105 Techera (n 101) 166.
106 *Ibid*, 227.
107 *Ibid*, ch 7.
108 Chang (n 101) 431–32; Techera (n 101) 167; Antony Anghie, 'Imperialism and International Legal Theory' in Anne Orford and Florian Hoffman (eds), *The Oxford Handbook of the Theory of International Law* (OUP, 2016) 166.

simply recognising Indigenous legal orders is not enough; measures to revitalise them and empower the culture that sustains these orders are needed. Notably, states need to recognise and grant customary tenure of the land (inclusive of adjacent marine areas) given the strong link between Indigenous laws and the land.[109] The revitalisation of Indigenous legal orders in marine areas under the jurisdiction of states could positively influence the development of the law of the sea away from anthropocenic constitutive processes.

For marine areas not covered (or potentially covered) by Indigenous law, the concept of the public trust doctrine offers a potential strategy.[110] The public trust doctrine originates from the understanding that some natural resources are 'so vital to public welfare and human survival that they cannot be exclusively exploited through private property ownership and control'.[111] As such, the trustee must manage the trust (the oceans) for the greater benefit of the beneficiaries (humanity, inclusive of future generations). The public trust underlines any private land title or rights allowing for greater public interference with its use either through governments or through private actions to force the trustee to perform its fiduciary duties.[112] The concept originates from the common law (based on a Roman law concept) and exists in various forms in other legal orders. Elements of it are even found in international law; for examples in Article 4 of the World Heritage Convention and in the deep seabed mining regime of UNCLOS.[113] The public trust doctrine could be used to insert in the law of the sea—the future BBNJ agreement's ABPMM could be used as an entry point for example—a paramount duty to preserve marine biodiversity and ensure that activities damaging it, like fishing, are done only to the extent they are needed within ecological limits and considering future generations.[114] Given the inherent destructive nature of the economic growth paradigm, the management of the ocean-trust by the international community would need to exclude purely economic considerations to ensure the fulfilment of fiduciary obligations.

Another strategic approach would be to implement measures based on Earth Jurisprudence. Earth Jurisprudence tries to eliminate anthropocentrism from law, inspired both by Indigenous worldviews and the more liberal concept of 'rights for nature'.[115] It thus has the advantage of being capable of bridging Indigenous and western legal theories. Earth Jurisprudence

---

[109] Chang (n 101) 439–41; Techera (n 101) 165–67, 169–71, 246–47.
[110] Mary Turnipseed et al, 'Using the Public Trust Doctrine to Achieve Ocean Stewardship' in Christina Voigt (ed), *Rule of Law for Nature: New Dimensions and Ideas in Environmental Law* (CUP, 2013).
[111] Mary C Wood, 'You Can't Negotiate with a Beetle: Environmental Law for a New Ecological Age' (2010) 50 *Natural Resources Journal* 167, 200.
[112] Turnipseed et al (n 110) 369–70.
[113] See *ibid*, 372–74.
[114] See for eg *ibid*, 375–78.
[115] De Lucia (n 99) 176, 184–85; Cormac Cullinan, *Wild Law: A Manifesto for Earth Justice* (Green Books, 2nd edn 2011) 88–84.

constituting principle is the Great Law, a set of unifying principles derived from our understanding of the Earth and the universe.[116] The Great Law acts as a framework limiting human actions. Within it is the Earth Community, the interdependence and the subjectivity of natural entities. Each entity has rights according to their needs (eg the ocean would have ocean rights).[117] Bender proposes the adoption of an Earth Law framework for Marine Protected Areas (MPAs).[118] This would entail giving legal recognition and rights to MPAs as a whole and to each ecosystem elements encompassed by a particular MPA, and consequently moving away from viewing marine biodiversity simply as a resource or as potential property. The right to life of the MPA and its components can be based on ecological health—ie the ability of the ecosystem to function and species to thrive within it. A guardian can act as the voice of the MPA to ensure the respect of its rights through conservation measure and through legal actions when needed. As a rights-based approach, an Earth Jurisprudence strategy has the advantage of resonating with the current politico-legal context and, thus, of being capable of undermining the constitutive process of economic growth from inside.[119]

Each of these examples has the benefit of fostering a sense of responsibility (ie *responsabilisation*) towards the ocean and marine life: Indigenous relational responsibility, fiduciary duties, and rights-based responsibility. Each should be strategically implemented when an opportunity arises that best suits the characteristics of the approach. For example, the ABPMM of the BBNJ draft agreement offers an opportunity to integrate Bender's proposal. Strategic revolution, the middle way, allows for a flexible path towards new constitutive processes and a responsible law of the sea in this age of the Anthropocene without the need for unlikely immediate radical social changes.

V. Conclusion

Humanity is now bearing the heavy burden of being a geological agent. In this Anthropocene era, we are becoming more conscious of our collective ability to shape geology, including the oceans. The consciousness of our geological agency needs to be accompanied by an equivalent understanding of our anthropocenic responsibility. Law can and should be used to that end; that is, to impose a framework on our agency that is reflective of our destructive capacity and of the needs of the biosphere. In other words, law can act as a means of anthropocenic *responsabilisation*. Nonetheless, law is not a neutral institution. As the evolution of the law of the sea regarding the

---

[116] De Lucia (n 99) 173–76.
[117] See Michelle Bender, *The Earth Law Framework for Marine Protected Areas: Adopting a Holistic, Systems, and Rights-Based Approach to Ocean Governance* (Earth Law Center, 2018) 16.
[118] *Ibid*, 14–20.
[119] De Lucia (n 99) 189–90.

protection of marine biodiversity demonstrates, the role, or responsibility, of law in bringing forth the Anthropocene is far from passive. The law of the sea —embedded in and constricted by the same liberal constitutive processes associated with the Great-Acceleration, namely economic growth—is indeed an active participant in the rapid decline of marine life. Achieving the *responsabilisation* of the law will require the strategic shedding of the liberal paradigm—particularly its economic profit and territoriality aspects —to move towards new ways of imagining the law of the sea. It is not an easy path forward, but it is a necessary one since, as affirmed by Vidas, '[t]he need of our time is *responsibility for* the seas'.[120]

Acknowledgements

I am very grateful to the Kent Summer School in Critical Theory and its 2019 seminar 'An Anthropogeology of Law', which helped me establish the theoretical foundation of this article. I particularly thank Professor Alain Pottage, the seminar's conductor, and all my friends and colleagues who participated in the seminar. I am also grateful for the comments and suggestions of the peer reviewers and the editors. All potential errors and omissions are mine.

Disclosure statement

No potential conflict of interest was reported by the author(s).

[120] Vidas (n 35) 922.

Regimes of waste (im)perceptibility in the life cycle of metal

Tina Beigi and Michael Hennessy Picard

ABSTRACT

The transnational legal landscape governing waste management, recycling, and disposal remains narrowly focused on the economic possibilities of 'end-of-life products', while paying little to no consideration to the much greater quantities of waste generated at the beginning of the product's lifecycle. We explore the existing regulatory framework through the duality of (in)visibility: whereas the circular economy of recycling increasingly integrates synthetic waste into the visible, the extractive industry buries biophysical waste into a 'cradle-to-grave' economy. We argue that waste becomes a perceptible matter of concern when commodified into a new cycle of wealth accumulation. By contrast, when waste is abandoned on mining sites, it becomes an imperceptible matter of fact. Mining risks, although perceptible to the industry and affected communities, are rendered less visible to the administrative bodies in charge of regulating them. Therefore, waste (im)perceptibility is industrially manufactured according to the commercial aspects of a product, rather than its toxicity.

When crimes start to accumulate, they become invisible. Berthold Brecht[1]

1. Introduction

At the turn of the century, Chile's National Commission of the Environment (CONAMA) gave permission to the Canadian mining corporation Barrick

[1] Brecht Bertolt, *Bertolt Brecht Poems* (vol 1, Eyre Methuen 1976).

Gold to move three glaciers out of the Pascua Lama gold-mining site. Though the project was soon cancelled out of the sheer impossibility to physically relocate the century-old glaciers, it glaringly exposed how nature is rendered politically invisible in the Global South in response to foreign mining interests.[2] Around the same time, the first comprehensive reports on discarded electronics started to raise awareness of their environmental and social impact, which provided the context in which the need to regulate e-waste emerged. Today, consumers in shopping malls around the world are invited to drop their old cell phones in dedicated recycling bins, as part of an increasingly popular waste management strategy known as the 'circular economy'. At the forefront of such initiatives, the European Commission's *Circular Economy Action Plan* intends to 'close the loop' by incorporating electronic wastes within existing recycling markets and 'help consumers choose sustainable products'.[3] However, the waste and substances identified in such circular economy regimes represent only a tiny fraction of the chemical, toxic, and hazardous products generated by the global supply chain of electronics. Since most of the toxic waste arising from electronics production occurs before consumers even purchase the commodity, household recycling programmes and zero-waste initiatives—commendable as they may be—will do little to mitigate industrial-scale waste generation. The Canadian geographer Josh Lepawsky offers one revealing example of the disproportionate amount of waste generated at the pre-consumption stage: one single smelter producing metals for electronics in Mexico generates almost twice the amount of e-waste exported by the United States annually. As a result, 'waste arising from electronics manufacturing vastly exceeds that arising from postconsumer discards'.[4]

These examples demonstrate a fragmented political economy of waste, where some peripheral sources of environmental degradation become 'sights unseen',[5] while others are commodified, valued and made visible. Regulatory concern is generally addressed by post-consumption recycling policies and rarely tackles the problem directly at the *source* of mineral extraction.[6] Could it be that the cosmology of industrial waste is split into two

[2] Javiera Barandiarán, *Science and Environment in Chile: The Politics of Expert Advice in a Neoliberal Democracy* (MIT Press 2018) 127.

[3] For more information, see the European Commission's portal on the circular economy, <https://ec.europa.eu/environment/circular-economy/index_en.htm>.

[4] Josh Lepawsky, *Reassembling Rubbish: Worlding Electronic Waste* (MIT Press 2018) 142.

[5] Scott Frickel and James Elliott, *Sites Unseen: Uncovering Hidden Hazards in American Cities* (Russell Sage Foundation 2018).

[6] In this article, the *source* refers to the waste generated by transnational industrial conglomerates, which are logistically designed to extract, store, refine, manufacture, and distribute minerals. Primary sources of upstream pollution are attributed to any matter, whether liquid, solid, gaseous or radioactive, which is discharged, emitted, or deposited in the environment in such volume, composition or manner as to cause an alteration of the environment.[6] Examples include mining waste (waste rock, mineral, processing chemicals), gas and petroleum waste from extraction (drilling fluids and cuttings like complex mixtures of clays and chemicals) as well as CO_2 emission, water pollution, for example. There are also

opposites, the invisible life and the visible life, which co-evolve dialectically across global chains of production and consumption? If so, what are the laws and dynamics ruling over the *invisible life* and the *visible life*? How is the material world of mineral and electronic discards normatively (dis)ordered?[7] Our research wishes to call the reader's attention to the making and un-making of these (in)visible spheres. We further investigate the blind spots, ambiguities and contradictions created by the legal categories of waste in the life cycle of metal.

In an influential article,[8] Bruno Latour voices his concern about climate change scepticism, which questions the reality of global warming. He laments the fact that sceptics now use the very argument of 'social construction', tools of epistemological doubt, and flawed objectivity, which Latour himself had developed—which he dubs matters of concern—to wage a war against hard-won evidence that could save our lives. At first, Latour's critique of science had called on scholars to question the presumption of naturalised objectified facts. Yet, at the turn of the twenty-first Century, such a critique was becoming instrumentalised by vested interests in Washington to deny the best available scientific data on environmental boundaries—considered *matters of fact*—upon which the Anthropocene is encroaching.[9] Latour suggests that, for the critical mind to become relevant again, scholars must attempt to deal with matters of concern. To be critical is not to debunk, but to assemble and reassemble.[10]

Following Latour's theory of assemblage, we intend to start collecting fragmented knowledges and norms about hazardous waste and focus on the sets of regulations and policies, which organise and sustain the (in)visibility of waste. According to our binary classification, what we call 'matter of fact' is the volume of toxic extractive waste and the materiality of its distribution, whereas the phrase 'matter of concern' refers to the relevant laws of waste management and mitigation. As demonstrated by the chart below, there is an inverted correspondence between the seriousness of a privately manufactured hazard and the amount of public attention it receives. The *legality* (matters of concern) does not only fail to reflect the *materiality* of waste (matter of fact), it also obscures its

secondary sources of downstream leakage (which, for the purpose of our study, is concerned with—but not limited to—the postconsumer stage), such as recyclable solid waste containing plastic, cardboard, glass, paper, aluminium, and minerals such as e-waste.

7 Neil Walker, 'Beyond Boundary Disputes and Basic Grids: Mapping the Global Disorder of Normative Orders' (2008) 6(3–4) *International Journal of Constitutional Law* 373.

8 Bruno Latour, 'Why has Critique Run Out of Steam? From Matters of Fact to Matters of Concern' (2004) 30 (2) *Critical Inquiry* 225; for recent discussion see Gareth Leng and Rhodri Ivor Leng (eds), *The Matter of Facts: Skepticism, Persuasion, and Evidence in Science* (MIT Press 2020).

9 Will Steffen et al, 'Planetary Boundaries: Guiding Human Development on a Changing Planet' (2015) 347 (6223) *Science* 1259855.

10 Latour (n 8).

uneven distribution.

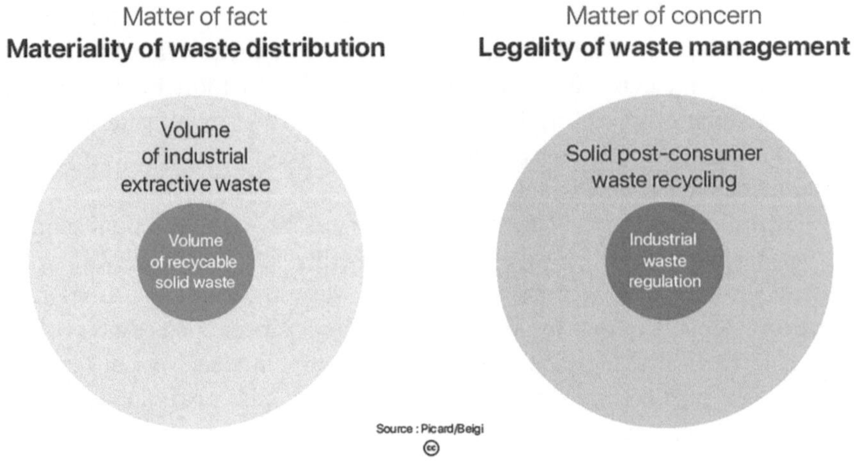

The chart above illustrates the classification of imaginaries in global waste management. On the left hand, the volume of industrial extractive waste is shown by the larger circle to demonstrate its significantly massive scope, globally 100 billion tonnes per year compared to only 500 million tonnes of recyclable e-waste represented by the smaller circle. On the right hand, the legality of waste management shifts societal concerns to e-waste by producing more and more stringent laws and regulation pertinent to this type of discard as it gains more and more economic value. By contrast, laws rulings over industrial waste are represented in the smaller circle depicting the dearth of rigour to mitigate environmental pollution at the source.

In other words, the current matter of concern *foregrounds* postconsumer waste, while simultaneously *backgrounding* the fact that industrial waste is far more voluminous and toxic than postconsumer waste. Visibility and invisibility are co-produced, as one illuminated feature of the e-waste mining economy simultaneously obscures other features of the mineral supply chain. Waste becomes a perceptible matter of concern, when commodified into a new round of wealth accumulation. On the contrary, when waste is abandoned on mining sites or spread as microparticles in the atmosphere, it becomes an imperceptible matter of fact.

A growing body of scientific literature known as 'agnotology'—the study of ignorance—points to the socially constructed blindness towards ecological hazard manufactured by powerful industries, such as the tobacco, petrochemical and mining sectors.[11] Active ignorance is deliberately orchestrated by

[11] Janet Kourany and Martin Carrier (eds), *Science and the Production of Ignorance: When the Quest for Knowledge Is Thwarted* (MIT Press 2020).

'science wars'[12] to forestall regulation of polluting industries, 'jam the scientific airwaves', produce uncertainty and divergent interpretation of evidence, which question scientifically established consensus by setting up impossible standards of proof. As we shall see, mining risks, although perceptible to the industry and affected communities, are rendered less visible to the administrative bodies in charge of regulating them.[13]

Powerful lobbies work hard to keep the hazardous industrial pollution outside the purview of global regulatory reform, while highlighting their otherwise voluntary participation in municipal e-waste recovery schemes.[14] For instance, though toxic nickel sulphates may be regulated and controlled by a 2007 European Union regulation, their widespread usage is still allowed and facilitated by a close association between industrialists and regulators.[15] Transnational governance relating to waste internalises the managerial logic of the market, by rejecting mining waste as a 'negative externality' at the source of extraction and monetising it as recoverable e-waste at the sink of consumption.[16] As a result, waste (im)perceptibility is manufactured according to the commercial aspects of a product, rather than its toxicity.[17]

Before addressing the specific legal regimes of e-waste management (3) and mining waste evacuation (4) in the life cycle of metal, the following section provides theoretical insights on the asymmetry of waste perception framed by legal (dis)orderings (2).

2. Asymmetry of perception framed by legal (dis)orderings

Discard Studies reveal that transnational laws[18] pertaining to waste management disproportionally address the household and municipal solid waste,

[12] The term *science wars* refer to a complex of intellectual exchanges and strong polarization over questions of intellectual legitimacy and scientific authority in the mid-1990s.

[13] Kourany and Carrier (n 11).

[14] François Jarrige and Thomas Le Roux, *La contamination du monde. Une histoire des pollutions à l'âge industriel* (Le Seuil 2017).

[15] Council Regulation (EC) No 1907/2006 of the European Parliament and of the Council on the Registration, Evaluation, Authorisation and Restriction of Chemicals (REACH) [2006] OJ L 396/1. See Henri Boullier, *Toxiques légaux: comment les firmes chimiques ont mis la main sur le contrôle de leurs produits* (La Découverte 2019) 115.

[16] Because this article focuses on the life cycle of minerals, *the sink* refers to the growing trade of electronic waste, containing valuable elements, including gold, silver, palladium, platinum, aluminium, copper, yttrium, lanthanum, terbium, neodymium, gadolinium, praseodymium, etc. For a general discussion on sinks, see Jennifer Gabrys, 'Sink: The Dirt of Systems' (2009) 27(4) *Environment and Planning D: Society and Space* 666.

[17] Olga Kuchinskaya, *The Politics of Invisibility: Public Knowledge about Radiation Health Effects after Chernobyl* (MIT Press 2014).

[18] *Transnational law of waste* is an umbrella term for all environmental and trade laws regulating waste, which transcend national frontiers and include but are not limited to public and private international law. Transnational investment law, for instance, implies that regulation pertaining to mineral waste management can be diffused globally without necessarily involving traditional international law between Nation States. See Terence Halliday and Gregory Shaffer (eds), *Transnational Legal Orders* (Cambridge University Press 2015) 4.

which amounts to less than 10% of all waste created, while seldom tackling the majority, some 90%, of upstream industrial pollution.[19]

> Typically, the problem of e-waste is cast as a post-consumption disposal issue. Yet formatting it that way brackets out all the practices of resource extraction, design, manufacturing, distribution, and use from which far more waste arises. Postconsumer recycling will never solve the problem of waste arising from electronics production.[20]

This asymmetry of perception is framed by legal (dis)orderings.[21] Transnational laws, such as bilateral investment treaties, protocols regulating global pollution and regional regulatory mechanisms,[22] organise the political economy of waste according to industrial policies, vested interests and political priorities, which carry the bulk of toxic waste 'out of sight and out of mind'. The classification of waste across asymmetric legal spaces is central to the circulation of some types of waste and the immobilisation of other types of waste across the life cycle of metal. Because of the importance of mineral extraction for global value chains, transnational law fragments regimes of environmental responsibility by rendering mineral waste relatively invisible, while concentrating regulatory efforts on the recovery of electronic waste.

International Law has an equivocal definition of waste, drawn from the general understanding of waste as a 'substance' or 'object' to be 'discarded' or 'disposed of'.[23] A first definition of waste, derived from continental civil law, suggests that a disposable object may be synonymous to an abandoned object: once the classic trilogy of *usus*, *fructus*, *abusus* is consummated, the object becomes *res nullius*.[24] Industrial and mining waste is often left abandoned on site, dumped in the peripheries of the extractive economies: *res*

---

[19] Lepawsky (n 4). See also the research network *Discard Studies Social Studies of Waste, Pollution & Externalities* <https://discardstudies.com/>.

[20] *Ibid*, 10.

[21] See Halliday and Shaffer (n 18).

[22] See Protocol on Civil Liability and Compensation for Damage Caused by the Transboundary Effects of Industrial Accidents on Transboundary Waters (adopted 21 May 2003) ECE/MP.WAT/11-ECE/CP.TEIA/9; Basel Protocol on Liability and Compensation for Damage Resulting from Transboundary Movements to the Convention on the Control of Transboundary Movements of Hazardous Wastes and their Disposal, (adopted 10 December 1999) UNEP/CHW 1/WG/1/9/2; Council Regulation (EC) 166/2006 of 18 January 2006 Concerning the Establishment of a European Pollutant Release and Transfer Register and Amending Council Directives 91/689/EEC and 96/61/EC [2006] OJ L 33/1, Article 11.

[23] Basel Convention on the Control of Transboundary Movements of Hazardous Wastes and Their Disposal (adopted 22 March 1989, entered into force 5 May 1992) 1673 UNTS 57 (Basel Convention), Articles 2(1) and 10(2); Bamako Convention on the Ban of the Import into Africa and the Control of Transboundary Movement and Management of Hazardous Wastes Within Africa (adopted 20 January 1991, entered into force 13 December 1998) 2101 UNTS 177, Artcile 1(1); Convention to Ban the Importation into Forum Island Countries of Hazardous and Radioactive Wastes and to Control the Transboundary Movement and Management of Hazardous Wastes within the South Pacific Region (adopted 16 September 1995, entered into force 21 October 2001) 2161 UNTS 91, Article 1.

[24] Martine Rémond-Gouilloud, *Du droit de détruire: essai sur le droit de l'environnement* (Presses Universitaires de France 1989) 107.

nullius, res derelicta. As we shall see, this 'linear' definition corresponds to the negative externalities of foreign extractive corporations operating in the Global South.

By contrast, a second definition of waste, derived from English common law, claims that what can be 'disposed of' includes *the selling for gain*, which subjects the disposable object to mercantile transactions and economic exploitation.[25] This 'circular' definition pertains to the worldwide commodification of recyclable waste in industrialised economies.

This article thus relies on a binary definition of waste as the disposable residue of our activities, which is either *abandoned and forgotten* or *converted into a positive value.*[26] Once we accept the binary definition of waste, we realise that transnational governance co-produces a soft law of ecological imperceptibility, while simultaneously promoting a perceptible regime of recyclable commodities. Depending on market preference, the transnational governance of waste is either a 'negative' concealment tool or a 'positive' lustration tool.

Each year, mining operations generate extreme volumes of mineral waste, which are unknown in detail. According to the Mining, Minerals, and Sustainable Development Project, there are approximately 3,500 active mining waste sites worldwide, consisting of waste rock dumps and tailing dams.[27] The estimated worldwide generation of solid wastes from the primary production of mineral and metal commodities is over 100 billion tonnes per year,[28] compared to the 500 million tonnes of e-waste produced annually.[29] Statistically, the amount of e-waste generated at the sink of the life cycle of metal corresponds to 0.5% of the total volume of mining waste generated at the source.

And yet, the scope and stringency of e-waste legislation worldwide is far greater than the regulations on waste generated by the mining sector. In 2017, 66% of the world population was already covered by e-waste management laws, an increase from 44% that were covered in 2014.[30] By contrast, the mining industry lacks stringent international mining and environmental standards. Though the 1996 Aarhus Convention calls on all parties to establish national pollution registers, there is no internationally agreed upon

---

[25] Nicolas de Sadeleer, 'The Concept of Waste' in Thomas Ormond, Martin Führ and Regine Barth (eds), *Environmental Law and Policy at the Turn to the 21st Century – Liber Amicorum Betty Gebers* (Lexxion 2006), 243, 249–50.

[26] Jean-Jacques Laffont, 'Externalities' in Steven Durlauf and Lawrence Blume (eds), *The New Palgrave Dictionary of Economics* (Palgrave Macmillan, 2nd edn, 2008).

[27] International Institute for Environment & Development, 'MMSD [Mining Minerals and Sustainable Development Project], Final Report' (Earthscan Publications Ltd 2002) <www.iied.org/mmsd-final-report>.

[28] John Rankin, *Minerals, Metals and Sustainability: Meeting Future Material Needs*, Commonwealth Scientific and Industrial Research Organisation (CSIRO 2011).

[29] Silpa Kaza et al, 'What a Waste 2.0: A Global Snapshot of Solid Waste Management to 2050' (World Bank Publications 2018).

[30] Cornelius Baldé et al, 'The Global E-waste Monitor 2017' (United Nations University, International Telecommunication Union and International Solid Waste Association) <www.itu.int/en/ITU-D/Climate-Change/Documents/GEM%202017/Global-E-waste%20Monitor%202017%20.pdf>.

strategy for the collection of mining emission data.[31] The erosion of the efficacy of the information disclosure obligations reflects the dominance of market liberal perspectives over social welfare in environmental law.[32]

Moreover, the Protocol on Pollutant Release and Transfer Registers, signed by 38 States and in force since 2009, is not designed to reduce pollution levels, but to enhance public access to information through the establishment of coherent, integrated, nationwide pollutant release and transfer registers. Resource-rich countries of the world, specifically Canada, the United States, China, Latin American and African states, are not parties to the Protocol.[33] Finally, many voluntary initiatives void of legal stringency, such as the Extractive Industries Transparency Initiative,[34] illustrate the weakness of public governance structures and their numerous failings at documenting, coordinating, and policing wrongful environmental behaviours at the local, national, regional, and global levels.

Mining waste regulation rests on definitional misunderstandings, miscalculated environmental costs, and methodological inconsistencies. The lack of full disclosure of mining flows is one of the most crucial limitations in advancing towards a comprehensive regime of mining pollution law. Without knowledge of the volume and spatial distribution of mining leakage, it is impossible to develop coherent strategies to mitigate ecological harm. Whereas e-waste management reforms have taken place at the international level (Basel technical guidelines and Ban amendment of 2019[35]), the regional level (the 2012 European Union (EU) Waste Electrical and Electronic Equipment Directive (WEEE) directive[36]) and domestic level (Canadian E-waste Stewardship programme and United States legislation, for example[37]), the mining waste reforms on the contrary have been frozen in time by the transnational legal activism of mining corporations.

[31] Convention on Access to Information, Public Participation in Decision-Making and Access to Justice in Environmental Matters (adopted 25 June 1998, entered into force 30 October 2001) 2161 UNTS 447; Kristina Saarinen, 'A Method to Improve the International Comparability of Emission Data from Industrial Installations' (2003) 6(4) *Environmental Science & Policy* 355.

[32] Michael Mason, 'So Far but No Further? Transparency and Disclosure in the Aarhus Convention' in Aarti Gupta and Michael Mason (eds), *Transparency in Global Environmental Governance: Critical Perspectives* (MIT Press 2014) 83, 85.

[33] Protocol on Pollutant Release and Transfer Registers to the Convention on Access to Information, Public Participation in Decision-Making and Access to Justice in Environmental Matters (adopted 21 May 2003, entered into force 8 October 2009) 2626 UNTS 119.

[34] Extractive Industries Transparency Initiative, <https://eiti.org/>.

[35] Technical guidelines on transboundary movements of electrical and electronic waste and used electrical and electronic equipment, in particular regarding the distinction between waste and non-waste under the Basel Convention (E-waste) (10 July 2015) UNEP/CHW.14/7/Add.6/Rev.1, adopted by the Conference of the Parties to the Basel Convention on the Control of Transboundary Movements of Hazardous Wastes and Their Disposal, Fourteenth meeting Geneva, 29 April–10 May 2019.

[36] Council Directive 2012/19/EU of the European Parliament and of the Council of 4 July 2012 on Waste Electrical and Electronic Equipment (WEEE) [2012] OJL 197/38.

[37] See Electronics Product Stewardship Canada, <https://epsc.ca/>; California Electronics Waste Recycling Act 2003, 14 CCR [18660.5] (US).

Canadian historian Michelle Murphy frames the ways in which the politics of knowledge production and the process of materialisation render certain things obscured while others acquire and retain visibility within scientific communities and society.[38] Murphy also examines this concept in relation to industry-funded research, which produces what she calls 'regimes of imperceptibility' that obscure and entrench the power of corporations over local communities and remove them from visible scenes. Inspired by her work, we share the view that various regimes of transnational law design the circular economy as a 'regime of perceptibility' at the sink, while perpetuating a 'regime of imperceptibility' at the source of the linear extractive economy.[39] In the following sections we address the production and reproduction of regimes of (im)perceptibility both at the source and the sink of linear and circular economies.

3. Regimes of e-waste perceptibility in circular economies

E-waste is an amorphous legal category that sits uneasily between conflicting transnational legal regimes. On the one hand, e-waste has been globally traded as the main ingredient of the circular economy.[40] On the other hand, the Basel regime on the transboundary movement of waste defines e-waste as a discarded object to be managed by sound environmental practices. Over the last three decades, as the market for second-hand electronic equipment soared, e-waste has progressively garnered public attention and been subjected to the legal scrutiny of formal transnational regimes. Therefore, e-waste has been encased into two parallel dynamics of market externality and market commodity, fragmenting as well as expanding the legal consciousness of the e-waste problem between two legal orders: the legal space of environmental law represented by the Basel Convention, and the legal space of market commodities adjudicated by the circular economies. Initially conceived as an environmental problem to be addressed (matter of concern), e-waste has now entered the global metal supply chain (matter of fact).

3.1. Matter of concern: the perceptibility of e-waste regulation

Historically, the e-waste regime emerged as an international problem to be addressed with the entry into force of the Basel Convention in 1992.[41] Though the Basel Convention is not a specialised international treaty pertaining to e-waste, it nonetheless framed the debate and controversies around the

[38] Michelle Murphy, 'Uncertain Exposures and the Privilege of Imperception: Activist Scientists and Race at the US Environmental Protection Agency' (2004) 19 *Osiris* 266.

[39] Sara Ann Wylie, *Fractivism: Corporate Bodies and Chemical Bonds* (Duke University Press 2018).

[40] E-waste has been historically dominated by the criminal underworld of 'midnight movers', which evacuated two thirds of e-waste on the informal market economy. See Rémond-Gouilloud (n 24).

[41] Basel Convention (n 23).

management of e-waste. The Convention does not determine a legally binding cap on waste transfer across jurisdictions. Provided the host State consents and is notified by the exporting State, hazardous waste may legally be traded on the international market. In short, there is no ban of waste transfer, rather a regulatory platform for exchange. The Convention imposes on member states a duty of reporting their levels of hazardous wastes (Article 13.3), yet never achieved its general aim of 'eliminating the generation of hazardous wastes ... in an environmentally sound manner'.[42]

At the Basel Conventions Conference of the Parties (COP), member States long failed to adopt universal technical guidelines on the definition of electronic discards, partly because of disagreements over their material complexity.[43] E-waste often evaded the category of hazardous waste and fell outside the purview of the Basel Convention.[44] This meant that sovereign states, following the World Trade Organization rules of free trade, were able to claim the legality of their e-waste export and import with minimal oversight. The e-waste trade economy revealed what was 'hazardous' in some European countries was elsewhere—in Egypt or China for example—defined as a 'recyclable' commodity or a 'reusable object'.[45]

These definitional inconsistencies and loopholes in the transnational regime of e-waste regulation magnified the importance of tackling the e-waste problem from a sturdier environmental perspective. It is crucial to remind the reader about the dual regime of (im)perceptibility here. The international effort to address the growing worldwide e-waste trade further drove the concern about the mineral waste to the background of international legal consciousness.

Thus, when the Ban amendment annexed to the Basel convention finally entered into force in 2019, the legal perceptibility of e-waste was inflated once more. The amendment essentially bans the export of hazardous waste from 'developed countries' (Organisation for Economic Co-operation and Development, EU member states, Liechtenstein) to 'developing countries'.[46] Thus, additional bureaucratic conflict over the interpretation of key defining terms of e-waste generated a new round of debate, substantiated by heavy lobbying by the industry to shelter e-waste from the Ban amendment. The same year, the Basel convention technical guideline on transboundary movement of electronic waste was adopted by the COP. Pursuant

42 *Ibid*, Art 10(2)(c).

43 Sabaa Ahmad Khan, 'E-products, E-waste and the Basel Convention: Regulatory Challenges and Impossibilities of International Environmental Law' (2016) 25(2) *Review of European Comparative & International Environmental Law* 248.

44 Josh Lepawsky, 'Are We Living in a Post-Basel World?' (2015) 47(1) *Area* 7.

45 Jamie Furniss, 'Alternative Framing of Transnational Waste Flows' (2015) 47(1) *Area* 24.

46 Amendment to the Basel Convention on the Control of Transboundary Movements of Hazardous Wastes and their Disposal (adopted in 22 September 1995, entered into force 5 December 2019) UNEP/CHW.3/35.

to paragraph 32(b) of the guidelines, used electronic equipment can still move across jurisdictions when the equipment is destined for failure analysis, or for repair or refurbishment by the same owner.[47]

As a result of these technical and legal restraints, e-waste as a commodity has been diverted towards regional and domestic circular economies. After the 2019 entry into force of the Ban amendment and Technical guidelines on e-waste, the Basel regime prompted a heightened perception of the e-waste issue within national boundaries, where large industrial manufacturers aimed to economically and politically capitalise on urban e-waste mining.

By diverting the issue of waste regulation to the technical expertise of e-waste, sovereign States and corporations have espoused a managerial ethos, which distracts 'civic epistemologies' from the attention that mineral production deserves.[48] Initially conceived as a response to a growing environmental concern over the increasing volume of toxic waste trade, the Basel Convention and its additional protocols internalise an economic rationale as the underlying functional logic of the global waste management system.[49]

3.2. Matter of fact: the implementation of the regime of e-waste perceptibility

The implementation of the regime of e-waste perceptibility was the result of the significant rise in transboundary e-waste commodity transfer. Between 1992 and 2019, the average life of consumer electronic devices progressively decreased as a result of changes in equipment features, capabilities and planned obsolescence.[50] This created a large stream of obsolete electronic equipment, which is expected to reach 500 million tonnes by the end of 2020.[51] In response to the rise of post-consumer waste, the waste management sector developed greater waste recycling capacity.

E-waste tracking and participatory sensing projects render urban waste management more visible.[52] High-tech monitoring techniques are now used to track and manage e-waste at the sink of global consumption, such as 'automated means of cellular scanning, drones, cameras, sensors combined with

---

[47] Technical guidelines (n 35).

[48] Sheila Jasanoff, *Designs on Nature: Science and Democracy in Europe and the United States* (Princeton University Press, 2011).

[49] Freyja Knapp, 'The Birth of the Flexible Mine: Changing Geographies of Mining and the E-waste Commodity Frontier' (2016) 48(10) *Environment and Planning A: Economy and Space* 1889.

[50] Sabine LeBel, 'Fast Machines, Slow Violence: ICTs, Planned Obsolescence, and E-waste' (2016) 13(3) *Globalizations* 300.

[51] Kaza et al, (n 29); Baldé et al, (n 30).

[52] Monitour E-trash Transparency Project, 'How does E-waste Travel Across the World after Disposal?' (Basel Action Network and MIT Senseable City Lab, 2012) <http://senseable.mit.edu/monitour/>.

actuators, and robotics in the recycling warehouses. They assist with inventory assessment, classification, and sorting'.[53]

Parallel to the technical innovations in the circular economy, new regulations have created a new infrastructure of e-waste monitoring, which include a trail of contractual papers, certification, evaluation, invoices and safe packaging, which all guarantee the formal handling of the hazardous material.[54] To illustrate such a regime of e-waste perceptibility, we focus on two regions that have undergone the highest levels of circular integration, Europe and Asia.

3.2.1. Europe

Electronic waste is currently governed by a European Community directive, the WEEE Directive.[55] The Directive is a broad framework for the re-use, recycling and recovery of e-wastes for the benefit of European manufacturing.[56] In 2016, circular activities such as repair, reuse or recycling generated almost €147 billion in value added, while standing for around €17.5 billion worth of investments.[57] The EU has recently adopted a revised legislative framework to modernise waste management systems, which entered into force in July 2018.[58] The Directive harmonises definitions and calculation methods and clarifies the legal status for recycled materials and by-products. The following quote conveys the heightened regime of perceptibility at the EU level:

> The Commission is supporting and engaging with Member States in the implementation of the waste legislation *to increase visibility* and understanding of circular economy opportunities in those Member States that have the biggest challenges in meeting their recycling targets.[59]

The same year, the Urban Mine Platform was launched to help build a centralised database of information on stocks, flows and treatment of WEEE. Increased recycling targets for municipal waste encourage circularity of electronics metals. Many States have supported initiatives of urban mining, which endeavour to extract and purify precious metals taken from waste streams.

---

[53] Rolien Hoyng, 'Aggregations of the Opaque: Rethinking Datafication and E-waste' (2019) 24(4) *First Monday* 1.

[54] See Technical guidelines (n 35).

[55] WEEE (n 36).

[56] Nicky Gregson and Mike Crang, 'From Waste to Resource: The Trade in Wastes and Global Recycling Economies', (2015) 40 *Annual Review Environment and Resources* 151.

[57] See European Commission, 'Private Investments, Jobs and Gross Value Added Related to Circular Economy Sectors' (*Eurostat*) <https://ec.europa.eu/eurostat/tgm/refreshTableAction.do?tab=table&plugin=1&pcode=cei_cie010&language=en>.

[58] Directive (EU) 2018/851 of the European Parliament and of the Council amending Directive 2008/98/EC on waste [2018] OJ L 150/109.

[59] Report from the Commission to the European Parliament, the Council, The European Economic and Social Committee and the Committee of the Regions on the implementation of EU waste legislation, including the early warning report for Member States at risk of missing the 2020 preparation for re-use/recycling target on municipal waste, COM (2018) 656 final. Emphasis added.

The e-waste recovered from one million smartphones is estimated to deliver 34 kg of gold, 14,000 kg of copper, 15 kg of palladium, and 350 kg of silver. To further put this into perspective, one tonne of smartphones can yield up to 300 times more gold than one tonne of gold ore.[60] Considering the high stakes, EU Member States incorporate the new closed-loop business model by modernising their recycling capabilities. For example, a major smelter company Umicore, headquartered in Belgium, turned its business model from highly polluting smelting to an e-waste-processing urban mining operation.[61]

3.2.2. Asia

In Asia, the post-consumer waste transfer and waste mining economy has led to the establishment of International Recycling Zone, where certified tax-free recycling plants process post-consumer waste in EcoParks. As the circular economy gains traction, solid waste management at the sink of the economy is made visible by transnational industrial cooperation, involving States, corporations and municipalities. Underlining this evolution, a new generation of preferential waste-trade regulations has emerged in the Pacific. In the last decade, Japan has concluded a series of bilateral treaties with Asian countries (Singapore, Malaysia, the Philippines, Thailand, Vietnam), and most recently with China. An agreement between Tokyo and Beijing was formalised on 7 May 2008, which forged an economic partnership on waste transfer and mining. The agreement set up an International Recycling Zone in the Ziya Circular Economy Industrial Park, which unites the Eco-Cities of Kitakiyushu (Japan) and Tianjin/Guangdong (China). Under the joint venture, Chinese companies salvage the embedded value from Japanese discards, reprocess them and send them back to Japanese manufacturers.

At the Chinese national level, urban mining schemes are designed to reclaim secondary resources from urban wastes and obsolete materials and mitigate China's resource scarcity. The Government initiated an Urban Mining Demonstration Bases (UMDBC) programme in May 2010 to operationalise urban mining.[62] It is estimated that the annual recycling capacity is reaching 45 million tons, which significantly increases the rates of e-waste collection and recycling.[63] One flagship UMDBC is the Tianying Industrial Park located in Jieshou, Anhui Province, recovering lead from monitors

---

[60] Bianca Nogrady, 'Your Old Phone is Full of Untapped Precious Metals' *BBC Future* (18 October 2016) <www.bbc.com/future/article/20161017-your-old-phone-is-full-of-precious-metals>.

[61] Nigel Roome and Victoria Jadot, 'A Case of Radical Reinvention: Umicore' in Gilbert Lenssen and Craig Smith (eds), *Managing Sustainable Business* (Springer 2019) 519.

[62] Hua Zhou, 'Urban Mining Demonstration Base: The Development Trend of Recycling industry' (2014) 7 *Recyclable Resource Circular Economy* 21.

[63] Yuan Hu and Mark Poustie, 'Urban Mining Demonstration Bases in China: A New Approach to the Reclamation of Resources' (2018) 79 *Waste management* 689.

and TVs with Cathode-ray tube displays. Elsewhere, in Jinsheng Industrial Park in Linyi of Shandong Province, the amount of copper and metal collection reaches 1.74 million tons annually.[64]

As the establishment of international and domestic recycling zones in Europe and Asia demonstrates, the circular economy emphasises waste management at the sink of the metal life cycle. Transnational law has legalised a regime of perceptibility of e-waste, yet by the same token has rendered invisible other types of waste generated by the electronics sector. While the volume of e-waste recovery is on the rise, as a matter of fact it still pales in comparison to the level of mineral production at the source, which provides the essential ingredients to manufactured electronics.

4. Regimes of industrial waste imperceptibility in linear economies

The same transnational legal system that at the sink rendered post-consumer waste visible, by contrast, keeps extractive waste at the source 'out of sight, out of mind'.[65] Since the establishment of the Convention on the Settlement of Investment Disputes in 1966 and the subsequent adoption of free trade policies in Latin America by what came to be known as the Washington Consensus, the investment in mineral extraction has created a surge of transnational extractive operations across the world.[66]

4.1. Matter of fact: the volume and toxicity of extractive waste at the source

4.1.1 Volume

Hard rock metal mining waste commonly consists of overburden (surface vegetation and soil that covers an ore body), waste rock (rock that needs to be removed to access the ore) and tailings, the finely ground remains of crushed ore from which the target mineral has been removed. Waste to product ratios, or 'stripping ratios', vary by ore body. They can be as high as 99 tons of waste per ton of copper, and 91 tons of waste for an ounce of gold.

On average, for each ton of metal extracted from ores, 2–12 tons of overburden material is removed as waste. In Chile, 1.5 million tons of tailings are produced every day.[67] South African mining companies in 2013 produced

---

[64] *Ibid.*

[65] Susan Marks, 'Law and the Production of Superfluity' (2011) 2(1) *Transnational Legal Theory* 1.

[66] Maristella Svampa, 'Commodities Consensus: Neoextractivism and Enclosure of the Commons in Latin America' (2015) 114(1) *South Atlantic Quarterly* 65.

[67] 'Chile's Mining Waste Poses Silent Threat to Humans on Multiple Fronts' *France* 24 (25 July 2019) <www.france24.com/en/20190725-chiles-mining-waste-poses-silent-threat-humans-multiple-fronts>.

562,000 times as much waste as gold.[68] According to the EU Data Centre on Waste for 2010, around 60% of the waste generated by 29 European countries consisted of mineral waste and soil, mainly from activities in the mining sector.[69]

4.1.2. Toxicity

Mine waste is environmentally hazardous by virtue of its volume, often causing siltation or smothering of surface water sources. A further source of toxicity for surface and ground water derives from sulphides as well as metals—such as cadmium, copper, iron, lead, manganese, mercury and silver—that may occur naturally in the ore body. Oxidised sulphides in contact with water produce sulfuric acid and accelerate metal leaching from mine waste.

Dumping mine tailings into rivers and streams causes increased sedimentation, turbidity, flooding, contamination of floodplain sediments, and in some cases the burial of large swaths of tropical lowland rainforests and mangroves with a veneer of waste, causing dieback of vegetation on a large scale.[70]

4.2. Matter of concern: the regime of imperceptibility at the source

International norms in general, and international environmental law in particular, have proven ineffective in monitoring the dissemination of mining waste across ecosystems. Firstly, this is because many conventions governing liability for the transboundary movement of waste have not yet entered into force.[71] Secondly, even when conventions are in place, substantial limitations exist regarding their scope. For instance, the UN Convention on the Law of the Sea, which protects coastal States against risks posed by High Risk Vessels, does not effectively protect marine life from the pollution dumped by coastal States.[72] Similarly, the *International Convention for the Prevention of Pollution from Ships* (MARPOL) is ill-equipped to tackle the mining problem at the source simply because it overlooks the metabolic rift of tailing ponds, which—inadvertently or by design—travel from the telluric source to the thalassic sink.[73]

---

[68] See South African Chamber of Mines, <www.mineralscouncil.org.za/>.

[69] European Environmental Agency, 'Waste: A Problem or a Resource?' (2014) <www.eea.europa.eu/signals/signals-2014/articles/waste-a-problem-or-a-resource>.

[70] Bernd Lottermoser, *Mine Wastes: Characterization, Treatment, and Environmental Impacts* (Springer, 3rd edn 2010) 229–33.

[71] See: Protocol on Liability and Compensation for Damage resulting from Transboundary Movements of Hazardous Wastes and their Disposal (n 22); Protocol on Civil Liability and Compensation for Damage Caused by the Transboundary Effects of Industrial Accidents on Transboundary Waters (n 22).

[72] United Nations Convention on the Law of the Sea (adopted on 10 December 1982, entered into force 16 November 1994) 1904 UNTS 320.

[73] Protocol of 1978 relating to the International Convention for the prevention of pollution from ships, 1973 (with annexes, final act and International Convention of 1973) (adopted 17 February 1978, entered into force 2 October 1983) 1340 UNTS 61 (1983).

Although the 1996 London Protocol to MARPOL effectively prohibits dumping of mine tailings at sea, the Protocol does not prohibit Submarine Tailings Disposal (STD), which is a discharge from land. The International Maritime Organization has issued guidelines to prevent land-based marine disposal, but STD has become a common practice throughout the mining industry worldwide. As early as 1971, coastal mining companies have submerged pipes to dispose of their mine tailings into the sea.[74] Since then, the mining industries from the capital-exporting States have increasingly used the coastal regions of host States as mine waste dumps.[75] Active mines using STD are located in Papua New Guinea, Turkey, Indonesia, Chile and Norway. STD occurs routinely off the coast of developing countries by companies headquartered in developed countries, where such disposal methods would be politically unacceptable.[76] One example is the 'world class' Ramu nickel–cobalt mining operation led by a consortium of Canadian, Australian and Chinese companies on the coast of Papua New Guinea, which disperses its tailings in the sea and causes toxic exposure to ecosystems and marine life in multiple ocean layers, introducing to the sea and marine biota toxic metals and chemicals.[77]

Current STD incidences show the insufficient national and transnational environmental regulation to effectively prohibit mining pollution at sea. Even some environmental research bodies such as the Scottish Association for Marine Science are actively paid by the World Bank to produce a set of guidelines to assist governments in setting conditions for marine dumping of mine waste.[78] The extractive industry has 'created a regime of imperceptibility in which the tools and infrastructures of environmental protection actually function to make hazards less perceptible.'[79]

Even when primary pollution sites are bound by environmental laws, they may be difficult to monitor. In Canada, home to 75% of the world's mining company headquarters, the Metal and Diamond Mining Effluent Regulations are designed to limit the environmental impact of mining operations. However, the limited scope of these mechanisms has resulted in weak governance of mining waste at the industrial and federal levels. This can be detected in regulators' over-reliance on 'scientific' models, 'technical guidelines' and arguments developed by industry consultants.[80] In 2019, Canada's

[74] Catherine Coumans, 'Into the Deep: Science, Politics and Law in Conflicts Over Marine Dumping of Mine Waste' (2018) 68 *International Social Science Journal* 303.
[75] *Ibid.*
[76] *Ibid.*
[77] Mining Data Solutions, 'The Kurumbukari (Ramu) Mine' <https://miningdataonline.com/property/3323/Kurumbukari-(Ramu)-Mine.aspx>.
[78] Lindsay Vare et al, 'Scientific Considerations for the Assessment and Management of Mine Tailings Disposal in the Deep Sea' (2018) 5 *Frontiers in marine science* 17.
[79] Wylie (n 39) 286.
[80] Coumans (n 74).

environment commissioner found Canada's federal environment departments failed at monitoring the waste dumps of domestic mining companies.[81]

In addition to the weak governance of mining waste at the national level, a double standard of enforcement has allowed Canadian companies to benefit from lax environmental regulations abroad, extracting sizable profits while causing environmental and social harms on a scale rarely seen in Canada itself.[82] Outcomes are likely to differ when extractive operations are located in jurisdictions with substantially different levels of transparency, public accountability, and corruption.

4.2.1. The imperceptibility of mining waste under investment regimes

Whereas the Mining Codes of the investor state are legally transplanted in the extractive host states, the environmental safeguards—usually more stringent in the investor State's jurisdiction than in the host State's—are not transplanted. As the leading State in mining investment abroad, Canada signed free-trade agreements with host mining States, such as Chile (1997), Peru (2009), Columbia (2011), Columbia (2011) and Honduras (2014). Despite reference to principles of corporate social and environmental responsibility, these free-trade and investment treaties do not impose obligations on mining companies to minimise pollution.[83]

One clear example of this asymmetry is the Free Trade Agreement signed between Canada and Honduras. Before signing the agreement, Canada offered 'technical assistance' to reform Honduras' Mining Code which entailed recommendations to simplify regulatory processes, reduce environmental standards and limit the consultation rights of affected communities. According to Mining Watch Canada

> the new law left water sources largely unprotected, allowed open pit mining even though it was opposed by 91% of Hondurans, provided for consultation only after concessions had been granted, denied public access to information about the technical and financial aspects of the mining projects, and allowed forced evictions resulting in the destruction of entire communities.[84]

Canada and Honduras later signed the Free Trade Agreement, which upon examination, does not implement environmental review standards or detail

[81] Office of the Auditor General of Canada, *Spring Reports of the Commissioner of the Environment and Sustainable Development to the Parliament of Canada, Report 2: Protecting Fish From Mining Effluent* (April 2019) <www.oag-bvg.gc.ca/internet/English/att__e_43314.html>.

[82] Jordan Ardanz and Chris Fukushima, 'Deviations and Double Standards: Canadian Mining Practices at Home and Abroad' (International Justice and Human Rights Clinic, University of British Columbia School of Law 2019).

[83] Linda Reif, 'Canada and Foreign Direct Investment in Latin America and the Caribbean: Evolution of an International Investment Agreement Framework' (2010) 13 *International Trade and Business Law Review* 86, 113.

[84] Mining Watch Canada, 'Honduran Mining Law Passed and Ratified But the Fight is Not Over' (24 January 2013) <www.miningwatch.ca/news/honduran-mining-law-passed-and-ratified-fight-not-over>.

precise mining waste management processes, rather 'endeavours to encourage voluntary best practices of corporate social responsibility by enterprises … to strengthen coherence between economic and environmental objectives'.[85]

Another neglected factor that contributed to the invisibility of pollution embodied in trade is the incomplete waste assessment from official reports on the economic impact of free trade agreements. As a result, a comprehensive understanding of pollution driven by production at the source is currently limited. Although various environmental footprint databases and methods have been developed by academia, statistical offices, and international organisations to assess pollution and resources embodied in trade, they are still at their infancy and certainly not implemented by trade agreements.[86] One important cause of this lack of monitoring is what scholars refer to as a 'race to the bottom', which implies competitive deregulation among host States with regards to environmental standards.

Furthermore, most of the environmental assessment is practiced on a voluntary basis by foreign corporate enterprises in the Global South, which increase the risk of submitting incomplete information on waste monitoring. In Honduras, major gaps in mining regulation have led to accusations by local communities of pollution by foreign companies, such as Canadian mining giant Goldcorp.[87] Insufficiency of waste monitoring is not limited to Honduras. Throughout Latin America, the environmental regulation on waste monitoring is performed by for-profit consultants. Market-based science has repeatedly bred public distrust about the objectivity of information contained in the environmental reports drafted by corporations.

Since a substantial amount of waste is made invisible by official and corporate mining data, secondary accounts by community organiser, local advocacy platforms and non-governmental organisations can give an approximate idea of the magnitude of waste produced at the source. One such noteworthy effort is a report entitled 'Extractive casino', which illustrates the surge of lawsuits filed by corporations against Latin American states to limit their environment oversight over their own domestic extractive sector.[88] Over the last two decades, global mining corporations have used the mechanism of the International Centre for Settlement of Investment Disputes (ICSID) against Latin American governments to demand compensation for public

[85] Agreement on Environmental Cooperation Between Canada and the Republic of Honduras (adopted 5 November 2013, entered into force 1 October 2014) <www.canada.ca/content/dam/eccc/documents/pdf/international-affairs/compendium/2018/batch-11/agreement-environmental-between-canada-republic-of-honduras.pdf> Article 10.

[86] Arnold Tukker, Stefan Giljum and Richard Wood, 'Recent Progress in Assessment of Resource Efficiency and Environmental Impacts Embodied in Trade' (2018) 22(3) *Journal of Industrial Ecology* 489.

[87] See: Inter-American Commission on Human Rights, 'The Impact of Canadian Mining in Latin America and Canada's Responsibility' (2014).

[88] Jen Moore and Manuel Perez Rocha, 'Extraction Casino: Mining Companies Gambling with Latin American Lives and Sovereignty Through Supranational Arbitration' (CIEL, IPS, April 2019) <https://ips-dc.org/wp-content/uploads/2019/05/ISDS-Mining-Latin-America-Report-Formatted_April29.pdf>.

environmental policies that they claim reduce the value of their investments. This aggressive litigation tactic ensures that the State's response to waste generated within its boundaries subsides under the superior interest of foreign direct investors' right to extract resources.[89]

Whereas International Environmental Law emphasises rules of cooperation, International Trade Law has a more stringent level of legalisation, marked by a combination of binding rules and delegation to international arbitration, which overlook contamination at the source.[90] The environmental annexes to free-trade agreements lack enforcement mechanisms and advocate instead for a non-binding managerial ethos of care, by promoting 'the trade and investment of environmental goods and services'.[91] On the one hand, financial disputes arising from bilateral investment treaties are to be adjudicated by international arbitration. On the other, disputes arising from parallel environmental cooperation treaties are only to be resolved through 'consultation' between countries, without recourse to an independent arbitrator.[92]

In this context, the 1994 *North American Free Trade Agreement* (NAFTA) entrenches an investment regime, which invisiblises corporate liabilities and their waste production.[93] Ever since its entry into force, NAFTA's Chapter 11 on foreign investment rights has allowed Canadian and US companies to pocket millions of dollars using this mechanism against the Mexican State. One case is the Canadian mining company Blackfire, which in 2009 was faced by strong opposition to its presence in Chicomuselo, Mexico. Community members were speaking of broken promises, little or no consultation, social division, intimidation, violence, environmental degradations such as soil erosion, silt and mud contamination, dried up rivers, and dead cattle as more and more pastures were compromised downstream of the mine.

Under Chapter 11, only corporate entities are allowed to take action against the State, which effectively prevents States from seeking punitive damages from such corporation before an international court. As a result, victims of mining pollution may only resort to domestic courts in developing countries, where the judicial branch has systematically been accused of siding with big

---

89 *Ibid.*

90 Kenneth Abbott et al, 'The Concept of Legalization' (2000) 54(3) *International organization* 401.

91 See: Canada-Peru Environmental Cooperation Agreement, (adopted 29 May 2008, entered into force 1 August 2009) <www.canada.ca/en/environment-climate-change/corporate/international-affairs/partnerships-countries-regions/latin-america-caribbean/peru/full-text.html> signed in parallel to the Free Trade Agreement, Article 2 [6].

92 *Ibid*, Article 12.

93 North American Free Trade Agreement (NAFTA) (adopted 17 December 1992, entered into force 1 January 1994) 107 Stat 2057, 32 ILM 289. On November 30, 2018, Canada, the United States, and Mexico signed an agreement to replace NAFTA with the Canada-United States-Mexico Agreement (CUSMA). This agreement renews the investor-State arbitration regime in Chapter 14. See United States-Mexico-Canada Agreement Implementation Act, HR 5430; Public Law 116–113; 19 USC January 29, 2020 (US).

business. When the local municipality of Chiapas demanded the Mexican Federal Government to act immediately to cancel the mining concessions given to Blackfire, the Canadian State mounted a defence to support its national corporation. Instead of directing its resources to obtain a third-party perspective on the matter, the Trade Commissioner provided Blackfire with advice about how to sue the Government of Chiapas under NAFTA for having suspended mining operations.[94] An attrition of judicial avenues exists for States from the Global South, which are highly exposed to foreign mining waste dumping.

To conclude this section, foreign mining companies skilfully use transnational economic laws to keep national environmental regulators at bay. As a result of lobbying and international arbitration, public policies largely immunise the mining sector from the legal adoption of production restrictions, environmental taxation and sanitary regulation.

5. Conclusion

Our examination of transnational legalisation reveals a hierarchical architecture of (im)perceptibility between the sources of waste production and sinks of waste distribution. When waste acquires commodity value, transnational trade regulation renders it visible; yet when waste becomes an environmental hazard, the transnational legal order renders it invisible.

However, most visible mineral solid e-waste embodies a certain ratio of invisible industrial waste and a certain ratio of industrial mining waste is increasingly rendered visible as a recyclable commodity.[95] This paradoxical co-production of waste (im)perceptibility is observed in the mining industry, where recent technological advancements increase the capacity to recycle tailing products such as minerals contained in waste rock.[96] In the same vein, it can be said that environmental market incentives, such as carbon tax or cap and trade schemes, play a role in commodifying—hence visualising—waste at the source, the same way that waste is monetised at the sink. Nevertheless, by no means are these respectively recycling and commodification schemes addressing the magnitude of waste produced at the source. Admittedly, the production of industrial and mining waste shows no sign of decline since the introduction of such technologies.[97]

---

[94] Jennifer Moore and Gillian Colgrove, 'Corruption, Murder and Canadian Mining in Mexico: The Case of Blackfire Exploration and the Canadian Embassy' (Mining Watch Canada, 2013).

[95] Erica Schoenberger, 'Environmentally Sustainable Mining: The Case of Tailings Storage Facilities' (2016) 49 *Resources Policy* 119.

[96] Vladimir Golik, Vitaly Komashchenko and Vladimir Morkun, 'Innovative Technologies of Metal Extraction from the ore Processing Mill Tailings and Their Integrated Use' (2015) 3 *Metallurgical and Mining Industry* 49.

[97] Daniel Hoornweg et al, 'Environment: Waste Production Must Peak This Century' (2013) 502(7473) *Nature News* 615.

Innovations to recycle mining operations' tailings are constrained and marginal, notwithstanding the funnel of endowment by the industry in marketising its progress. Similarly, while cap and trade is a fast-growing regional market, it has been proven ineffective in visualising carbon dioxide emissions at the source.[98] Although scrutinising these policies is beyond the scope of this article, failure of these schemes in reducing carbon dioxide emissions can be attributed to weak legalisation.[99] When the carbon trade initiative is designed according to the invisible hand of the market, it resonates with prior pledges which have produced dubious results in the past.[100] At the postconsumer sink, some residual unprocessed waste is impossible to recycle or commodify and is buried under another layer of imperceptibility. One example from the margins of the informal economy is the untreated waste generated by the circular economy itself, creating a feedback loop of waste accumulation in the periphery of high-tech recycling plants.[101]

Although further investigation is encouraged to disentangle the uncertainties and contradictions of the recycling economy, we hope this study contributed to raising awareness of the shifting boundaries of transnational waste regulation. The study of transnational law calls to attention the blind spots created by the legal categories of mining and electronic waste. Some recent policy recommendations have attempted to address such blind spots, calling for the creation of a specialised UN agency for strategic minerals.[102] Another possible avenue of change recently suggested by a policy report of the OECD would be to ecologically tax transnational electronics corporations, instead of subsidising them.[103]

This special issue of *Transnational Legal Theory* called for an engagement with environmental law in the Anthropocene. The Anthropocene typically refers to a new geological epoch where humanity is '*literally making*' the planet.[104] Rather, we wish to argue that hierarchical and fragmented regimes of transnational law conceal the *littering and breaking* of the planet by *some members* of humanity.[105] The Molysmocene[106] is a corollary

---

98 Rahel Aichele and Gabriel Felbermayr, 'Kyoto and Carbon Leakage: An Empirical Analysis of the Carbon Content of Bilateral Trade' (2015) 97(1) *Review of Economics and Statistics* 104.

99 José Granados et al, 'Policies to Reduce CO2 Emissions: Fallacies and Evidence from the United States and California' (2019) 94 *Environmental Science & Policy* 262.

100 Peter Dauvergne and Jane Lister, *Eco-Business: A Big-Brand Takeover of Sustainability* (MIT Press 2015).

101 Carl Benedikt Frey, *The Technology Trap: Capital Labor, and Power in the Age of Automation* (Princeton University Press 2019).

102 Massachusetts Institute of Technology, 'Mission 2016: Strategic Mineral Management', <https://web.mit.edu/12.000/www/m2016/finalwebsite/solutions/protocol.html>.

103 Organisation for Economic Co-operation and Development, 'Taxing Energy Use 2019: Using Taxes for Climate Action' (15 October 2019) <www.oecd.org/tax/taxing-energy-use-efde7a25-en.htm>.

104 Simon Dalby, 'Environmental Geopolitics in the Twenty-First Century' (2014) 39(1) *Alternatives* 3.

105 Giles Slade, *Made to Break: Technology and Obsolescence in America* (Harvard University Press 2009).

106 *Molusma* means 'filth' or 'stain' in Greek (μολυσμός). The Molysmocene was coined in the 1960s by French marine biologist Maurice Fontaine to refer to a future wasteland, an era which we now live in. See Tina Beigi, Olivier Barsalou and Michael Hennessy Picard, 'Welcome to the Molsymocene' (2017) *Critical Legal Thinking* 1.

neologism to the Anthropocene, which defines the permanent state of exceptional toxicity that we live in. Stratigraphically, anthropogenic deposits form a new layer of the earth crust on the top of the lithosphere. This crust of civilizational waste, we call the *littersphere.*[107] Rather than proposing a new stream of environmental law in the Anthropocene, we call for ecological law to radically address the systemic and institutional flaws of the littersphere. Ecological law offers a more responsive, sustainable, and just system of governance that better protects our interconnected, interdependent world.[108]

Ecological law is in line with structural reforms focused on strategies of degrowth, which gain traction in periods of global meltdown when critical inquiry into the vulnerability of free market societies becomes a public necessity. One such degrowth strategy would be to propose financial divestment from mass electronics manufacturing, henceforth reducing global mineral demand at the source of the global supply chain, which uninterrupted would exhaust the sink capacity of the earth. Furthermore, a reconsideration of 5G technology, which would require an overhaul of the entire electronic grid to satisfy this new high-speed communication platform, is essential. Such policy reforms require a serious reconsideration of the transnational legal structure, which has imposed a market-based approach to environmental concerns for the benefit of the mining and electronics industries.

Disclosure statement

No potential conflict of interest was reported by the author(s).

[107] Justin McBrien, 'Accumulating Extinction: Planetary Catastrophism in the Necrocene' in Elmar Altvater et al, *Anthropocene or Capitalocene? Nature, History, and the Crisis of Capitalism* (Pm Press 2016) 116. Michael Hennessy Picard and Tina Beigi, 'Stains of Empire: Accumulation by Contamination in the Middle East' (2020) *Journal of Energy History, Special Issue on Energy Imperialism.* (to be published).

[108] Carla Sbert, *The Lens of Ecological Law: A Look at Mining* (Edward Elgar 2020); Ecological Law and Governance Association, *Oslo Manifesto for Ecological Law and Governance* (2016) <www.elga.world/oslo-manifesto>.

Index

Footnotes are indicated by the page number followed by "n" and the number of the footnote e.g., 162n123 refers to note number 123 on page 162.